EDUCATION AND THE CULTURAL COLD WAR IN THE MIDDLE EAST

EDUCATION AND THE CULTURAL COLD WAR IN THE MIDDLE EAST

The Franklin Book Programs in Iran

Mahdi Ganjavi

I.B. TAURIS
LONDON • NEW YORK • OXFORD • NEW DELHI • SYDNEY

I.B. TAURIS
Bloomsbury Publishing Plc
50 Bedford Square, London, WC1B 3DP, UK
1385 Broadway, New York, NY 10018, USA
29 Earlsfort Terrace, Dublin 2, Ireland

BLOOMSBURY, I.B. TAURIS and the I.B. Tauris logo are
trademarks of Bloomsbury Publishing Plc

First published in Great Britain 2023
This paperback edition published 2024

Copyright © Mahdi Ganjavi 2023

Mahdi Ganjavi has asserted his right under the Copyright, Designs and
Patents Act, 1988, to be identified as Author of this work.

For legal purposes the Acknowledgments on pp. vii–viii constitute an
extension of this copyright page.

Series design by Adriana Brioso
Cover image: A member of the Army of the Savior during class.
(© Paul Almasy/Corbis/VCG/Getty Images)

All rights reserved. No part of this publication may be reproduced or transmitted
in any form or by any means, electronic or mechanical, including photocopying,
recording, or any information storage or retrieval system, without prior
permission in writing from the publishers.

Bloomsbury Publishing Plc does not have any control over, or responsibility for,
any third-party websites referred to or in this book. All internet addresses given in this
book were correct at the time of going to press. The author and publisher regret any
inconvenience caused if addresses have changed or sites have ceased to exist,
but can accept no responsibility for any such changes.

A catalogue record for this book is available from the British Library.

A catalog record for this book is available from the Library of Congress.

ISBN: HB: 978-0-7556-4342-4
PB: 978-0-7556-4346-2
ePDF: 978-0-7556-4343-1
eBook: 978-0-7556-4344-8

Typeset by Integra Software Services Pvt. Ltd.

To find out more about our authors and books visit www.bloomsbury.com
and sign up for our newsletters.

CONTENTS

Acknowledgments	vii
A Note on Transliteration	ix
List of Abbreviations	x

Chapter 1
A COLD WAR HISTORY OF BOOKS AND EDUCATION ... 1

Chapter 2
CULTURAL IMPERIALISM: WHY FRANKLIN BOOK PROGRAMS MATTERS ... 13

Chapter 3
FRANKLIN BOOK PROGRAMS: TRANSLATION, PUBLICATIONS, AND BOOK DISTRIBUTION DURING THE COLD WAR ... 19
    Origins, Policies, and Structure ... 21
    Categories of Title Listing and Process of Title Selection ... 28

Chapter 4
HISTORY AND INTERNATIONAL EVOLUTION OF THE FRANKLIN BOOK PROGRAMS (1952-77) ... 33
    Early Years and Early Success (1952-6) ... 34
    Moving away from Translation Programs toward Educational Projects (1956-68) ... 43
    Reintroduction as an International Educational Development Program (1968-75) ... 52
    Years of Decline (1975-7) ... 62

Chapter 5
FRANKLIN BOOK PROGRAMS IN IRAN: CONTEXT, ESTABLISHMENT, AND REGULAR TRANSLATION PROGRAMS ... 65
    Soviet-US Rivalry in Iran during the Cold War and the Role of the Iranian State ... 65
    Soviet-Iran Cultural and Educational Relations ... 68
    US-Iran Cultural and Educational Relations ... 72
    Tehran Branch: Establishment and National Development ... 76
    Publishing Industry in Iran ... 81
    Regular Translation Program ... 86

Chapter 6
FRANKLIN BOOK PROGRAMS IN IRAN: SPECIAL EDUCATIONAL
PROJECTS, REACTIONS TO THE TEHRAN BRANCH, AND DEMISE   93
    Production and Publication of the *Persian Encyclopedia*   94
    Development of the Printing Plant (Offset Printing House)   96
    Mass Distribution of Books in Iran (*kitābhā-yi jībī* Project)   97
    Workshops for Publishers   99
    Development of the Paper Production Company (Pars Paper Company)   99
    Afghanistan Textbook Project   100
    Technical Aid to the Printing Plant of Afghanistan's Ministry of
        Education   103
    Iran Textbook Project   104
    Publication of Children's Literature and *Payk* Magazines   111
    Relations with Other Organizations in the Field of Education   123
    Reaction to the Tehran Branch: The Case of Jalal Al Ahmad   125
    Demise of the Tehran Branch   131

Chapter 7
THE COLD WAR, KNOWLEDGE PRODUCTION, AND THE MIDDLE EAST   135

Appendix I: The Presidents of the FBP and a List of FBP Local Branches   146
Appendix II: Local Participation by Civic and Intellectual Leaders   149

Notes   154
References   176
Index   186

ACKNOWLEDGMENTS

This research is a scholarly travelogue, a product of eight years of historical and intellectual journeying to the world of education and knowledge production during the Cold War. This investigation could not have been fulfilled without many people who assisted me in different ways in my long inquiry. Years ago, Mahmoud Daqaqi, a librarian and former friend of Homayun San'atizadeh, manager of the Tehran Branch of Franklin Book Programs (FBP), first introduced me to the Tehran Branch. Almost a decade later, in the second year of my master's in Near and Middle Eastern Civilizations (University of Toronto) when I undertook an investigation of the Tehran Branch, Daqaqi was also the first librarian I advised with.

Professor Amir Hassanpour was crucial in shaping my theoretical understanding of imperialism and my historical understanding of the Cold War era. Moreover, I assisted Professor Hassanpour with his historical investigation into the Kurdish peasant movement of the 1950s, a research project that helped me significantly in obtaining a deep and critical perception of archival research.

I had the chance to discuss the Tehran Branch with a few people formerly affiliated with it and also with staff. I am thankful to Tom Ricks and Mahdokht San'ati for sharing with me their insights. I thank Dr. Himani Bannerji, Dr. Angela Miles, and Dr. Kanishka Goonewardena for reading and commenting on early drafts of this research. Fereshteh Molawi and Dr. Amir Kalan assisted me in presenting my early findings. I also have to thank Stephan Dobson for all his comments on an early draft of this book. A sincere thank-you to Sara Magness for her diligent copy-editing of the full manuscript.

This book is primarily based on my PhD thesis at the Department of Leadership, Higher and Adult Education (OISE/University of Toronto). I am thankful to my supervisor Dr. Shahrzad Mojab; to my committee members, Dr. Mohammad Tavakoli-Targhi and Dr. Aziz Choudry; to the external examiner, Dr. Afshin Matin-Asgari; and to the internal-external examiner, Dr. Jamie Magnusson. I have benefited from Dr. Mojab's comments many times and in all aspects of this research, and beyond. Her insights, resources, and intellectual and moral support were essential throughout. Dr. Tavakoli-Targhi helped me with his comments and resources to dig deeper into the dynamics of the Tehran Branch and contextualize it within US–Soviet rivalry in Iran. Dr. Choudry, a brilliant and inspiring mind to whose intellectual and moral support I am so indebted, also generously helped me in globalizing the FBP, contextualizing it within wider networks of US knowledge production during the Cold War. The heartbreaking news of his passing away has marked 2021 with a deep sense of grief. I also have to thank the anonymous reviewers of my manuscript for their constructive comments and suggestions.

Finally, this research journey could not have been fulfilled without the moral support of my partner, Mehrnaz Mansouri. Her never-ending kindness, patience, and love were vital. She has listened to hundreds of questions and concerns I have had during this intellectual journey, and she has assisted me in many ways in administering the research. I am further indebted to my parents, Mohammad and Parvin, and my father- and mother-in-law, Ali and Anis, who through all these years have been kind, patient, and lively supporters.

I would like to acknowledge that this research was supported by two Ontario Graduate Scholarships that I received for 2017–19 and by a Social Sciences and Humanities Research Council Doctoral Award in 2019–20.

A NOTE ON TRANSLITERATION

I have used the Library of Congress standardization for transliterating Persian and Arabic words. When possible, Persian words that appear in this work are transliterated into their most common English forms. Works quoted in this book use differing systems of transliteration, and direct quotes are represented as they originally appeared.

ABBREVIATIONS

AAUP	Association of American University Presses
ABPC	American Book Publishers Council
AFME	American Friends of the Middle East
ALA	American Library Association
APOC	Anglo-Persian Oil Company
ASCD	Association for Supervision and Curriculum Development (United States)
ATPI	American Textbook Publishers Institute
BYU	Brigham Young University
CCF	Congress for Cultural Freedom
CET	Center for Educational Technology (Iran)
CIA	Central Intelligence Agency (United States)
CIS	Confederation of Iranian Students
CUTC	Columbia University Teachers College
CWIHP	Cold War International History Project
DRL	Bureau for Democracy, Human Rights and Labor (United States)
EML	Educational Materials Laboratory (United States)
EPC	Educational Publications Center (Iran)
FBP	Franklin Book Programs
IIA	International Information Administration (United States)
IIDCYA	Institute for the Intellectual Development of Children and Young Adults (Iran)
IIE	Institute for International Education (United States)
INCINC	International Copyrights Information Center
ICS	Information Center Service (United States)
NED	National Endowment for Democracy (United States)
NSA	National Security Archive
OECD	Organization for Economic Cooperation and Development
PSB	Psychological Strategy Board (United States)
SAVAK	National Organization for Security and Intelligence (Iran)
Society	Society for Cultural Relations between Iran and the Soviet Union (Iran)
Tehran Branch	Tehran Branch of the Franklin Book Programs

UPenn	University of Pennsylvania
USAC	Utah State Agricultural College
USAID	United States Agency for International Development
USIA	United States Information Agency
USIS	United States Information Service
VAID	Village and Industrial Development (Pakistan)
VOKS	All-Union Society for Cultural Ties with Foreign Countries (Soviet Union)

Chapter 1

A COLD WAR HISTORY OF BOOKS AND EDUCATION

Franklin Book Programs (FBP) was a private not-for-profit US organization founded in 1952 during the Cold War. It was funded by the United States' government agencies as well as private corporations. The FBP initially intended to promote US liberal bourgeois values through the translation of US books and also to create appropriate markets for US books in "Third World"[1] countries (Robbins, 2007). However, from this initial objective of exporting US culture to rival the influence of Soviet socialism, the FBP evolved into an international educational development program publishing university textbooks, schoolbooks, and supplementary readings (Laugesen, 2012). As the FBP moved to become one of the most significant international organizations of the Cold War era with a global focus on the production of educational materials, its activities broadened from those specifically related to translation. It started to develop printing, publishing, and bookselling institutions. Moreover, it undertook the training of local teachers as textbook writers and also sponsored the publication of reading materials for newly literate children, teens, youth, teachers, and parents.

This book explores the role of the FBP (1952–77) in the print publishing industry, in book translation, in textbook writing, and in the educational policies of the Middle East, with a specific focus on Iran. Through archival study and historical analysis of the international role of the FBP, this book examines the interrelations between imperialism, the state, and knowledge production. Criticizing the prevalent understanding of imperialism as an economic system, this research explores and historicizes the ideological functioning of imperialism through its cultural and educational policies. I will show that the printing, translation, production, and widespread distribution of books, literacy and school texts, and supplementary readings throughout the Middle East were a continuation of the anti-communist policies of the United States during the Cold War era. Notably in Iran, the wide distribution of these texts was facilitated and sponsored by the pro-US regime of Pahlavi. In historicizing the effects of the FBP in Iran, where the Pahlavi regime cooperated with it in its various projects and initiatives, this study also contributes to a Marxist conceptualization of imperialism, the state, and knowledge production.

Historically, this book is an exploration of the twenty-five-year operation of the FBP, from 1952 when the FBP was first established in the United States to 1977 when it was dissolved due to a lack of financial resources. I will examine the FBP in the context of various US international educational initiatives and policies and their developments during these decades (the 1950s to the 1980s). This requires a study of the role that educational and technical assistantship programs played in the US policy of containment, once the defeat of fascism at the end of the Second World War ended the strategic alliance between the Allied forces. This historical investigation extends to cover the three decades of the consequent Cold War rivalry between the capitalist and socialist blocs, in its international ideological and cultural manifestations.

In its course of operations, the FBP functioned in as many as seventeen countries in the Middle East, Asia, and Latin America. Its overall purpose in all of its international cultural and educational operations was the same, but the method, scope, and length of its operations differed in some aspects between regions. A brief comparison between FBP operations in the Middle East and Latin America is helpful. In the Middle East, the FBP was active for twenty-five years and established several local offices to pursue its projects, such as the Cairo Branch (1953–77) and the Tehran Branch (1954–77). The Latin American division, however, was primarily active for only five years (1963–8). The FBP never had an office in Latin America, but carried out its programs through associated organizations in Buenos Aires, Rio de Janeiro, Sao Paulo, and Mexico City. Moreover, the Ministries of Education in Iran, Egypt, Pakistan, and Afghanistan worked closely with the FBP's local branches in their various operations. In the case of Iran and Afghanistan, the governments of these countries financially sponsored several of the projects of the FBP; but in Latin America, the FBP's funding sources were mainly limited to special-purpose grants from foundations and other not-for-profit organizations, the most important of which was the W.K. Kellogg Foundation.

This book particularly focuses on the role of the FBP on the print publishing, translation, and textbook writing of Iran, where the FBP was most "successful" in fulfilling its objectives and most varied in the operations it undertook (Smith, 2000). While I will explore the FBP in the context of the history of the Cold War and its cultural and ideological manifestations, I will remain focused on the FBP's role and operations as an organization. A detailed historical account of the Cold War is not the subject of this study. Also, while the operations of the FBP in Iran and FBP's various affiliations with Iran's publishing industry and its Ministry of Education will be historicized, this research is not an extensive history of print publishing and education in modern Iran.

Since the mid-twentieth century, the Middle East, with its vast supplies of hydrocarbons, has been a crucial zone within the wider global economy. Thus, control of the Middle East has been a long-standing crossroads of global conflict (Hanieh, 2013). Several countries in the Middle East were within the spheres of influence of foreign powers from the beginning of the rise of imperialism (the late 1870s). However, it was mainly after the Second World War that the Middle East's geopolitical importance significantly intensified; by the end of that war, the world witnessed "a qualitative leap in the internationalization of capital" (Hanieh, 2013, p. 20). Internationalization resulted in a large increase in energy use. Following a wave of discoveries during the 1920s and 1930s, it came to be known that "the world's largest supplies of cheap and easily accessible hydrocarbons" were in the Middle East (Hanieh, 2013, p. 21). In light of the Middle East's geopolitical position, and its important energy resources, this region was crucial during the Cold War both for the US policy of containing communism and also in establishing an anti-communist alliance. However, this highly crucial region lacked a US-affiliated local publishing infrastructure and mass book distribution system and in most areas was totally devoid of any US literary, educational, or cultural influence.

By the end of the Second World War and the intensification of the conflict between the capitalist and socialist blocs, Iran as the southern neighbor to the Soviet Union was the most crucial Middle Eastern country for the US policy of containment. In 1953, fearful of the oil nationalizing efforts, the Central Intelligence Agency (CIA) sponsored a coup against the nationalist prime minister, Mohammad Mosaddeq. Subsequently, the post-coup regime repressed the socialist and nationalist political groups and gradually reshaped and developed Iran's educational system in line with the US educational structure and curriculum, as part of a state-based educational reform, officially celebrated as the "Educational Reform." The FBP's Tehran Branch soon became the main educational and publication corporation behind this initiative (Filstrup, 1976, p. 440).

The Tehran Branch translated more than 800 books, sponsored the establishment of the largest printing house in the Middle East (1958), published the textbooks for the first four grades of Iranian primary schools (1958–77), and joined the Iranian Ministry of Education to establish the most widely circulated educational magazines Iran had ever witnessed, a series entitled *Payk* (Courier). According to internal reports, the "dream" of the FBP was to see the "amazing" success of its Tehran Branch replicated in other developing countries. To analyze this "success," this book historicizes the important geopolitical role of the Middle East, and especially Iran, in the US policy of containment, as well as the history of Iran–US relations and its educational and technical assistantship manifestations during the Cold War.

A critical investigation of the FBP operations will make a notable interdisciplinary contribution to the fields of book history and print culture, cultural imperialism studies, comparative global education, Cold War studies, and modern Iranian cultural and political history. Although the FBP functioned for twenty-five years (between 1952 and 1977) and in seventeen countries on three continents (Asia, Africa, and South America), its global role in the development and transformation of literacy programs, in modernizing the print and publishing industry, and in translating US books and training textbook writers has remained understudied.

In terms of analysis, most of the literature on FBP (Smith, 1956; Smith, 1963; Hemphill, 1964; LeClere, 1973; Filstrup, 1976; Yadegar, 1979; Smith, 1983; Smith, 2000) heavily builds on the analytical frameworks used and promoted by the architects of the FBP itself. This is to say that this literature mainly historicizes and analyzes the FBP through the discourse and analytical framework of modernization theory, celebrating the FBP's achievements by means of reiterating the statistics and information reported by FBP's board of directors and promoted by the local managers and branches. Datus C. Smith, the FBP's first president, wrote four articles on the program, two of which (1956 and 1983) provide an overview of the FBP and two of which focus particularly on the Tehran Branch (1963 and 2000). In 1963, Smith wrote the first article on FBP operations in Iran and its accomplishments there. In this article, "Ten Years of Franklin Publications," Smith provides an overview of the structure and internal history of the FBP. His account, as the FBP president, is written for informative and promotional reasons rather than for the purposes of analytic or scholarly investigation. Smith also wrote the entry for the FBP published in *Encyclopaedia Iranica* in 2000. The fact that this entry is written by a former president of the organization of course undermines its scholarly objectivity. In the absence of a historical investigation, either of the social history of Iran or Cold War geopolitics or of the history of Iran–US relations, the entry fails to analyze why among all the FBP branches, Tehran became the most efficient and financially successful local office.

In 1964, Ruth R. Hemphill wrote a master's thesis on the role of the FBP in book development in the Middle East and Southeast Asia between 1952 and 1963. It is primarily based on Hemphill's correspondence with the FBP staff in New York and Tehran and celebrates the FBP for its modernizing role in the Third World. In 1973, the Tehran Branch published LeClere's *Let Us All Share in the World of Books* (1973), which is also a descriptive and promoting account of the Tehran Branch's achievements based on the modernization theory. Another article on the FBP, by J.M. Filstrup, was written in 1976 when the Tehran Branch was still operating. Filstrup's article reports on the educational strategies and operations of the FBP in Iran, pointing to the importance of the Shah's "Educational Reform," which brought the FBP into the mainstream (Filstrup, 1976, p. 440). Filstrup's article relies heavily on LeClere's book and on reports from the FBP's architects, and correspondence and interviews with a few FBP founding board members and Tehran Branch staff. In 1979, just two months after the revolution in Iran, Zhaleh Yadegar defended her master's thesis on FBP operations in Iran. Yadegar's thesis is a general overview of the Tehran Branch's operations, primarily based on her personal interviews with the former Tehran Branch staff.

In the last few years, there has been a rise in the study of the FBP in the context of the cultural Cold War. Louise S. Robbins provides a brief account of the establishment and history of the FBP (2007). While Robbins's attempt at contextualizing the FBP within the context of the Cold War ideological rivalry is noteworthy, she draws mainly on the archival documents of the FBP held at Princeton University and admittedly neglects the literature of the target countries, writing, "without more extensive reading of the current literature of the target countries, and without interviewing people who live, or perhaps lived in Iran and other target countries, any realistic estimate of FBP's impact will be virtually impossible" (Robbins, 2007, p. 648). Amanda Laugesen first wrote a concise investigation of several Cold War-era book programs implemented by the United States, in which she also touched on the history of the FBP (2012). Later, Laugesen devoted a monograph to the FBP (2017), which remains a significant contribution to our understanding of this program, through the lens of cultural imperialism.

Laugesen has specifically studied the role of American publishers within the FBP and chronologically detailed the FBP's functions. A thorough discussion of the FBP's operations in Iran inevitably complements Laugesen's study.

One specific aspect of the FBP's operations—that is, the FBP's Regular Translation Programs—has been the subject of a few recent scholarships in the field of translation studies. Arrabai (2019) and Asiri (2021) have contributed the most detailed studies of the FBP's Regular Translation Programs in the Arab world. Arrabai's study is based on an investigation of two sets of archives: the FBP records with regard to its Arabic program and more than a hundred introductions in Arabic written for the FBP-sponsored translations. Arrabai contextualizes the FBP within the US cultural Cold War and as part of the networks of US "image building" efforts in the Arab world. Asiri, on the other hand, particularly investigates the extent of direct US involvement in the FBP Regular Translation operations in Egypt. These studies contribute significantly to our knowledge of the FBP's Arabic translations.

Haddadian-Moghaddam (2016) discusses the political factors in the circulation of world literature during the Cold War and explores the Tehran Branch-sponsored literary translations into Persian. Through a brief discussion of selected copyright negotiations between the FBP and its local branches, and the role of local staff in the title selection process, Haddadian-Moghaddam argues that the "propaganda reading" of the FBP is a useful contextual tool, but not "sufficient" (Haddadian-Moghaddam, 2016, p. 386). Limiting his points of reference to a few examples of the role of local staff, Haddadian-Moghaddam claims that this staff, at least in the case of the Tehran Branch, "transformed" a "propaganda foreign program" into something "useful" (Haddadian-Moghaddam, 2016, p. 386). This line of argument, while an exception in the recent scholarship in English, has been echoed frequently in literature published in Persian.

The current literature rarely analyzes the long-term results and consequences of the operations of the FBP or how it was perceived or criticized by local intellectuals. After the Second World War, with the rise of US imperialism and several newly formed nationalist states, an extensive anti-US imperialism literature appeared in the Third World countries. In the case of Iran, such criticism of US imperialism can be traced in prose, poetry, films, and in various labor and student movements. With the radicalization of student organizations during the 1960s and 1970s in Iran, this anti-imperialism movement with its internationalist perspective also built a transnational network and influenced the formation of the culture of dissent in Europe and the United States in the late 1960s (Nasrabadi & Matin-Asgari, 2018). An extensive study of anti-US cultural imperialism in Iran is important, but this book will detail the criticism specifically directed toward the FBP's operations in Iran. In particular I will shed light on the importance of re-reading Al Ahmad's writings in light of his personal engagement with and reflections on the Tehran Branch.

Disillusioned with the Tehran Branch, Jalal Al Ahmad (1923–69), the prominent intellectual and former translator for the Tehran Branch, wrote harsh personal attacks against Sanʿatizadeh and also criticized the hegemonic role that the Tehran

Branch was playing in Iran's cultural and educational spheres. Al Ahmad went on to write *Westoxification* (*qarb zadigī*) in 1962, a foundational text for Iran's anti-Occidental, anti-imperialist discourse. I will show how Al Ahmad's personal and intellectual affiliation and later disillusionment with the Tehran Branch have contributed to the formation of the theory of westoxification. Al Ahmad argued that translation projects had failed in the process of "conquering" Western culture and that publishers were collaborators with imperialism and the autocratic Pahlavi regime. As I will discuss in Chapter 6, Al Ahmad suggested that religion and religious clergies (*'ulamā*) could revive to become the political force and agents capable of fighting against cultural imperialism. While it can be argued that Al Ahmad's ideas changed and developed in the course of his life, still the above-mentioned suggestion contributed to the formation of the Islamic anti-Occidental and anti-imperialist discourse during the Iranian Revolution of 1979. As I will also discuss in Chapter 6, soon after the 1979 revolution in Iran, the remaining properties and offices of the Tehran Branch were confiscated by the Islamic state. The office was restructured and reopened as the Organization for Publication and Education of the Islamic Revolution.

For the purposes of this book, I have studied a variety of archives in order to contextualize the FBP within US Cold War cultural diplomacy, as well as to historicize the role of the US government agencies in sponsoring and directing the FBP—including the corporate records of the FBP, the declassified documents accessible through the Cold War International History Project (CWIHP), the CIA archives, and the National Security Archive (NSA) at George Washington University. Notably, in the case of the Tehran Branch, this study has entailed a critical investigation of the archives of Iran's Organization of National Intelligence and Security (known as SAVAK) and the records of the US embassy in Tehran to analyze the "cultural diplomacy" of the competing capitalist and socialist blocs in Iran during the Cold War. The study of these archives aids in revealing how these cultural, educational, and knowledge production activities were received, supported, or blocked by the Iranian state and its intelligence service. Memoirs, interviews, and reflections of the local staff, publishers, writers, and intellectuals are also examined to give a detailed and multilayered understanding of the Tehran Branch operations. Below I will discuss the various sources of this study.

(1) Corporate records of the FBP: The FBP's complete corporate records are held in the Department of Rare Books and Special Collections at Princeton University Library's Archives of American Publishing. These archives contain the program's administrative records and include the minutes, correspondence, memoranda, reports, contracts, and photographs spanning the twenty-five years of the FBP's functioning. The documents are mostly in English; however, some of them are in Persian, Arabic, French, Spanish, and Urdu. The FBP donated this archive to the Princeton University Library in 1978. It contains 249 archival boxes, four half-size archival boxes, twenty-eight 8x10" photograph boxes, six 5x8" boxes, two 5x7" boxes, two 9x12" boxes, one 14x18" box, two microfiche boxes, one phonograph box, and three custom-made boxes.

This archive sheds light on the relation between the FBP and civic and intellectual leaders of local countries and helps us to document and historicize the relationship between the FBP and prime ministers, presidents, cabinet ministers, ambassadors, senators, judges, educational leaders, and literary standings in Iran, Egypt, Indonesia, Lebanon, Pakistan, and so on. It also includes correspondence with associations and consultants on international projects. Among the FBP's consulting associations were the following: Adult Education Association (1961–71), American Council on Education (1953–67), American Friends of the Middle East (AFME) (1951–68), American Textbook Publishers Institute (ATPI) (1952–66), Association for Supervision and Curriculum Development (ASCD) (1969–71), Association of American University Presses (AAUP) (1953–76), Council on Books in Wartime (1965), Education and World Affairs (1964–8), International Youth Library (1957–71), and UNESCO: Economics of Book Publishing in Developing Countries (1965–77). The collection further includes correspondence between the FBP and several foundations such as the Ford and Rockefeller institutes and helps provide detail on the relationship between the FBP and the United States Agency for International Development (USAID), and the United States Information Agency (USIA). The financial relation that FBP had with USAID and the USIA, the role of the USIA in title selections, and also the role of USAID in the FBP's teacher-training projects are also documented in the archives.

The FBP has not been very consistent in its archiving, especially in terms of the placement of its items. According to the description of these records provided by the Princeton Library, former FBP executive director Jack Kyle has admitted to misfilings and attributed them to FBP staff.[2] Here, it is noteworthy that in studying the FBP's archives, especially its annual reports, I have been mindful of the modernization discourse in which they were produced. As such, in extracting the masses of historical information contained within the archive, my study does not submit to and repeat the self-promotional and heroic account of the organization's board of directors. Moreover, as I will expand on later in Chapter 2, I have benefited from Dorothy Smith's Marxist feminist approach to the textual analysis of organizational relations to analyze the role of discourse in institutional texts (Smith, 1999). In this study, in citing FBP records, I have used "FBPR" (Franklin Book Programs Records), followed by the title and date of the relevant document.

(2) National Security Archive/Cold War International History Project/Central Intelligence Agency Archives/Psychological Strategy Board: The two key archives for the study of Cold War history are the NSA at George Washington University, founded in 1985, and the CWIHP, established at the Woodrow Wilson International Center for Scholars in 1991. Both have archived and made accessible declassified documents related to the Cold War era. Several of the NSA declassified documents dating back to the 1950s reveal historical information on the nature and scope of the relations between the Department of State, the Information Center Service (ICS), and the FBP. The CWIHP sheds light on the Soviet Union's sensitivity about the FBP and its operations. In citing the NSA, I have used "NSA" followed by the title and date of the relevant document. The same formula has also been used for CWIHP documents. Other archives useful in investigating the FBP include the CIA's archives and the Psychological Strategy Board File. Where I cite CIA sources, I have used "CIAA" followed by the number and date of the document. The Psychological Strategy Board Files are held with the Harry S. Truman Papers, cited in this book as "PSB" followed by document title and date.

(3) Archive and records of the Tehran Branch: The Tehran Branch was dissolved two years before the 1979 revolution. The remaining properties and offices of this branch were also confiscated once the revolutionaries had prevailed. Soon after the revolution, Homayun Sanʿatizadeh (1925–2009),[3] the first manager of the Tehran Branch, was imprisoned for possible ties with the CIA and later convicted by the Islamic Revolutionary Court, accused of "promoting and publishing American culture." The anti-US sentiments of the revolutionaries, along with the fact that the Islamic Revolutionary Courts convicted a few of the major publishers working during the last decade of the Shah's regime, had quite a negative effect on the process of preserving the Tehran Branch records. Several of the records were destroyed either during the days of revolution or by the frightened publishers themselves. In a recent development, as I was finalizing this book, the Museum and Document Center of Scientific and Cultural Publications (*muzah wa markaz asnād intishārāt ʿilmī va farhangī*) was launched (on May 24, 2021)—which, more than four decades after the dissolving of the Tehran Branch in 1977, has made a collection of Tehran Branch documents available. The launching of this center will open up new areas of research, especially for those interested in the history of modern print in Iran. This center also holds more details for future studies on the operations of the Tehran Branch.

(4) SAVAK/US embassy in Iran: Two sets of archives released and made accessible after the revolution of 1979 proved valuable for this study: the archive of the Pahlavi regime's SAVAK, and the records of the US embassy in Iran, which were confiscated by the Muslim Student Followers of the Imam's Line when they occupied the embassy in Tehran in 1979. A critical and skeptical evaluation of these two sets of archives assists in historicizing and analyzing the "cultural diplomacy" of the United States and Soviet Union in Iran, as well as how these cultural and educational activities were received and addressed by SAVAK. The SAVAK archives have been published in several volumes in Iran by the Center for Historical Documents Survey, a post-Revolution state-affiliated organization; each volume includes a set of documents under a certain subject (for instance, the relations between Iran and Soviet Union). The challenge with using SAVAK documents arises from concerns regarding original order and respect given to the archives. These documents have been confiscated, sorted, and selectively published in the context of the establishment of a revolutionary anti-US Islamic regime. Still, this valid critical concern should not eliminate them from the study, as many scholars of the history of Iran are working with these documents to investigate student and social movements, the history of the left, and many other subjects. For the purposes of this book, I have referred to these documents very cautiously. The SAVAK documents referenced in this book are used to show either the Iranian state's concerns over the distribution of leftist materials in Iran or the relation between San'atizadeh and the court. Such policies and relations have been described in other sources as well. Another key consideration when examining documents was whether a specific record might have been selected and decontextualized by the authorities to defame certain groups or people in line with the official state historiography. The Muslim Student Followers of the Imam's Line has also published the US embassy's confiscated records in ten volumes, translated into Persian. Some of these translations are published along with a copy of the original document, and in several cases the original document by now has been declassified by the US Department of State.

(5) Memoirs and reflections on the FBP's Tehran Branch: There are a few memoirs by former staff of and persons affiliated with the Tehran Branch, which have discussed the organization, most notably the memoir of Abdulrahim Ja'fari, manager of Amīr Kabīr publishers, one of the most prestigious publishers of the time closely affiliated with the Tehran Branch. Branch staff who have reflected on their affiliation in articles and memoirs include Najaf Daryabandari (Tehran Branch editor-in-chief), Karim Emami (Tehran Branch editor-in-chief), Abdulhussain Azarang (editor, Tehran Branch), and Pirouz Kalantari (book designer, Tehran Branch). There are also several published interviews with the staff of the Tehran Branch, most notably those that Sirous Alinejad conducted with Homayun San'atizadeh, the first manager of the Tehran Branch, during whose management it developed to become the FBP's most successful branch. While Sirous Alinejad has not sought to critically engage with San'atizadeh's responses, still these interviews reveal San'atizadeh's detailed narrative of the establishment and development of the Tehran Branch. Alinejad has also conducted interviews with four other staff of the Tehran Branch, which provide us their account of the economical, administrative, and intellectual history of this office.

(6) Textbooks, translations, and journals sponsored or produced by the Tehran Branch: As mentioned above, during its operation over a quarter of a century, the FBP's Tehran Branch translated more than 800 books. The FBP also cooperated with Iran's Ministry of Education to establish the Educational Publications Center (EPC), the goal of which was the preparation, production, and distribution of wholesome, inexpensive supplementary readings for children, teenagers, and youth. It also intended to train teachers in education methods, all of which resulted in several school magazines under the name of *Payk*. These educational and supplementary magazines were at the time the only reading materials for children in the smaller towns and villages, with a distribution of 11,000,000 copies in 1971 according to the FBP's annual report. For this study, I have obtained 550 issues of these *Payk* magazines, published between 1963 and 1977. The section on these journals in Chapter 6 is based on a survey of this collection. Textual analysis of these journals, textbooks, and translations is crucial for a critical evaluation of the FBP's Tehran Branch, and the knowledge, which it produced and distributed for Iran's state-sponsored mass literacy program during these two decades.

This book is a study of the FBP and the knowledge that it produced and distributed during its twenty-five years of operation. I will ask: What were the social and political conditions that facilitated the establishment of the FBP? What were the cultural, educational, and political goals of the FBP, and how did these goals inform and shape the FBP's structure and policies? How did the FBP evolve in the course of its history, in terms of its scope and function? How did the FBP affect Iranian education and textbooks? Why was the FBP most "successful" in Iran, and what role did the Iranian state play in this "success"?

This book is structured chronologically, moving from a general history of the FBP to specifically address and analyze the FBP in Iran. After this introductory chapter, I will discuss the theoretical concepts of this study in Chapter 2. The FBP's history and legacy will then be discussed in the four following chapters. Chapters 3 and 4 will detail the FBP's international history. Chapter 3 will contextualize the origin and early development of the FBP in the international contestation between the United States and the Soviet Union during the Cold War. This chapter shows how the FBP's origins in the Cold War shaped its policies and structures. It further studies the logic behind the title listing for the FBP's Regular Translation Programs and points to the importance of the local participation of political, intellectual, and educational leaders. It also discusses the importance of rural and regional distribution for FBP objectives, and the challenges the FBP faced in developing mass distribution systems in the Middle East.

Chapter 4 presents a general history of the FBP in its years of operation on three continents. To this aim, this long and multifaceted history has been divided into four periods of time, beginning with the FBP's early years of operation (1952–6) and then chronologically tracing how it gradually moved away from its early Translation Programs toward Special and Educational Projects (1956–68). By the late 1960s, the FBP was facing structural and then later financial challenges, which pushed it to undergo restructuring; the FBP ended up reframing itself as an international educational development program (1968–75). This chapter ends with a discussion of the reasons for the FBP's decline and its final dissolving in 1977.

Chapters 5 and 6 aim to historicize and analyze the operations and achievements of the FBP's Tehran Branch during the course of its operation (1954–77), and detail its relations and affiliations with the Iranian state and Iran's Ministry of Education. Chapter 5 contextualizes the establishment of the Tehran Branch within the cultural and ideological contestation between the United States and the Soviet Union in Iran and historicizes the branch's legacy and achievements in its Regular Translation Programs.

The operations of the Tehran Branch of the FBP were not limited to the Regular Translation Programs. The Tehran Branch also conducted a variety of Special and Educational Projects. Notably, under contracts with the ministries of education in Iran and Afghanistan, it played a significant role in textbook production in these two countries. The history of the Tehran Branch's Special and Educational

Projects is studied in Chapter 6, followed by a discussion of the Tehran Branch's eventual demise in 1977. Chapter 7 presents a historical summary of the study and concludes the analysis of the FBP in a discussion of the relations between imperialism, state, and knowledge production.

Chapter 2

CULTURAL IMPERIALISM: WHY FRANKLIN BOOK
PROGRAMS MATTERS

In the last few years there has been a renewed interest in the theory of "cultural imperialism," after a few decades in which this theory had been pushed aside by the discourses of globalization, hybridity, and transculturalism (for instance, Salih, 2020; Boyd-Barrett, 2015). The rising interest in the historical study of the cultural Cold War also invites an exploration of the methods, policies, and social networks of US cultural imperialism. Through historicizing the FBP, we can investigate some of the measures, methods, policies, principles, and objectives of the United States in its cultural Cold War. Furthermore, studying this book program expands our understanding of the role of the state in assisting or resisting the cultural Cold War. It shows how in actual practice, to assert their domination of the "Third World," the United States needed to build relations, transfer technology, work regionally, and most importantly connect with the state, which, in some cases such as Iran, meant incorporating the state's particular monarchical ideology into certain publishing projects.

The term "cultural imperialism" dates back to the 1920s but gained an intellectual popularity via the works of various scholars of the 1960s, including Galtung. Since that time it has been widely employed by scholars in different disciplines (Schiller, 1976; Fejes, 1981; Said, 1994; Kraidy, 2005). The variance in this term's usage arises from the different articulations of the two concepts of "imperialism" and "culture" that have come together to constitute it (Tomlinson, 1991).

The concept of imperialism arose in the context of specific social relations and is also affected by the historical developments of these relations. The words "imperial" and "imperialist" have been in use respectively since the fourteenth and seventeenth centuries, but the word "imperialism" developed during the second half of the nineteenth century, especially after 1870. This is to say that "imperialism" should not be mistaken with or reduced to the older definitions/usages of the words "imperialist," meaning the adherent of an emperor, or "imperial," meaning of the supreme power. The word "imperialism" developed late in the nineteenth century in the context of the social relations of colonial trade and organized colonial rule. By the early twentieth century, this term took on a new connotation in the works of a number of authors, namely Hobson, Luxemburg, Bukharin, and Lenin. These authors in different ways articulated modern imperialism as a phenomenon related to a particular stage of the development of the capitalist system—that is, the rise of finance capital (Williams, 1983). All viewed the rise of imperialism as linked to the expansion of capitalism in Europe and the United States. According to their historical analysis, as a result of the expansion of capitalism, the machinery of production in developed states became increasingly in need of raw materials and also access to new markets that would buy the surplus commodities.

Yet there were quite important differences between Hobson and Lenin in terms of their thoughts on the relation between imperialism and capitalism. Hobson, in his book *Imperialism: A Study* (1902), conceptualized imperialism as a foreign policy and criticized it by arguing that the markets that this policy provides for the imperialist country are of the poorest kind of goods while simultaneously intensifying antagonism with industrialized nations, who are more reliable trading partners. Therefore, according to Hobson's theory, imperialist practices are not an essential function of capitalism. For Hobson, "[i]mperialism was a set of misguided state policies that needed to be, and indeed could be, rejected and reversed" (Saccarelli & Varadarajan, 2015, p. 35). This articulation suggests that capitalism can undertake national redistribution policies in order to avoid resorting to imperialist foreign policies. This is a reformist view, which argues that capitalism can correct and reform itself.

Lenin, however, took a revolutionary stand in theorizing the imperialism of his era. Lenin, in his influential article "Imperialism, the Highest Stage of Capitalism," argued that imperialism is the outcome of the merging of banks with the industrial cartels, resulting in finance capitalism. He wrote:

> Capitalism only became capitalist imperialism at a definite and very high stage of its development, when certain of its fundamental characteristics began to change into their opposites, when the features of the epoch of transition from capitalism to a higher social and economic system had taken shape and revealed themselves all along the line. Economically, the main thing in this process is the displacement of capitalist free competition by capitalist monopoly.
> (Lenin, 1962, p. 127)

In this study I employ imperialism with this latter connotation and as the latest stage of capitalism. Imperialism is different from previous stages of capitalism in terms of "[t]he predominance of monopolies in major industries, the formation of 'financial capital' through the merging of industrial and bank capital, the predominance of the export of capital, the formation of international monopolies that divide the world among themselves, and the scramble of imperialist powers to re-divide the world into 'spheres of influence'" (Mojab, 2011, p. 167). Therefore, in this conceptualization imperialism is not merely a set of foreign policies, but rather a set of social relations deeply embedded in contemporary capitalism and directly tied up with strategies of capitalist accumulation (McNally, 2005).

Historically, the end of the Second World War marks the initial growth and consolidation of imperialism as an international system. However, as with the initial growth of previous phases of capitalism, this consolidation was not at all a peaceful one; it was only achieved once 37 million people had been killed or injured, and four empires—the Austro-Hungarian, the Ottoman, the Russian, and the German—had tumbled (Saccarelli & Varadarajan, 2015).

Developments after the Second World War (the formation of the United Nations, the end of colonial rule, and the recognition of the right to self-determination) reformulated and restructured imperialism. Furthermore, the situation of the United States immediately after the war was unique in the history of imperialism, marking a dramatic shift. While prior to this period, the history of imperialism was a history of competition among a handful of states of rather proportional economic, political, and military power, now there was a state that was an unchallenged economic and military power (Saccarelli & Varadarajan, 2015). After the Second World War, the United States possessed almost half of the world's wealth, and it produced almost "half of the world's steel, cotton, rubber, and electrical energy." It also produced "60 per cent of all manufactured goods, 70 per cent of oil, and over 80 per cent of all automobiles" (Saccarelli & Varadarajan, 2015, p. 143). The only state power that soon started to confront it was the Soviet Union.

Post–Second World War, the Soviet Union, which had relinquished its initial internationalist and communist policy (Saccarelli & Varadarajan, 2015), evolved into an imperialist power dictating its own national benefits to the developing countries and even weakening proletarian movements in several cases. The Cold War US–Soviet confrontation was global and had many manifestations, including cultural battles. However, even though the US–Soviet confrontation was depicted very much as an ideological one by both sides, "the interest over strategic issues and resources" was the crucial drive for both (Khalidi, 2009, p. 5).

Let us now turn our attention to the "culture" in "cultural imperialism" and the ways in which the relation between these two has been theorized. "Culture" is also among the most contested and challenging concepts. Raymond Williams argues that this is partly because of the intricate historical development of the word in several European languages, but mainly because "it has now come to be used for important concepts in several distinct intellectual disciplines and in several distinct and incompatible systems of thought" (Williams, 1983, p. 87). Williams points to three broad categories of usage for the word "culture": (1) a general process of intellectual, spiritual, and aesthetic development; (2) a particular way of life, whether of people or communities; and (3) the works and practices of intellectual and artistic activity (Williams, 1983). In the discourse of "cultural imperialism," it is the second and third usages of culture that are dominant (Tomlinson, 1991).

In the last fifty years, a variety of theorizations of cultural imperialism have been suggested. Here, before discussing the Marxist conceptualization which I have used in this research, I will briefly discuss the limitations of the structuralist (e.g., Galtung) and post-structuralist (e.g., Tomlinson) theories. Galtung's structural theory of imperialism was articulated in the context of the social relations of the Cold War as experienced by the late 1960s (Galtung, 1971). Galtung's theory separated imperialism from capitalism, arguing that imperialism is a structural dominance and violence empowered by the harmony between the interests of the center within the center nations, and the center in the periphery. According to Galtung, cultural imperialism is one of the five types of imperialism. The other four types are economic, political, military, and communicative. These types are conceptualized as different dimensions of the same structural imperialism, in which cultural imperialism creates monopolized structures of scientific knowledge, creative activity, and learning (Milan, 2016). I contend that the structural theory not only divorces imperialism from capitalist social relations but also violently abstracts the dialectics of base and superstructure, which results in the detaching of culture from the spheres of the economy, the military, communication, and politics. Therefore, in not understanding imperialism as consisting of social relations, the structural theory is unable to shed light on the internal relations between these apparently separate types of imperialism and is unable to analyze the role of ideology and educational systems (as parts of the superstructure) in strengthening and sustaining the social relations of imperialism (Ganjavi, 2017).

Tomlinson's post-structural theory of cultural imperialism argues that imperialism ended in the 1960s and that we are now living in "globalization," which he describes as the "end of organized capitalism." "Globalization," writes Tomlinson, "suggests interconnection and interdependency of all global areas which happens in a far less purposeful way" than capitalism (Tomlinson, 1991, p. 175). He criticizes neo-Marxists for their limitations in mapping state–imperialism relations. He writes: "Neo-Marxists rightly wish to emphasize the enormous and globally integrated and integrative power of capitalism, but they face problems in 'mapping' this system on to the 'political existence' of the world as nation-states" (Tomlinson, 1991, p. 25). Tomlinson criticizes neo-Marxists for "the functional role" they attribute to cultural imperialism in the spread of capitalism as an economic system and a set of class relations. Tomlinson further stresses mediation and interpretation of cultural commodities by the receivers to counter this "functional" role.

However, while Tomlinson criticizes the neo-Marxists for not having a theory of the state, he does not offer such a theory himself—instead, by means of introducing a concept of globalization, his post-structural theory implies the end of both imperialism and state. Therefore, his theory of cultural imperialism dismisses the state's important role in preserving the imperialist social order and organizing educational and cultural policies. Moreover, while the emphasis this theory places on the interpretation of cultural commodities by the receivers assists us in understanding the process of cultural transmission (and in certain cases the process of daily resistance), this emphasis on individual interpretation fails to take into account all the social and structural relations of dominance, which form the social context in which individual interpretation takes place. The glorification of interpretation does not allow us to see the extensive role of private and public institutions, states, and mass media in knowledge production and knowledge dissemination. For instance, a mere focus on receivers' interpretations would provide a fragmented analysis for our purposes, as it fails to analyze the international role that the FBP played for more than two decades in knowledge production. The historical materialist theory draws our attention to discovering the process of consciousness in the everyday organization of learning, rather than placing a simple stress on an individualized process of interpretation.

In this book I employ a Marxist conceptualization of cultural imperialism, which is based on a dialectical understanding of the relation between social formation and ideas produced to sustain it. A Marxist approach examines who produces what for whom, and where the social forms of consciousness originate. In Marxism, culture is conceptualized as part of the superstructure and thus has a dialectically internal relation with the base. The superstructure consists of phenomena—such as the state, ideology, education, mass media, science, art, etc.—that are dialectically interrelated and historically determined by the base, and which in turn determine the base in a specific historical period. While many conceptualizations of culture conceal the central question of the relation between social formation and production of ideology, the dialectical conceptualization explores the dynamic of interrelation between the two rather than a mechanical separation of them. Therefore, the dialectical understanding of the relation between base and superstructure assists us to theorize the relation between ideology and imperialism. Following Bannerji (2015), by "ideology" I mean a form of thought, which mediates and textualizes the social relations of capitalism by means of masking their true essence. Ideology, in other words, produces justification for the ruling relations.

Marx's theory of ideology was first expressed in *The German Ideology*, written in 1846 in collaboration with Engels. According to Marx and Engels, the ruling ideas in every historical period reflect the ideas produced and distributed by the ruling class. When the capitalists rule as a class, they do this also in the realm of knowledge, "hence among other things rule also as thinkers, as producers of ideas, and regulate the production and distribution of the ideas of their age: thus their ideas are the ruling ideas of the epoch" (Marx & Engels, 1998, p. 67). Marx defines ideology as a distorted consciousness produced under capitalist social relations, a consciousness that serves to mask the essence of capitalist relations. Ideology explains reality in a fragmented and partial way. It inverts "the historically specific/dialectical contradiction of capitalism" (Allman, 2007, p. 77). Ideology veils the relation between ruling class and ruling ideas. Ideology violently abstracts, decontextualizes, and separates ideas from their social origins. In other words, it also separates ruling ideas from the ruling class. Ideology further produces justifications for ruling relations. It mediates and textualizes the social relations of capitalism by means of masking their true essence.

Marxist feminists such as Smith, Bannerji, Mojab, and Carpenter have employed Marx's critique of ideology in their scholarship, to expand on the role that ruling patriarchal and racial ideas have in mediating and textualizing the ruling relations of capitalism (Smith, 1987; Bannerji, 2003; Bannerji, 2015; Carpenter & Mojab, 2017). Following Marx and Engels's theorization, Smith's institutional ethnography (IE) is an approach to inquiry, which begins in the material processes of life. She proposes that a social inquiry should "begin with individuals and their actual experiences and practice in relation to others" (Carpenter & Mojab, 2017, p. 99). An important component of this study is how Smith analyzes discourses and texts in institutional ethnography. In addition to the common Foucauldian understanding of discourse, which is useful in an analysis of the forms of power embedded in language and texts, Smith also emphasizes the role that discourse and texts play in mediating social relations. Therefore, for Smith discourse is not only a body of knowledge outside individuals, but "a particular arrangement of social relations in which people are active participants" (Carpenter & Mojab, 2017, p. 101). In an organization, this means that discourses and texts act to "coordinate" individuals' activities and also to "organize" the relations "between individuals and knowledge." While Smith's theorization is intended for institutional ethnography, such a historical materialist understanding of texts and discourses is quite helpful for an archival study of an organization and its role in knowledge production. The archives of an organization make the discourse and ruling relations in that organization visible. Institutional and organizational texts further help to see the ways in which individuals are tied to certain social relations. In other words, such texts work "as organizer and coordinator of social relations" (Carpenter & Mojab, 2017, p. 102).

There are two other important analytical aspects of a Marxist conceptualization of cultural imperialism. Firstly, it enables us to historicize schooling and developments in the educational systems within the social relations of imperialism. Secondly, it allows us to theorize the relations between the state, education, and imperialism. Historically, the spread of schooling was carried out in the context of imperialism, colonialism, and nation-state building. Schooling in its present form and purpose cannot be separated from this context, neither in industrialized countries nor in the Third World. Western formal education came to many countries as part of imperialist domination (Carnoy, 1974, p. 3).

The main institution linked to education is the state. Thus, having a theory that articulates this relationship is fundamental for theorizing the relation between education and imperialism. This examination sheds light on the important relation between the structure of social power and education (Mojab, 1991). Liberal educational theory depicts the state as an institution autonomous from class structure, a neutral institution that enhances and reflects the common good or general interest of all the citizens. Marxist educational theory, on the other hand, contends that states in capitalist societies are fundamentally class-based, and "educational systems are structured in such a way as to perpetuate state power and the economic system on which it is based" (Mojab, 1991, p. 3).

The growing interest of states in enhancing literacy programs is the result of the development of capitalism and its need for further division of labor. The development of literacy programs in capitalist societies is an attempt to internalize capitalist social relations. The development of capitalism is the precondition for and also the result of division of labor. In this process, education plays a crucial role in both the stabilization of the social formation and the process of capital accumulation.

Historical investigation should substantiate and inform the dialectical material conceptualization of the relations between imperialism, the state, and education. The history of the FBP assists us in looking at these relations during the Cold War.

Chapter 3

FRANKLIN BOOK PROGRAMS: TRANSLATION, PUBLICATIONS, AND BOOK DISTRIBUTION DURING THE COLD WAR

The mobilization of culture through the expansion of book publishing, libraries, and reading was an essential part of the Second World War (1939–45). The US government, publishers, librarians, and intellectuals used books to fight against fascism. In the aftermath of the Second World War, and with the polarization of the world between the capitalist bloc under US leadership and the communist bloc, the mobilization of bourgeois knowledge continued as part of US cultural diplomacy in the Cold War era (Laugesen, 2012). As the threat of the Soviet Union and the ideology of communism became the center of this US cultural diplomacy, a newly established organization called the United States Information Agency (USIA) inherited book programs established by the United States during the Second World War. By the early 1950s, the USIA was in charge of over two million volumes of books in about 196 information libraries in 64 countries (Laugesen, 2012, p. 129).[1]

For decades scholars have mostly focused on economic, political, and military aspects of US Cold War foreign policy. Since the 1990s, however, several studies have turned toward culture and discussed the Cold War in terms of the dimensions of cultural diplomacy and cultural exchange policies. Walter L. Hixson's *Parting the Curtain: Propaganda, Culture and the Cold War, 1945–1961* (1997), Liping Bu's *Making the World Like Us: Education, Cultural Expansion, and the American Century* (2004), and Victor Rosenberg's *Soviet–American Relations, 1953–1960: Diplomacy and Cultural Exchange during the Eisenhower Presidency* (2005) have studied the subversive use of cultural exchange programs by the United States to undermine the Soviet Union and to fight communism.

Some scholarship has studied the political and ideological reasoning behind specific artistic tours, exhibitions, and artistic mediums during the Cold War. Marilyn S. Kushner (2002) shows how the American National Exhibition in Moscow in 1959 was planned and used by the United States to depict itself as devoid of racial discrimination and inequality. Naima Prevots (1998) focuses on the role of dance as part of the US ideological and cultural competition against the Soviet Union. Andrew J. Falk (2010) investigates the developments in the socio-cultural role of Hollywood and US television during the Cold War and the transformative restructurings each went through to align with US ideological objectives. Greg Barnhisel (2015) discusses how the United States employed modernist art and literature in its cultural Cold War to construct an intellectual image of the United States as having the ability to lead progressive aesthetics.

The role of sport and especially the Olympics in US–Soviet cultural diplomacy is studied by Toby C. Rider (2016). Rider's study not only details the relation between US sport and the US state during the Cold War but also reveals how the clandestine establishment of a state–private network was a crucial aspect of US cultural diplomacy. In these state–private networks, while private networks were funded primarily by the state, and sometimes through the Central Intelligence Agency (CIA), their relations had to remain hidden to give the impression that the US public was independent of the US state in their disdain for communism (Rider, 2016).[2]

Clearly, the United States was not the only side in this ideological battle that mobilized culture for its international policy. The study of the Soviet side of the cultural Cold War dates back to Frederick C. Barghoorn's *The Soviet Cultural Offensive: The Role of Cultural Diplomacy in Soviet Foreign Policy* (1960) and Baruch A. Hazan's *Soviet Propaganda: A Case Study of the Middle East Conflict* (1976). There has been a rise of interest in the subject in recent years. Cadra Peterson McDaniel (2015) specifically attends to the role of the arts as a propaganda tool in Soviet foreign policy. McDaniel's study historicizes and investigates the Bolshoi's American tour, the ballet's music and choreography, to examine the Soviet Union's use of ballet as an instrumental weapon in spreading communist ideology. In addition to McDaniel, Christina Ezrahi (2012) has focused on the role of dance in Soviet cultural diplomacy.[3]

In a conversation with the above scholarship, the focus of the present volume is on the role that books, publishers, libraries, and the production of educational texts played as an essential aspect of the US ideological battle during the Cold War. Through investigating the FBP, which had offices in seventeen developing countries as well as conducting surveys and operations in several more, this study supplements the increasing literature that discusses the US network of ideological operations in Western Europe. As recent scholarship has shown, the centerpiece of the US covert cultural campaign in Western Europe was the Congress for Cultural Freedom (CCF, 1950–67).

Frances Stonor Saunders, in her groundbreaking investigation into the US secret cultural propaganda programs in Western Europe, *Who Paid the Piper? The CIA and the Cultural Cold War* (2000), studies the CCF, which was managed by the CIA.[4] The CCF was a transnational organization of intellectuals founded in the name of freedom of expression. The CCF's mission was to direct the intelligentsia of Western Europe away from its interest in Marxism and communism and toward a more "accommodating" view of the "American Way." Its inaugural conference was held in West Berlin on June 26, 1950 (Scott-Smith & Lerg, 2017). The conference intended to organize opinion in Western society in favor of the capitalist path and soon led to the establishment of a permanent organization in Paris. Initially the CCF was directed toward Western Europe. However, by the late 1950s, it had extended its reach into Africa, the Middle East,[5] and the Asia-Pacific region. The CCF had offices in thirty-five countries, published over twenty magazines, held international conferences, and awarded prizes to artists and musicians (Stonor Saunders, 2000).[6]

The FBP can be seen as comparable to the CCF in its missions and objectives. However, while their missions were rather similar, their primary areas of operation, structures, and networks of people involved were substantially different. In terms of area of operation, the FBP was mainly directed toward the Middle East. In this sense, a study of the FBP complements the few studies of the cultural Cold War in the Middle East, most notably Vaughan's *Failure of American and British Propaganda in the Arab Middle East, 1945–1957: Unconquerable Minds* (2005). Vaughan discusses British and US propaganda during the Cold War in the Arab countries of the Middle East, between 1945 and 1957. He has studied the history of the "psychological dimension" of US foreign policy toward the Middle East and historicized the operation of the USIA in this region. His extensive archival investigation into official Western government documents shows the ties between British and US "psychological strategies" and their policy making around their national interests in the Middle East (Vaughan, 2005, p. 4). However, while Vaughan in a few short instances refers to the FBP's early history, he does not undergo a detailed study of the FBP. Also, Vaughan's research is focused on the Arab countries of the Middle East and during a time period that ends in 1957.

In sum, in the past few years the scholarship on the Cold War has explored this historical period in its ideological manifestations and contestations. However, most of the research is on US–Western Europe cultural relations, and in the case of a few explorations of US–Middle East relations, the FBP has remained understudied.

Origins, Policies, and Structure

The Franklin Publications, Inc.,[7] a non-profit membership corporation, was founded in June 1952 under the laws of New York State.[8] The organization's name was an allusion to Benjamin Franklin (1706–90) as the first successful American publisher-printer.[9] The FBP board of directors consisted of US book publishers, librarians, scholars, scientists, and corporate representatives. According to the FBP's charter, its board had twenty-five members, fifteen of whom had to be book publishers and ten of whom had to be non-publisher representatives of the "public interest."

The US Department of State assisted the FBP financially with a seed grant of $500,000 when it was established in June 1952. The FBP had advised the Department of State that it would also seek financial support from foundations and other non-government sources to carry on a broader program of book publishing and distribution. However, its operations remained "in general accord" with the department's objectives.[10]

On July 22, 1952, the Department of State sent a classified letter for the information of the officers in charge, in particular the public affairs officers at each of the posts in Amman, Ankara, Baghdad, Cairo, Damascus, Tehran, and Tripoli. The letter informed the public affairs officers of the FBP's establishment and that the FBP would seek their advice concerning its plans for operations and other details. The Department of State requested that public affairs officers at each of the aforementioned posts send written reports back to the department on the following issues: (1) a brief description of the nature, structure, and extent of the book trade in the country, including any generalization about special interest in Soviet-sponsored books; (2) a short description of the educational structure of the country, on its literacy and languages of instruction; (3) a statement about any laws that would affect the FBP's operations; (4) suggestions of the kinds of books that the officers thought would be most readily accepted by the people of the country; and (5) commentary on the ways "anti-American feelings" might express themselves around such a program—that is, whether there might be any "booksellers' boycott." The Department of State later transmitted the public affairs officers' responses to the FBP. This letter also emphasized that "the Department's role in the undertaking outlined is not to be mentioned outside the missions or consulates."[11]

A few months later, on October 30, 1952, the Department of State notified its missions that three members of the FBP's executive board were to soon leave for the Middle East. These members were Datus C. Smith, Jr., first president of the FBP, who was on leave from his position as the director of Princeton University Press; Malcolm Johnson, chairman of the FBP board and vice-president of Van Nostrand Company, Inc.; and Francis St. John, director of the Brooklyn Public Library.[12] The US missions were informed that although the FBP operated to "a large extent" with funds appropriated by the department, its members had to be treated as "private businessmen," which meant that there had to be no official welcome at the airport or any hotel reservations made by the embassy officers. However, soon after their arrival, the FBP's executive board members called on the US public affairs officers and sought their help in arranging a schedule of people to be interviewed as possible local managers and advisors (and also on other details) and stated they would keep the officers informed of the substance of all their interviews. The department requested full cooperation on the part of the missions' staff.[13] The three FBP members had all been completely cleared by the Department of State for all classified material, including Top Secret.[14] These processes were planned so that, with the covert advice and assistance of the US public affairs officers in each of the countries concerned, the FBP's executive board members could select the local managers and advisors for the establishment of the FBP's local offices.

The International Information Administration (IIA) was established in January 1952 with the purpose of conducting the US Department of State's international information and educational exchange programs.[15] The IIA provided the FBP with a document entitled "Guidance for Franklin Publications." On October 27, 1952, Dan Lacy, director of the ICS,[16] addressed Datus C. Smith, the first president of the

FBP, and provided "guidance" in the FBP's publication and distribution of works in Arabic using funds granted by the Department of State.[17] This letter first discussed the "psychological and ideological problems" faced by the United States in the Arab area of the Middle East and asserted:

> The primarily negative reaction against the West with which we need to deal therefore revolves around the belief that the West has over a long period sought to exploit the people and the resources of the Arab world for its purposes, that this exploitation has involved the deliberate continuation of a quasi-colonial political status [...] To this set of attitudes has been added a hostility arising from religious sources—perhaps no longer primarily a zealous detestation of the infidel but rather resentment of the contempt or indifference with which the West is thought to view Islam and Islamic civilization; coupled with a conservative aversion to what are thought to be the materialism, godlessness, and immorality of Western and particularly American life.
> (NSA, "Guidance for Franklin Publications," 1952)

The letter noted that the conviction that the West was prepared to "use" the Arab world for its own ends was held because twice in a generation the Arab area in the Middle East had been the theater of hostilities between Western powers, in which Arabs felt they had no stakes. The support of Israel was also highlighted in this letter as more evidence in the mind of the Arabs that American leadership was ready to sacrifice vital Arab interests for its own advantage. The director of ICS argued, "In contrast, though most Arabs dislike Russia and detest Communism, they are inclined to dismiss the Soviet threat as one remote and unfamiliar in comparison with what they hold to be the known and present evils of Western control."[18]

This "Guidance for Franklin Publications" next pointed to economic and political instability as the internal factors complicating the above-mentioned international considerations in the Middle Eastern countries. It asserted, "It is not, of course, our responsibility to deal with this economic situation directly, but insofar as its causes and consequences are psychological, they lie within our sphere." It concluded its socio-political introduction to the Middle East by saying that US and Western interests should more immediately fear the "negative" collapse of economic and political order in the Middle East than the "positive" success of communist doctrine. Therefore, while an "awareness" of the dangers of Soviet communism was considered a desirable psychological goal,

> an even more urgent psychological objective is the establishment of such attitudes toward the West and toward the internal problems of the area as may permit a close collaboration between the West and the Arab area in the strengthening the economy of the latter, in aiding it toward the achievement of political stability, and in establishing a joint defense of the area.[19]

In the face of the above-mentioned objectives, not only was the content of the books published by the FBP important, but also "the character and the tone" of its operations. Therefore, the FBP in its local contracts and affiliations had to carefully attend to establishing reciprocal "good faith" in its broadest sense. In order to do so, the FBP had to avoid the kind of association with US political and information activities that would aggravate suspicion as to its motives. While the FBP had to admit to the contributions that it had received from the Department of State, it had to "picture" them as similar to the state's aid to the Institute for International Education (IIE),[20] as "a desire" by the US government to forward "a worthy effort at international understanding."[21]

Although the FBP had to avoid a certain degree of association with the US embassies, which would have tended to establish it in the eyes of the developing countries as a mere "tool" of the Department of State, it necessarily had to maintain "a close liaison" with public affairs officers in the missions concerned. The FBP had to seek the advice of public affairs officers on the current "psychological" problems in the country where their mission was situated and request information about the local nationals with whom the FBP would be dealing. The IIA asserted: "No publications should be produced or distributed in a country against the wishes of the public affairs officer for that area." Public affairs officers at most major posts, especially in Cairo, had already made contracts with local publishers for the production of desired translations. These and other contracts and commitments were to be transferred to the FBP. The public affairs officers, then, had to limit their publication channels to only those that would call "undesirable attention" to the FBP's association with the department.[22]

The IIA asked the FBP to pursue the establishment of a close working relationship with the "effective foci of opinion formulation and dissemination" in the regions concerned, such as ministries of education and universities—as such relationships could open the way to returns "incomparably more important" to the United States than any operation that would incur the resentment and distrust of these institutions.[23] Also, close cooperation with and utilization of local publishers, printers, and distributers were desirable as a means of assuring the FBP's goodwill and avoiding the resentment or suspicion that it was an instrument of competitive commercial intrusion.

One of the principal reasons for the establishment of the FBP, as viewed by the Department of State and the IIA, was the inadequacy of existing local publishing, manufacturing, and distributing facilities. Therefore, while it was highly desirable for the FBP to make the maximum possible use of local publishing, manufacturing, and distributing facilities in order to avoid commercial competition, the FBP's operations also had to enlarge and improve existing publishing channels in the country concerned. This could be accomplished by advancing working capital to the local publishers with the prior approval of the department and with the provision of equipment and technical assistance. New channels of regional distribution and mass distribution had also to be actively sought and developed.[24]

The structure, audience, policy, and content of the FBP, therefore, were formed so that it could move toward the operational aims that the department was seeking. There were three main structural rules of the organization. First, the operating offices of the FBP had to be staffed entirely by local nationals, with no resident

Americans. Second, the local manager of the FBP chose the books to be translated; however, the choice had to be from a list of books the FBP offered to them. Third, the FBP was not to act as a publisher. It had to prepare the book, translate and edit the final manuscript, and then sell it to a local publisher to publish it; the local publisher was required to pay a royalty.[25]

This IIA guidance further expanded on the issue of the audience for whom the FBP had to envision publishing. The intended audience was a broad one that included college and university students, the bureaucrats generally, government officials and employees, and the "conservative" intellectual community with a traditional Muslim education. The types of publications that the FBP had to concentrate on were textbooks; reference works with a political, social, and economic content; and trade books in an inexpensive format. For all these types of books, three possible levels of audience had to be aimed at: first, the university student and middle-level government officials; second, the high-school-educated level; and third, the juvenile level.[26]

The IIA further elaborated on the policies and categories, which had to govern the content of the FBP books offered to the local managers. Several types of books were prioritized—that is, works aimed at making Westerners and particularly Americans more familiar and understandable. Simple novels and simple poetry became good fits for this purpose. Emphasis had to be given to the egalitarianism of American life, to family stability, and to its moral, idealistic, and cultural qualities. A second category was aimed at emphasizing the specifically liberal, democratic, and humane aspects of US government and economic order. A third had to emphasize "the independence of American economic development from imperialism."[27]

IIA considered the question of whether the FBP could sponsor technical and scientific publications as a difficult one. It was not considered appropriate to use IIA funds for this sort of publication unless it could carry a "psychological" purpose, which meant that such sponsorship could affect "the attitudes on public issues of the people of the area." For these kinds of technical and scientific publications, the FBP had to consult very closely with the US Point Four mission in the field. Although spending a large amount of IIA funds on such publications was not desirable, if the countries concerned were to co-fund such projects, the FBP was encouraged to pursue collaboration. The publication of suitable writings by local authors and publications from other countries, to the extent that they would serve the above objectives, was also encouraged.[28]

One of the first collaborations between the FBP and the IIA took place in early February 1953, when the FBP offered to pay for the printing in Arabic of conference papers that were going to be presented at the Colloquium on Islamic Culture, which was sponsored by the IIA, to be held in September 1953 for American and foreign Muslim scholars.[29] Princeton University organized and administered this conference.[30] The Colloquium on Islamic Culture was to have the "impression" of an exercise in pure learning. However, the IIA financed and assisted it with $25,000, as it considered the organization of such conferences on Islam as an important "psychological approach" to the short- and long-term political objectives of the

United States in the "Moslem area." US government officials were also seeing a US role in guiding Islam's "revitalization and evolution."[31]

As discussed above, the first guiding instruction for the FBP came from the IIA. However, within a few months, the draft of "Memorandum for the Psychological Strategy Board" on the subject of the US "Doctrinal Program," dated May 5, 1953, clarified and established in an official, systematic, and comprehensive manner the "psychological and ideological interests" of the United States, in which the FBP was specifically referred to as pursuing this "Doctrinal Program." This memorandum further reveals the importance of the commercial distribution of books and the development of markets for US books, as well as the flexibility and minimum control over the production of materials, which the Psychological Strategy Board (PSB) suggested for practical reasons.

The PSB had been established by Presidential Directive on April 4, 1951. Its objective was to "authorize and provide for the more effective planning, co-ordination, and conduct within the framework of approved national policies, of psychological operations."[32] The "Memorandum for the Psychological Strategy Board" was prepared and unanimously approved by a PSB panel, established by the board at its fifteenth meeting on September 11, 1952, to study the problem of "doctrinal warfare" specifically "as directed against Soviet doctrine and to make recommendation for U.S. action."[33] To justify the necessity of a systematic and strategic Doctrinal Program, the memorandum pointed to the pattern of previous "national expansions"—the tripartite of rifle, plough, and Bible—to point out that the Soviet Union had already recognized that progress toward world domination requires equal emphasis on three basic factors—namely the military, the economic, and the ideological. The memorandum noted that the United States had already greatly strengthened the first two but had failed to do the same for the "ideological" basis for world domination.[34]

This memorandum argued that the US Doctrinal Program was "a belated effort—35 years late—to meet the Soviet influences in the doctrinal field."[35] The death of Stalin in March of 1953, according to this memorandum, had made it a "most appropriate" time for the United States to undertake a doctrinal program with "clarity, determination and energy." This memorandum emphasized that "an aggressive doctrinal program" cannot increase the threat of war.

The Doctrinal Program sought to create confusion, doubt, and loss of confidence in the accepted thought patterns of convinced communists and people under communist influence; to stimulate intellectual curiosity on political, scientific, and economic subjects; and to weaken objectively the intellectual appeal of neutralism and "predispose" its adherents toward the West.[36]

According to this memorandum, detailed government control over the production of "overt doctrinal material" was considered "repressive to creative thought." Therefore, a flexible and minimal control over the production of materials was suggested. This Doctrinal Program was not to "propagandize" the American people, but it had to be "a practical effort" to develop materials, which would be "acceptable to the world market" and which, "in their entirety, or with minor modification," could be widely distributed with an expectation of their doctrinal impact.[37]

The memorandum gave further details on the content, range, and producers of the ideas that had to be disseminated: new and stimulating ideas, even "contradictory ones," were described as desired. The doctrinal productions were not to be limited to political and philosophical analysis but were to encompass "all fields of intellectual and cultural interests." The Doctrinal Program was also not to be confined to the usage of American materials. Foreign production, if consistent with the doctrinal objectives, could be fostered, promoted, and distributed. For these non-American materials, "the acceptability to Western philosophy of life" was highlighted as the criteria of selection. The principal target audience of the Doctrinal Program was a "developed, articulate mind," as the PSB panel assumed that such an intellectual elite carries a weight and influence in forming, or predisposing, the attitudes of the opinion-making leaders in an area.[38]

The memorandum then pointed to the participating departments and agencies that were included in implementing these doctrinal plans. Among them was the Department of State, which, beside other initiatives, had to increase Voice of America's doctrinal inclusions, extensively increase book programs such as the FBP and Arlington Press, promote American publications through United States Information Service (USIS) libraries, and use its cultural and commercial attachés and mission chiefs to foster increased markets for American publications. The Department of State further had to attempt at all means to increase the distribution of American books. The CIA was also responsible for giving high and continuing priority to all activities supporting this Doctrinal Program.

The second proposal attached to the "Memorandum for the Psychological Strategy Board" specifically discussed the necessity of increasing the commercial distribution of American books. The proposal pointed out that almost everywhere, radio and television were novelties, and books were by far the most powerful means of influencing attitudes. Describing a book as "a window to the national soul," the proposal argued that most American publishers had been "unconcerned with the foreign market" and that until the time of this memorandum (i.e., 1953), few American books had been extensively distributed abroad through commercial channels.

To emphasize the necessity of commercial distribution of US books, the proposal reported on the achievements of the communists' book circulation policies and practices and argued that "the technique of the Communists" had not been to freely distribute their propaganda books but to "subsidize" the circulation of their books through the regular commercial trade of a given country. The proposal further observed that, in employing this "technique," the best-selling book in the world in recent years, with the possible exception of the Bible, had been the *Short History of the Communist Party of the Soviet Union*, with a circulation of more than 41,000,000 copies.[39] To illustrate the weakness on the part of the United States, the proposal pointed out that a reply to the *Short History* called *A Century of Conflict: Communist Techniques of World Revolution* (1953), written by Stefan T. Possony, had sold no more than 6,000 copies throughout the world.[40]

According to this proposal, the high price of American books compared to the price range in overseas markets, the lack of US distributing agents, the lack of overseas promotional activities, and currency exchange problems were the reasons behind the lack of a commercial distribution of American books that was capable of competing with the circulation of the communists' books. Commercial distribution was further recognized as better than "give-away" practices, both for financial reasons and because it would ensure greater and more permanent reader interest. The proposal stated: "Foreigners habituated to buying and reading American books cannot help but better understand America and the American way of life."[41]

Not only was the FBP included as one of the participating departments and agencies in implementing the PSB's doctrinal plans, its arrangement in working with the local publishers and developing commercial exchange of the books developed completely in line with the second proposal attached to this memorandum. The FBP made such strong business arrangements with local publishers that the latter's financial stake in a book remained substantially higher than the FBP's. This policy was aimed at ensuring a "continuing interest in the book on the part of the publisher."[42] This is to say that the FBP paid for translation rights, the cost of editing, and the cost of translation; the local publisher was then asked to pay for printing, paper, binding, and advertising costs. Under most of the contracts, the FBP received a royalty of 10 percent of the retail price of the book. The books were sold at prices within the range of locally produced books—that is, substantially below US prices at home.

Categories of Title Listing and Process of Title Selection

In August 1954, the FBP set out twenty-nine categories in which it intended to publish books and provided a brief explanation of each. This list was later closely followed by the book listings. This document clarifies the importance that the technique referred to as "local redaction" had for several of these categories. "Local redaction" means that a local scholar or writer—that is, "people of sophistication in the particular field but also with literary skill and a popular following"—should be chosen to "write a new book based on one or more" American works. This "technique" was used in cases in which a "simple redaction" of a book by a well-known popular writer would put the content at the disposal of a far larger reading public.[43]

The categories of book aimed at by the FBP were of several different types:

Encyclopedias and dictionaries: One of the goals of the FBP was to produce a one-volume general-knowledge encyclopedia for young people. The *Columbia-Viking Desk Encyclopedia* was chosen for this category, and Arabic, Urdu, Indonesian, Bengali, and Persian editions of it were published. In most of these languages, this FBP-sponsored volume was the first modern encyclopedia ever published.

Biographies and popular presentation of basic scholarships: While the need for simple biographies was suggested, it was also observed: "[s]traight translation is not as valuable as new books, written by local writers on the basis of existing

[American] literature but in terms that would be meaningful and interesting to local readers." The report pointed to Abbas Mahmoud al-Akkad's biography of Benjamin Franklin as an experiment in this line by the Cairo Branch. The technique of local redaction was also suggested for the books in the category of "popular presentations of basic scholarship." The FBP observed that a "realistic view of the world and of the particular country's place in it is most effective rather than tracts denouncing Communism in answering to the Soviet menace."[44]

Books on administration, business, and management: The FBP sought to translate texts in the field of public administration, as in almost every newly "independent" country the need for "training bureaucrats" was felt. In an Orientalist articulation, the FBP argued that the very concept of business was regarded as "eccentric" by Muslims. Therefore, it aimed to translate business education books "toward the objective of putting to useful work some of the thousands of Arabs and Asians with pretensions of higher education but no ability to do anything of any use to themselves or the world." The FBP also noted that publications in the field of personnel management were especially important for the two categories of "foremen" and "labor leaders."[45]

Scientific books: In this category, the FBP planned to publish books on health, intended for groups such as social workers, nurses, teachers, and minor government officials; nursing education in local languages; and books on agriculture, intended for students in agricultural schools, professional agricultural workers, government officials, and literate landlords. The FBP further intended to answer the demand for materials from the schools of social work that were developing in most countries of the Middle East and Asia.

Children's books and juvenile literature: In line with other US Department of State Cold War international cultural programs, the FBP also intended to target young people, as possible future leaders, through print.[46]

Another type of book that the FBP planned to publish was related to teacher training, the newly literate, and adult education. The need for teacher-training texts was widely felt throughout Asia; however, the FBP had recognized that its sponsorship of advanced works for teacher training was only feasible if the publishing project was sponsored by a local ministry of education that would offer assurance to FBP that the books would be distributed and used once published. This category was mainly pursued in the late 1950s with the rise of mass literacy programs in Asia and the Middle East. The FBP further intended to publish books for the newly literate, of whom there were enormous numbers in every Asian country as a result of government-sponsored literacy campaigns. Another FBP plan was to publish books for adult education, which presupposed a low level of literacy and not a large general knowledge.

There were two categories around which the FBP had serious questions and considerations: textbooks and military aid. For several reasons—such as the question of a "foreigner's competence for writing textbooks, resentment as a result of the local pride, and the possibility of fanatical xenophobia"—the FBP contended that it should not write textbooks unless under "the most exceptional circumstances."⁴⁷ However, it asserted that books for supplementary reading or for placement in school libraries would not entail the same "risk." To fulfill this category, cooperation with the ministry of education in each country had to be sought.⁴⁸

In the early years, the FBP also seriously considered whether it was a proper vehicle for publishing on military subjects, and the FBP rarely followed up on enlisting books in this category; however, in several cases the local branches invited military generals to translate or write introductions to the sponsored books. By the end of the 1950s, the FBP became "especially interested" in book purchases for army reading, as it considered the military as representing both an "elite" and a force for "political stability."⁴⁹ Consequently, the FBP undertook publication of supplementary readings for use in the army in a few of its local offices.⁵⁰

On January 9, 1957, the FBP reported that in "actual practice" its policies for title selection in its first five years of operation had resulted in a choice of books, which fell into the following categories:

1. Books of direct ideological value, as with F.L. Allen's *The Big Change: America Transforms Itself, 1900–1950* (1952); D.C. Coyle's *The United States Political System and How It Works* (1957); and S. Clough's *The American Way: The Economic Basis of Our Civilization* (1953).
2. Books providing the intellectual basis for anti-communism, as in G.H. Sabine's *A History of Political Theory* (1937) or E. Staley's *The Future of Underdeveloped Countries: Political Implications of Development* (1954).
3. Books conveying US ideas and ideals, especially as regards democracy, family life, education, and social equality—such as S.K. Bolton's *Lives of Poor Boys Who Became Famous* (1885) and E.R. Murrow's *This I Believe: Selections from the 1950s Radio Series* (1953).
4. Books showing impressive American contributions to culture, especially in relation to the areas where the FBP was operating, as with P.K. Hitti's *History of the Arabs* (1937) or A.U. Pope's *Masterpieces of Persian Art* (1945).
5. Some books without specific FBP content at all, but promoted with such force by some important person that the FBP as a whole would benefit from publication—such as B. Spock's *The Common Sense Book of Baby and Child Care* (1946), which in Iran was translated by the Shah's twin sister Ashraf Pahlavi.

This memorandum further expanded on the process of title selection and explained that while local advisors were permitted to take part in title selection for the purposes of "gaining their support" (i.e., the support of the local leaders), the FBP had a veto power, as its board of directors had to approve the budget of expenditures; therefore, the New York office retained technical veto power over title selection.⁵¹ According to this memorandum, "[t]he fact that the books do not contain short-run political propaganda, and that they appear with the endorsement of distinguished local leaders, assures them of a reception they could never have otherwise."⁵²

As the next chapter details, less than five years into its establishment, the FBP had developed to become an influential cultural organization with unprecedented achievements in transferring US books and culture to the Middle East. The main reasons for its effectiveness were largely the above-described sophisticated policies, procedures, and principles that the FBP followed in its title selection process and its relations with the local offices. In the heat of the Cold War, the question of "what kind of books" was "the most important of all," and the FBP had resolved this question through a combination of FBP bibliographical listings and selection from those listings by local advisors in the various countries. The FBP knew that any attempt by an American NGO or publisher to make up a list of hard-hitting pro-US or anti-communist books would have been immediately self-defeating, because "such books would be denied local endorsement by civic leaders or the willing participation of local publishers and booksellers."[53] Furthermore, such books would have labeled FBP as a propaganda tool.

The FBP's title selection policies and procedures resulted in the sponsorship of books that in practice followed the general aims of US doctrinal warfare during the Cold War. By pursuing the policy of letting locals select their final book based on the bibliographical information provided to them by the FBP, a list of books was chosen of which substantial numbers were "making precisely the points which an American would wish to have made."[54] The local advisors were usually unfamiliar with US books and were only able to suggest general categories. Thus, it was the FBP's headquarters that had to suggest specific book titles with the help of selected American specialists in different fields. The local advisors then would choose from this list those that they found desirable. Labeling this procedure as an attempt to avoid "ideological paternalism," the FBP noted that "it has thus frequently happened that, without dictatorship or even pressure from America, but on purely local initiative in the foreign country itself, some of the most important volumes, from America's own point of view," gained their place on the FBP list.[55] In another framing of the same argument, the FBP advised: "It should be stated here that American-compiled lists of anti-communist books, though presenting exactly the ideas we would like to see flourish, would in most cases make no headway abroad; but that books selected by the foreigners themselves will often contain those same ideas but also will reach the reading public."[56]

The FBP's principle of working with local publishers was also an important factor behind its early success because, devoid of commercial competition, this collaboration resulted in the publishers having the private-enterprise stimulus of gains from books that would sell. The other principle that resulted in success was the FBP's decision to use local nationals rather than Americans to staff its field offices. This policy, as the FBP reflected, was very important in persuading the most distinguished civic and educational leaders of the countries concerned to contribute to the FBP or to endorse it. This policy also resulted in many breakthroughs for the FBP, as the creativity and energy of the local managers assisted it in developing its projects in ways it would not have been able to do otherwise. This was especially true in the ways local managers found new methods of distributing the books, such as the efforts that Homayun Sanʿatizadeh made to sell Persian-sponsored books to Afghanistan's Ministry of Education.[57]

Chapter 4

HISTORY AND INTERNATIONAL EVOLUTION OF THE FRANKLIN BOOK PROGRAMS (1952-77)

Historicizing the operations and developments of a program that had a wide range of activities in numerous countries for a period of twenty-five years is an entire area of study, rather than something achievable in one book. Therefore, as I mentioned in Chapter 1, this exploration focuses primarily on the role of the FBP on the print publishing, textbook writing, and educational policies of the Middle East, with specific attention to Iran. Nonetheless, it is necessary to give a historical sketch of the FBP's functions in its entirety. This chapter is a modest attempt at this goal, providing some details on the developments of the FBP and its local offices.

Through a detailed study of the archives of the FBP, and paying attention to the FBP's changing focus and developments in its policies, finance, and structure, I have divided the FBP's history into four separate time periods. It should be noted that the focus of this chapter is a discussion of the FBP's operations in line with its objectives of establishing commercial distribution for US books and in building a US-affiliated infrastructure of modern publishing in areas of the world that were mainly devoid of American ideological influence. Therefore, the accounts of the "achievements" of the FBP are referring to its "success" in achieving its organizational knowledge production and dissemination objectives.

This chapter chronologically details the challenges and achievements of the FBP. This account includes certain important details in the text and some noteworthy activities in the notes. While such detail has made this chapter rather dry, I think it is only through an annual journeying through the operations of the FBP that we can obtain a nuanced understanding of its various and multifaceted challenges, how and when it pursued its diverse objectives, and the ways in which it aimed to fulfill its missions. Such details are crucial to go beyond generalizations and abstractions about cultural imperialism, and understand how cultural domination and influence were planned, and the measures for such cultural policies were reassessed and reorganized.

Early Years and Early Success (1952–6)

Early years (1952–4)

A year after its establishment, the FBP's first field office was opened in June of 1953 in Cairo, with the cooperation of the USIS in Egypt. The manager of the Cairo office was Hassan al-Aroussy, a lawyer, former diplomat,[1] and an author and translator.[2] According to the US Public Affairs Officer in Cairo, William Henry Weathersby, the USIS programs in Cairo continued "without any real" change in the first months of the revolution of July 1952. This is to say, both the Cairo Branch of the FBP and the Fulbright programs began and continued operations with the rise of Gamal Abdel Nasser to power in Egypt (Weathersby, 1989).

The Tehran Branch was the second FBP branch established in the Middle East, having been established nine months after the Cairo Branch. The first book that the FBP sponsored was published in Arabic in October 1953. By August 1954, the FBP had offices in New York (four employees), Cairo (six Egyptians), and Tehran (four Iranians), and had opened its third local office in Lahore (two Pakistanis).

Translation and book production: By August 1954, the FBP was sponsoring or aiding the publication of translations into Arabic, Indonesian, Persian, Urdu, and Turkish. It had already published twenty-six books in Arabic (a total of 264,000 copies or an average of 10,000 copies per title) and one in Turkish. Fifty-two books in Arabic, thirty in Persian, and thirteen in Urdu were in progress. The translations were of all kinds, excepting school textbooks and advanced books in science. While there were no copyright laws in any of the areas in which the FBP was working (i.e., in Iran, Egypt, and Pakistan), it had formally purchased the translation rights of its sponsored books, though at a nominal fee from the copyright proprietors.[3] The books appeared under the name of the local publisher, each copy bearing the designation "Published in Cooperation with Franklin Publications."

The FBP had found it "unexpectedly easy" to gain the eager participation of the local publishing industry. The books were printed in Cairo, Tehran, or Lahore. The illustrations, however, were still mostly done in the United States on account of technical considerations. Cover designs were usually original, yet with the exception of some local artwork, the illustrations inside the books were normally from the original US editions. In the Arabic program, very early on a competition for cover designs for FBP books was conducted by Egypt's College of Applied Arts and sponsored by the Egyptian Minister of Education. The best covers were then presented at the Cairo Museum of Modern Art in October 1953, where the Egyptian Minister of Education opened the session and distributed the prizes. FBP-sponsored books were priced substantially below US domestic prices and even further below the prices charged for US books abroad.[4]

Educational use of FBP-sponsored books: In its early years, as a matter of policy and because of "the likelihood of reprisals which would imperil the whole Franklin Program," the FBP did not publish regular elementary or secondary school textbooks unless in "the most exceptional circumstances."[5] However, the FBP from the outset was very supportive of and interested in the usage of its books for educational purposes. As early as August 1954 in Egypt, for instance, all FBP books intended for juvenile reading were on the approved list issued by the Ministry of Education. The Ministry of Education in Egypt paid for the purchase of any of those books by individual schools for collateral reading. The School of Education in the University of Beirut was also using all of the Arabic-language juvenile and educational books sponsored by the FBP.[6]

Local participation: The keystone of FBP policy, in its early years, was the development of local participation in any given country. Positions in FBP local branches were all filled by national staff. Moreover, the FBP sought the participation of the "most respected civic, educational, and literary figures" in its publications. From the time of its establishment, the FBP's president undertook survey trips to the Middle East and Asia to interview local intelligentsia, in search of local managers and advisors. With the covert assistance of the US embassies in each country, extensive use was made of special consultants and advisors to acquire expert advice and limit the size of permanent staff. The local managers of the FBP were chosen for "their personal qualities of integrity, energy, and vision and their patriotic devotion to the interests of their own countries."[7] This process of selecting managers, therefore, did not necessarily involve looking for individuals experienced in the techniques of publishing and printing—as clearly exemplified in the case of the selection of Homayun San'atizadeh, who had no experience in the publishing industry before managing the Tehran Branch.[8]

In addition to recruiting local staff, the FBP further developed its network of local advisors through its process of book selection. First, FBP survey teams received suggestions from local managers and local advisors to see what kinds of books were needed and in what particular fields. Next, the FBP's New York office commissioned a compiler to prepare a list of suggestions for the books in the given category. The FBP then shipped the suggested books by air to the field office, and local advisors were asked to examine them. The FBP further solidified its contacts with these local advisors by engaging them in the selection of a local translator, a reviser of the translation, and the author of the introductions.

Two years after the FBP's establishment, it was already "very proud" of the "national and international prominence" of the people who were contributing to its projects. "The cream of the intellectual and civic leadership" of the countries concerned was contributing to the FBP.[9] To point to the prominence of the Egyptian intellectuals who were already participating in the FBP, either as translators or local advisors, the FBP's report indicated that in the introductory article to the February 1954 special issue of *La revue du caire*, which surveyed the previous fifty years of Egyptian literature, the names of ten living writers were mentioned as contributors to the "Egyptian renaissance."[10] From these ten writers, eight were already active participants in the FBP (three as advisors and five as writers or translators): Taha Hussein (1889–1973), Mohammad Hussein Heikal (1888–1956), Abbas Mahmoud al-Aqqad (1889–1964), Tawfiq al-Hakim (1898–1987), Mahmoud Teymour (1894–1973), Aziz Abaza (1898–1973), Abdel Rahman Sidqy (1896–1973), and Ahmad Amin (1886–1954).[11] The importance that building these social and intellectual networks had for the FBP in following its ideological aims cannot be overemphasized.

As discussed in Chapter 1, this study focuses on the FBP's operations, objectives, and history. Therefore, I am not aiming at a detailed discussion of what motivated local authors, public intellectuals, and political officials to participate. There have been suggestions of different and distinct motivations, which should be studied through conducting interviews, and studying memoirs, as well as personal correspondences. As Laugesen put it, "it is possible to discern a variety of motives for embracing elements of American culture as well as the multiple uses to which such culture was put" (Laugesen, 2017, p. 5). Working with the FBP was an opportunity to network with American cultural elites and to learn about US publishing, bookselling, and editing techniques; some local affiliators were actually advocating for disseminating American books as an effort that could contribute to vitalizing and modernizing the national culture. Also, in some instances such collaboration was the most rewarding in advancing local individuals' own careers. The structure of the FBP and its sophisticated policies, however, were essential in attracting people with different motivations to working with it. Moreover, one cannot generalize on the reasons that locals in various countries endorsed the program. Specific historical conditions make the case of each country different. In the case of Iran, as I will discuss in Chapter 5, the Tehran Branch was established just a few months after the coup of 1953. In the context of the post-coup suppression of leftist and nationalist movements, the Tehran Branch was indeed one of the few cultural spaces that could offer working opportunities for many intellectuals and people of culture.

Reception: On January 1, 1955, the FBP reported on excerpts from articles written on the FBP's books. These reviews show that its books were mostly well received even in generally anti-American dailies, such as the Cairo magazine *Al-Ḥilāl*. *Al-Miṣry*, another generally anti-American Cairo daily, also praised the physical production of books sponsored by the FBP in Cairo, writing: "Arabic books for the first time look like European books in their printing and production." Critical appreciation of FBP-sponsored books had also appeared in *Al-Aḥrām* (a Cairo daily), *Al-Jumhūrriya* (a government-sponsored Cairo daily), *Akhbār Al-Yūm*, *Al-Anīs* (Tetoun, Morocco), and *Al-Dāwar* (the Muslim Brotherhood's journal, Cairo).

A negative reaction from the Arab world was noticed in two instances. The first one was a series of four articles published in the Cairo paper *Rose al-Yousef*, in what the FBP report labels "a sustained attack" on the FBP. According to this report, these series of articles charged FBP with being an imperialist effort to influence Arab minds, an attempt to destroy the Arab publishing industry by dumping books at less than cost, and as a project to make enormous profits for monopolist American corporations. The radical religious thinker Sayyid Qutb (1906–66), editor of the journal of the Muslim Brotherhood, was the author of the second article, in which Qutb attacked the local Egyptians who were contributing to the Cairo Branch.[12]

The FBP, however, was confident that none of these articles had been effective in "limiting the effectiveness of FBP's books, or in dissuading the best people in the Arab countries from participating fully" with the FBP. Even in the case of the Muslim Brotherhood, the journal of this religious group had also published a "warmly favorable full-page review to the FBP-sponsored Morrison's *Man Does Not Stand Alone*."[13] The reason for this warm review was that Shaykh Ahmed Hussein al-Bakuri, former leader of the Muslim Brotherhood, was the translator of the book.

Local redaction: The technique of local redaction was pursued from the early years, and it was one that worked in favor of the FBP's assigned ideological objectives—not only because the locally adapted editions were better received by the local readers, but also because this technique developed and solidified local participation and resulted in local endorsement of the edited books. Among the first instances of such books was Edward R. Murrow's *This I Believe*, which consists of a series of statements of personal philosophy. This book was edited in its Arabic version to include twenty-five statements by Americans and twenty-five newly written by famous Arab people, including President Mohammad Naguib of Egypt (during 1953–4), cabinet ministers, ambassadors, educators, and so on from several Arab states. The book sold out its 35,000-copy edition on the day of publication. Sarah Bolton's *Lives of Poor Boys Who Became Famous* was also heavily adapted in its Arabic edition. Half of the chapters were from the original American book (on figures such as Benjamin Franklin [1706–90], Giuseppe Garibaldi [1807–82], Abraham Lincoln [1809–65]), and the remaining half consisted of newly written biographies of poor Arab boys who had become famous. Both of these books were edited by prominent cultural figures, the first by the historian and writer Ahmad Amin, the head of the cultural section of the Arab League, and the second by Mohammad Farid Abu Hadid (1893–1967), Under Secretary of Education and a popular writer and historian of the time. The same plan was followed for Persian editions of both books, and the FBP's Tehran Branch acquired the monarch Mohammad Reza Shah's consent to write the biography of his father, Reza Shah, for Bolton's book.[14]

Distribution: The FBP's objective was to improve the distribution of its sponsored books, both inside each country, to be accessed in provinces, and internationally, to be accessed by other people of the same language. In terms of distribution, however, the FBP was facing two challenges: how to distribute its materials in provinces and rural regions and how to export its sponsored materials to other countries with the same language. As a result of poverty, an abysmal literacy rate, the distance between the main cities and villages, and the lack of distribution machinery, sales in rural areas were very low. The FBP soon observed that those newspaper and magazine publishers with a fairly good distribution system could be employed for sales in provinces where a US-affiliated distribution network was completely lacking.[15]

The second distribution problem that the FBP intended to address concerned book exports to other countries with the same language-speaking population; the challenge was that there was no US-affiliated pan-Arab or regional book distribution system in the Middle East and Asia. The FBP also found it very hard to arrange such pan-Arab book distribution because of government control over foreign exchange in Egypt, Jordan, and Iraq; French opposition to the import of Arabic books into North Africa; Saudi Arabia's religious objection to certain books; and nationalistic ideologies. Furthermore, the FBP had to find a wholesaler specialized and with experience in such regional distribution.

To build a US-affiliated pan-Arab book distribution network, the FBP encouraged export wholesalers in Egypt and Beirut to work closely with Cairo, as the leading publishing center of the Arabic-speaking area, in moving FBP-sponsored books across international boundary lines so that these became accessible in Jordan, Iraq, Beirut, Saudi Arabia, and North Africa. The FBP managed this to the extent that by August 1954, 500 copies of each of its sponsored books were automatically exported by an export wholesaler for non-Egyptian sale. Moreover, the books issued through the newspaper and magazine publishers had been successful outside of Egypt.[16] The FBP was further looking to find ways to build a transnational book distribution system for Persian and Urdu, so as to be able to export its Persian books to Afghanistan and to export its sponsored Urdu books to Urdu speakers in India.

Auxiliary activities: The FBP's early activities were not limited to sponsoring translations and developing a distribution system but also contained "auxiliary activities," meaning activities that were deemed worthy, were reasonably if indirectly contributing toward the FBP's ideological aims, and were low-cost. For instance, the FBP participated in arranging US representation in a large textbook exhibition sponsored by the Ministry of Education in Indonesia. In doing so, the FBP sent 400 textbooks, carefully selected to assure US representation in the particular exhibition and to show "goodwill" to the Ministry in Jakarta. The FBP was sure such an endeavor would result in a stimulus in Indonesia for the translation of US books and textbooks. Another common auxiliary activity of the FBP was to send a considerable number of US books to many individuals in several countries, as a method of building connections and as an acknowledgment of courtesies rendered. These auxiliary activities further expanded to include technical assistance to Egyptian, Lahore, Amman, and Tehran printers. The FBP also assisted the Iranian Ministry of Propaganda in learning how to obtain educational broadcast scripts from the United States for use on the state radio.[17]

Years of expansion and "success" (1955–6)

As early as 1956, the FBP was describing its operations as a success. It had already built a vast and growing network of US publishers and local Middle Eastern intelligentsia upon which it developed its programs for the next decade. In spite of the rise of anti-US sentiments in the Middle East, especially in Egypt, the FBP was functioning efficiently in line with its ideological goals, and it was crediting its policies and structures for its achievements in the region.

By May 1956, the FBP had opened two more offices with local staff in Dacca (East Pakistan) and Jakarta (Indonesia), making the total number of its local offices five. It had published 200 books in at least one of the languages of Arabic, Persian, Urdu, and Turkish (with the combined editions totaling over a million copies) and was in the process of sponsoring publication in Bengali and Indonesian. These six

4. History and Evolution of the FBP (1952–77) 39

languages at the time were the languages of about 250 million people in "perhaps the most critical areas of the world."[18] The FBP also had more than 350 additional books in progress. The number of readers in these languages was far in excess of the number of books; because of the scarcity of reading materials and high demand for them in underdeveloped countries, each volume was used over and over again.

Only four years after its establishment, the FBP was framing its operations as a "revolution" in the book trade of the Middle East and crediting its local managers and the technical advice of its US staff for enabling it. To support this claim, the FBP argued that during these years new techniques of advertising and promotion had been introduced and used and that some bookstore displays had been modernized. The effect of the FBP's printing and book production is clear in many reviews published in the Arabic, Persian, and Urdu world. *Al-Ḥurrīya*, published in Baghdad, stated in January 1955: "Franklin Publications has presented to the Arabic reader what no other publishing firm, even the strongest and most widely circulated, had ever been able to produce—in numbers, in versatility of subject matter, or in reasonableness of price [...] Franklin books reach the hands of the citizen as easily as his everyday requirements." Another journal published in Baghdad, *Jīl al-Jadīd*, again in January of 1955 reported: "Franklin has effected a revolution in the world of books. Any fear of a relapse to the tattered past is banished." Such praise of printing quality can also be seen in Egypt. For instance, *Al-Miṣry* in Cairo in January 1955 wrote: "The books presented by Franklin Publications have reached such a level that Arabic books for the first time look like European and American books in their printing production."[19] In a very short space of time, the FBP affected the physical appearance of most of the book trade in the countries concerned. When the FBP first introduced its design, especially their method of cover-printing, its books were distinctive in comparison to others published in Iran and Egypt. However, by 1957 most Arabic and Persian books looked like FBP ones. The methods of bookstore display and book promotion in both countries were notably Americanized, and the book trade in both countries was looking to the FBP for leadership and instructions in both these areas.[20]

During these years, the FBP improved the distribution of its sponsored titles in four ways: (1) by introducing the mass market approach, to make them available for those who did not normally go to bookstores; (2) by expanding the sales to provinces and rural areas; (3) by expanding sales to foreign sales—to do so, especially in order to create a pan-Arab distribution system, FBP entered into an arrangement with a wholesaler in which FBP took the wholesaler's post-dated checks and itself paid the publisher for the books delivered to the wholesaler for export sale; and (4) through the educational sales of its sponsored books, which were prompted through the use of examination copies accompanied by high-level endorsement.[21]

As a result of the above arrangements, FBP-affiliated book distribution systems developed to the extent that US books were being distributed in places where US books had rarely ever been seen. The FBP was proud to point to a report of a "Muslim friend" who had been in Mecca the previous year for the pilgrimage and who narrated that "FBP books were widely displayed in the holy city itself." The FBP's Cairo office had also developed a pan-Arab distribution plan to make

FBP-sponsored translations available throughout the Arab world, from Morocco to Baghdad.[22] The FBP had further developed its network of leading intellectuals and civic figures who endorsed or participated in FBP projects, to include three prime ministers of Egypt (Aly Maher Pasha [1881–1960], Mohammad Naguib [1901–84], and Gamal Abdel Nasser [1918–70]), and the Shah of Iran's sister Ashraf Pahlavi (1919–2016).

Sales: By January 1957, the FBP had sold 504,000 books in Arabic out of 116 titles published, 173,400 copies of its eighty-eight Persian published titles, 21,000 of its thirty Urdu published titles, and 27,000 of its seven Turkish published titles. It had published a total of 243 books and printed 1,155,000 copies of them, of which 725,400 were sold.[23] Not only had individual sales risen, but the institutional sales—especially to educational institutions—had also increased substantially.[24]

At the time, the average for book sales in Arabic was 2,000 copies, and less than 1,000 in Persian and Urdu. The FBP sales for each title amounted to two to three times the average in these languages. The Arabic edition of *This I Believe* had sold another 25,000 copies in addition to the 35,000 copies of its first edition, making this book one of the very few Arabic titles, excepting the Quran, that have sold in such quantities over two editions. The Persian edition of Sarah Knowles Bolton's *Lives of Poor Boys Who Became Famous* sold 25,000 copies, probably the largest number of sales at that time for a trade book in Iranian print history.[25] The Shah of Iran not only contributed a chapter on his father to this book but also offered a gift of $10,000 to aid the publication of an FBP-sponsored book dealing with Iran.[26]

By this time, press reviews of FBP-sponsored books were in the hundreds, appearing in the local press from Casablanca to Dacca. The FBP further pointed out: "To take notice of American books at all is a strikingly new development for nearly all of these journals. In most cases, no review or other notice of an American book had ever appeared before."[27] Radio broadcasting stations in Iran, Pakistan, and Egypt had given "generous attention" to FBP and FBP-sponsored books. In Iran, Princess Ashraf's translation of *The Common Sense Book of Baby and Child Care* was presented in serial form over a number of weeks. Another continuing program, entitled "Come Let's Build a Better World," had drawn its text entirely from the FBP-sponsored *Better Living Series.* Radio Pakistan had given attention to FBP books on several occasions from its stations in Lahore, Peshawar, and Dacca. Egypt's state radio broadcast had also reviewed most of the FBP books published in the country.[28]

In 1956, the Imperial Court in Iran awarded an FBP-sponsored book, George Sarton's *The Life of Science: Essays in the History of Civilization* (1948), as the best translation of the year. The two runners-up were also two other books sponsored by the FBP. "This was the first time that any American book had been so much as noticed, and one of the few times when a translation from the English language had been honored, the prizes in the past having generally gone to translations from the French and Russian," an FBP memorandum added, on the importance of this award. Very quickly, the FBP had been locally established "as one of the most important cultural facts in the Middle East in the last five years."[29]

Relations with publishers: By 1957, the FBP was in constant close association with about seventy-five publishing houses in five countries. In Iran, the Tehran Branch manager was responsible for organizing the Iranian Publishers Association and for the launching of the *Monthly Publication* (*kitāb-i māh*), which carried regular bibliographical information as well as articles about books. This association constantly turned to the FBP as its chief advisor on many publishing subjects. Further, the FBP frequently used *Publisher's Weekly* and other trade magazines in its offices. It arranged for several consulting services and advisory functions by visiting US publishers in Indonesia and other countries. It also placed articles by US publishers in the local press in Egypt, Lebanon, Iran, Pakistan, and Indonesia.[30]

Bookselling and promotion: In the book trade, the FBP worked to push its affiliated publishers away from their habit of increasing profits by withholding the books from competing publisher-booksellers. Instead, it directed them toward dynamic retail trade to support the widest possible development of retail bookselling. The FBP introduced or strengthened the following methods to develop the promotion and merchandizing of its books in Asia: catalogs, direct-mail circulars, newspaper and magazine advertising, wide distribution of review copies, examination copies for educators, endorsement by public figures, exhibits, radio, literary debates, display devices for bookstores, and development of an effective jobbing system. It also brought each of the field-office managers to the United States for a period of observation and study of US publishing and bookselling.

Direct-mail selling was introduced by FBP to the Persian book trade when, for Van Loon's *Story of Mankind* (1921), the Tehran Branch prepared circulars and shipped them to provincial booksellers together with names and addresses of literary people in their region. The Tehran Branch had acquired the names from the list of people who had sent fan mail to Radio Tehran. The idea was that if someone owned a radio and could write a letter they were a possible purchaser of books in Iran.

Analysis of the early success

The FBP's success in its translation, publication, and distribution missions was in spite of the rise of anti-US sentiments in some of the countries it was operating within. The FBP's success was especially "striking" in Egypt, where FBP books were being published and sold without interruption, even given the context of the anti-US political developments. The FBP had been able "to continue with local government support and encouragement in spite of successive political overturns in Egypt, Pakistan and Indonesia."[31]

At the beginning of January 1957, the FBP wrote extensively on its success in achieving its ideological and organizational objectives. The FBP president rhetorically asked how important it was that "attractive" children's books mirroring the "American way of life" had filled a need that would otherwise be filled by communist material. He further pointed out that FBP-sponsored translations were helping to build US cultural competence for "world leadership." Datus C.

Smith asked, "Who can assess the value of counteracting the Communist claim that America has only a 'bathtub civilization' and that its cultural vacuity makes it unsuited for world leadership?"[32]

Several factors contributed to the FBP's early "success." I have already discussed the importance of the sophisticated policies, procedures, and principles that the FBP followed in its title selection process, and its relations with the local offices, in the previous chapter. Here, I should also point to the role of the American publishing industry. The "open-handed cooperation given to the project by the American publishing industry" was a major factor in FBP's success.[33] Almost all US publishers whose books appeared in the list of FBP-sponsored titles accepted the relinquishing of their economic interest in the context of US doctrinal warfare during the Cold War. While historically the US publishers tended to fear translations as being a threat to the export sales of copies in their regular English-language editions, in this case the industry had "patriotically" assisted the FBP in its missions. The US publishers not only granted, almost for free, the translation rights of their books but also voluntarily supported the FBP with technical advice. By 1956, for instance, of the 500 FBP-sponsored translation projects, the publishers had granted rights of translation into a whole galaxy of Asian and African languages for a token fee (with the exception of three projects). As a result, the FBP paid a mere $4,400 in its first three years of operation for the token permission costs. Also, some of the most important executives of the US book industry gave an "astonishing amount of volunteer time" to serve on the FBP's board of directors, various committees, and worldwide survey teams. The US publishing industry also supported the FBP with technical advisory and consultative services, which otherwise would have cost this program thousands of dollars.

In discussing the effectiveness of the title selection process, the FBP points to Frederick Lewis Allen's *The Big Change: America Transforms Itself, 1900–1950* (1952), Shepard B. Clough's *The American Way: The Economic Basis of Our Civilization* (1953), and David Cushman Coyle's *The United States Political System and How It Works* (1957) as examples of books with straightforward political significance, which had been included in the FBP-sponsored listing. Another group of books selected through this process were those whose effect was not direct yet had "deeper and long-lasting influence" because they gave the "intellectual basis for anti-Communism." These included works such as Eugene Staley's *The Future of Underdeveloped Countries: Political Implications of Economic Development* (1954) and George Holland Sabine's *A History of Political Theory* (1937).

Most of the books were without direct political content but portrayed "American ideas and ideals in many fields such as democracy, family life, social equality, education, etc." The FBP emphasized that these books exhibited impressive cultural contributions that served to "combat the Communist charge that Americans can make atom bombs and automobiles but not works of literature or philosophy."[34] According to the FBP, the most useful and influential of these books were the ones that showed American interest in and knowledge of the areas where the book was being published, such as Albert T. Olmstead's *History of the Persian Empire* (1948) and Harry W. Hazard's *Atlas of Islamic History* (1952). The FBP further pointed out that in certain countries, the mere printing of non-communist books had been a valuable contribution, as it filled the vacuum that could otherwise have been exploited by the Soviet Union.

Another area that FBP-sponsored books were aiming at was to address the conservative Muslim sphere by showing US scholarly interest in the Middle East. Publications of books like M.S. Dimand's *A Handbook of Mohammedan Decorative Arts* (1947) were seen by the FBP as contributing to this interest. Such books could show that the United States had "humane" interests in the Middle East and that "oil and power" were not its sole concern.[35] The FBP was also confident that university students and possible future leaders in the Middle East reading D.C. Coyle's *The United States Political System and How It Works* (1957) or F.L. Allen's *The Big Change: America's Transformation, 1900–1950* (1952) in their own language should be seen as a success.

Moving away from Translation Programs toward Educational Projects (1956–68)

By the mid-1950s, the FBP had consolidated its early "success" in its Regular Programs (i.e., translation projects) and started to evolve its focus toward Special Projects—that is, publishing textbooks, sponsoring encyclopedias and dictionaries, village library development, and mass distribution operations. While in the early years, the FBP avoided textbook publishing, it soon developed toward educational publishing, through direct activity and through training textbook writers, consulting, and other forms of assistance to other organizations. This transition was also a response to the rise of literacy programs in Third World countries and resulted in the internationalization of the FBP as it opened new offices in Africa and Latin America and expanded its operations in the Middle East and Asia, into closer affiliations with national ministries of education. The FBP's international scope extended with its role in conducting book surveys in new countries and through making those surveys available to foundations, publishers, and government agencies. Moreover, the FBP pursued Special Projects in the field of school library development and in the production and distribution of supplementary-reading books for rural library development and school use.

In 1956, the FBP undertook to produce the textbooks for the first four grades of Iranian primary schools. The whole project was subsidized by the Imperial Organization for Social Services (*sāzimān shāhanshāhī khadamāt-i ijtimāʾī*). Furthermore, in response to a request from the Iranian Ministry of Education, the FBP also assisted this ministry in improving the content of the books. To do so, the FBP provided a training program for Iranian textbook editors, sponsored with a grant of $85,000 from the Ford Foundation. This training program will be discussed in detail in Chapter 6.

Another development in 1956 was the signing of a tripartite agreement between the Egyptian Ministry of Education, the American embassy in Cairo, and the FBP for the use of money from the 1954 Agricultural Trade Development and Assistance

Act known as Public Law 480.³⁶ The agreement was for the FBP to contribute to the translation and publication of any US school text or reference book recommended by interested bodies in Egypt. The FBP was nominated by the US government to carry out this project, in accordance with the requirements of the Egyptian government through its Ministry of Education. The Egyptian government had initiated a policy of Arabicizing scientific, engineering, and medical faculties in the universities, a move that was inspired by the Egyptian desire to follow Syria in using Arabic in all its university faculties as the medium of instruction. While the later break in US–Egypt diplomatic relations in 1967 terminated the funding, the books already in the process of translation were carried through to completion, the last of 138 university- and higher-institute-level books being published in 1972. Engineering and agriculture books made up the bulk of university-level translations.³⁷

The above two projects in Iran and Egypt demonstrate the FBP's gradual move after 1956 into the field of textbooks. Still, it is the Afghanistan textbook project (discussed further in Chapter 6) that is pointed to in the FBP's records as their grandest move. Moreover, at this point a substantial order of 5 to 100 copies per title for juvenile and educational books had come to the FBP from the ministries of education of Kuwait, Bahrain, Libya, Jordan, Tunisia, Saudi Arabia, and Sudan as well as the more predictable countries of Lebanon, Syria, Iraq, and Egypt. A thousand copies each of more than twenty-five titles of FBP-sponsored books had been purchased for schools by the Egyptian Ministry of Education.³⁸

By early 1959, the Soviet Union had become concerned about the FBP's operations, especially with regard to its influence in the Arab world. In a handwritten report dated January 13, 1959, from G. Zhukuv (Soviet general) to N.A. Mukhitdinov (Secretary of the Central Committee of the Communist Party of Uzbekistan), the direction of US propaganda in the East is described as follows: "the praise of American democracy, the American way of life and US foreign policy, the economic 'aid' of the US to poorly-developed countries, popularization of the so called 'people's capitalism' of the US, anti-Soviet propaganda in all its forms, and propaganda directed at discrediting Communist and worker's Parties." The document also reports on several severe attacks on the Soviet educational system as part of US propaganda efforts. The Soviet official was also concerned that one-third of the USIA's $32 million budget in 1957/8 was slated for propaganda abroad in Asian and African countries and that the US government was planning to increase these regions' propaganda funds by $2 million for the 1958/9 fiscal year, with a reduction in appropriations for propaganda in Western Europe. Pointing to the relations between US state and private foundations, Zhukuv wrote that the USIA also directed the activity of private US organizations such as the Ford Foundation, the Rockefeller Foundation, and the Kellogg Foundation, "which pursue propaganda work in Asia under the cover of cultural, scientific, or publishing activity."³⁹

This report specifically points to the FBP and asserts: "The Franklin Organization controls all American cultural activity in Arab countries and is one of the centers for the publishing of American propaganda literature, including anti-Soviet [literature]. Many publishers, newspapers, magazines, and also cultural and scientific organizations of the Arab countries are under the influence of the Franklin Organization." The report states that the USIA was mainly relying on local publishers to distribute books by US authors in the East in large quantities, books that "justify American policy and refute Communism, however in the appearance of an academic approach to the problems which is aimed at the local intelligentsia and students."[40]

By September 1959, the FBP had opened new offices in Beirut,[41] Baghdad,[42] and Kuala Lumpur, and a sub-office in the provincial city of Tabriz, Iran.[43] It had published 600 titles in editions totaling 10,000,000 copies. Only one quarter of this total number of copies (2,460,000) was published in the FBP's Regular Program. The remaining copies (7,540,000) were printed as part of its Special Projects, at this time in the textbook programs for Iran and Afghanistan.[44] Special Projects were not carried out at the expense of the Regular Program; rather, each had been financed ad hoc by a grant for that specific purpose by the self-liquidating character of the project itself or from surplus income from a related Special Project.

By the end of 1960, the combined population of countries where FBP books were distributed was 300,000,000.[45] All offices were in close contact with the New York office, with more than 20,000 numbered items of correspondence to and from operating offices extant up to this time. In addition, there were a total of 155 office visits by American staff members; six of the nine office managers had been to the United States for training and four of the five editors of the encyclopedia projects also. Fifteen Iranian textbook editors had also gone to the United States in 1960 under FBP sponsorship. Textbook projects by then had extended to include the United Arab Republic. A grant of Egyptian pounds under Public Law 480 was used to produce twenty-eight books largely in the technical fields. The largest program of educational publishing, however, remained in Iran, and it was funded by a grant from the Ford Foundation, grants in local currency under Public Law 480, and in far larger amounts by ones from the Iranian Ministry of Education and the Iranian Imperial Organization for Social Services. The Afghanistan project was funded completely by the Afghanistan government.

As is clear from the above, only a few years into the FBP's establishment, their Special Projects (a term used for textbook projects, encyclopedias, and other various special enterprises such as establishing printing plants) had dramatically gained in importance. The annual report of the FBP credited the Regular Program for creating such satisfaction that Special Projects had become possible. It stated:

> The sometimes more dramatic quality of certain of the Special Projects [...] should not make us overlook the rock-bottom essentiality of the Regular Program, without which nothing else would have been possible. For instance it was FBP's success in conducting its Regular Program which led to the history-making Afghan textbook program.
>
> (FBPR, Box 15, Annual Report 1960)

The FBP-sponsored encyclopedias were adapted editions of the *Columbia–Viking Desk Encyclopedia*. The Arabic edition was the FBP's first encyclopedia project and was financed by a grant of $192,300 from the Ford Foundation. The adapted Persian edition of the *Columbia–Viking Desk Encyclopedia* had been underway since 1956 with a grant from the Ford Foundation and Princess Ashraf of Iran (the Shah's twin sister) to a total of $50,000. The FBP also received a grant of $200,000 in rupees under Public Law 480 for adapted editions in Urdu and Bengali, and editorial work began in 1960. A grant of $100,000 in rupiahs under Public Law 480 was also approved for the Indonesian edition.[46] The editorial work on this edition was also launched in 1960.

The dictionary projects of the FBP also heated up in 1960, with the Rockefeller Foundation making a conditional grant of $115,000 for an English–Arabic dictionary to be prepared by the Beirut office. The condition for this grant, stipulated by the Rockefeller Foundation, was an equal grant from another source. The Ford Foundation was also preparing paperwork for a grant of $70,000 for a Persian dictionary project under the sponsorship of the Tehran office.[47]

One of the Special Projects was to assist financially and technically in the establishment of printing plants that could assist the FBP in answering its printing machinery needs for its textbook projects. In 1959, the FBP's board of directors authorized a FBP loan of $150,000 for use in the purchase of printing machinery from abroad to the Iranian Offset Printing House. This loan came from the profit of FBP's earlier textbook production projects. This will be discussed in depth in Chapter 6.

By the end of 1960, the village development libraries project was also commencing. The FBP was considering a large project in collaboration with the Iranian Ministry of Education. In both East and West Pakistan, with the assistance of the Asia Foundation and the Pakistan Village and Industrial Development program (VAID), several hundred collections of FBP books were selected from the Regular Programs in Urdu and Bengali and placed in villages in "box libraries." However, the FBP recognized that it needed to start preparing books especially for the newly literate in order to develop its educational reach in villages.[48]

In 1961, the Kennedy administration focused on "the importance of education and technical aid to help nations modernize" (Laugesen, 2012, p. 136). This articulation further assisted the FBP to focus its function specifically on education materials. Alongside a substantial rise in the publication of translations through the Regular Programs and the continuation of its textbook projects, the FBP started to enter the area of introductory literacy books.[49] A new Special Project producing materials for new literates had been undertaken in Iran, which was aided by a fund from Mrs. Ellen Clayton Garwood.[50] This fund was used to print introductory literacy books in substantial quantities.

In 1961, continuing its process of internationalization, the FBP began looking toward operations in Africa and Latin America due to "the great increase of public interest."[51] The FBP intended to study and examine Latin America and sub-Saharan Africa, even if only for informational reasons and without assuming new responsibilities.[52] A memorandum sent from the Deputy for Policy and

Plans, USIA to President Kennedy—dated April 16, 1962—shows that the survey conducted by the FBP in Latin America was at the USIA's request. This survey was later used in answer to President Kennedy's inquiry regarding US and communist book programs in Latin America.[53] The memorandum further shows the rise in USIA efforts in the early 1960s to overcome the "book gap" in Latin America and how the USIA framed its publications in Latin America within their use for the purposes of anti-communism.

Financially, 1962 marked a new era in FBP history. The FBP received a grant of $1,000,000 from the Ford Foundation that had to be spread over five years. This money was not to be used for the cost of operations but had to be assigned entirely to support the organization's headquarters in New York and its services in surveying, coordinating, consulting, and administrating. The FBP's annual report states: "FBP is in a better position than ever before to assume responsibility for projects, if they are properly financed within themselves, moving toward the idea of an effective book industry in each of the major 'new countries.'" The FBP also continued to receive major grants in local currency in the United Arab Republic, Pakistan, and Indonesia under Public Law 480. The Imperial Organization for Social Services in Iran in connection with textbook production and Princess Ashraf in connection with the costs of the *Persian Encyclopedia* project (*dāyirat al-maʿārif fārsī*) had also offered funds to the FBP's Tehran Branch.[54]

This new era began when two "new trends" absorbed increasing attention within the FBP. The first, while in its early years the FBP had avoided textbook publishing, involved the further development of its trend toward educational publishing, whether through direct activity or through training, consulting, and other forms of assistance to other organizations. The second new trend was "school libraries"—the FBP was trying to stimulate the entry of supplementary-reading books into these libraries, specifically in Pakistan and Iran.[55]

By the end of 1963, the FBP was placing more emphasis on projects for supplementary-reading books for in-school use through school libraries and for trade sale. With the rise of mass-literacy programs in many countries, the FBP was considering devoting major efforts to providing reading materials suited to the new readers' interests.[56] The FBP had already carried out its largest school library projects in East and West Pakistan, involving the presentation of several hundred thousand children's books in Urdu and Bengali that were paid for through grants received under Public Law 480.[57] In this year, the Literacy Corps (*sipāh-i dānish*) was established in Iran. Secondary school graduates subject to the draft, under the direction of the Iranian Ministry of Education and arrangements with the army, were assigned to rural areas as literacy teachers. The FBP's Tehran Branch was a publisher at the forefront of this state-led literacy campaign. The FBP sponsored the preparation of the *First Literacy Book*, which had an initial printing of 300,000. This book was the first reading material for Literacy Corps trainees in Iran. The project was funded by a gift from Mrs. Ellen Clayton Garwood.[58]

With the greater focus on books for supplementary reading, new literates, and vocational education,[59] the development of systems of mass distribution became even more important for the FBP. A mass distribution system for inexpensive books was developed in Iran, borrowing some of the techniques of American paperbacks. Pocket Books (*kitābhā-yi jībī*) was a broad-scale cooperative venture devised by the FBP in Tehran and carried out by a group of Iranian publishers. By this time, about 4,800 book display shelves had been placed at strategic points in the country (in the metropolis, provincial cities, market towns, and some villages), which were serviced at regular intervals.[60]

The year 1964 "was marked by noteworthy developments which extend the area of FBP's interest and widen the scope of its assistance to book industries in developing countries."[61] The FBP formally established a new training division, with Byron Buck as its director, which resulted in close collaboration with US government agencies, foreign governments, US foundations, non-profit organizations, professional and trade groups, and private companies. USAID had funded the establishment of this division, which was intended to undertake its own training programs as well as to assist professionally in the coordination of the training projects of US government agencies, foreign governments, foundations, and so on.[62]

In this year, the FBP moved toward further internationalizing its operations and also expanded its operations to the areas of children's education and literature. The four new operating offices established during 1964 were in Kabul, Afghanistan,[63] Lagos and Enugu, Nigeria,[64] and Buenos Aires, Argentina. The FBP's surveying practice expanded substantially in this year to include Nigeria, Liberia, Congo, Kenya, Uganda, Tanganyika, Argentina, and Brazil.[65]

Under contract to Afghanistan's Ministry of Education and aided by a loan of $100,000 from the Asia Foundation, in 1964, the FBP accepted the overseeing of the remodeling and re-equipping of the Ministry's printing plant, the training of its personnel, and the production of its textbooks in Persian and Pashto. Meanwhile, at a UNESCO conference on educational materials in Paris in the spring of 1964, two FBP operating directors (of the Tehran and Lagos branches) were their countries' representatives. The US delegation also included a FBP vice president from New York and two members of the board of directors.[66]

In 1964 alone, 8,100,000 textbooks were produced with FBP cooperation. About 6,600,000 copies were textbooks in Persian for Iranian schools and for the mass literacy project. Around 1,300,000 copies were for schools in Afghanistan. The remaining 200,000 copies were in Arabic for use as textbooks in Egyptian universities and technical schools. The FBP was also making an effort to introduce the policy of having teachers' manuals for all textbooks and to secure widespread distribution of simple books for parents and teachers on child guidance. More than a hundred of the titles published with FBP cooperation during this year were of the teacher-training category.

With the new financial resources received, and as a result of closer open affiliation with governmental and international agencies, the year 1965 was celebrated by the FBP as "the most distinctive" in its thirteen-year history. New activities were undertaken, operations were expanded to new geographical areas, and a "new emphasis" was also given to established projects. Up to this time, the great majority of books translated in the Regular Program were from American originals. Starting from 1965, arrangements were completed for the inclusion of books from some other Western countries, with financial assistance provided by those countries. While the FBP continued to focus on supplementary reading and school libraries, it further moved strongly into the field of materials for newly literate readers.[67]

By this time, FBP worldwide staff numbers stood at about 440, as it conducted its programs through offices in seventeen cities in twelve countries on three continents (in South America, through affiliated non-profit organizations). The gradual admittance of non-Americans to the board of directors of the FBP and its New York office continued with Dariush Homayoun,[68] who became a field consultant in Asia for the New York office, the first non-American member of the New York staff (and now surveying the distribution problems in Malaysia and Indonesia) following a year as a Nieman Fellow at Harvard.[69]

Including textbooks, the FBP had aided the publication of a total of 2,765 titles (50,000,000 copies in total). It had further pursued textbook projects in Lagos, Enugu, Kaduna, and Nairobi. The FBP's training division conducted textbook-writing programs for trainees who were "concerned with textbooks more than with any other kind of book."[70]

The FBP's dictionary projects were now expanded: there was a Persian dictionary (financed by the Ford Foundation and later under sponsorship of the Persian Culture Foundation of Tehran), an English–Indonesian dictionary (financed by Cornell University with the assistance of a Ford Foundation grant), and an English–Arabic dictionary (Lebanon; financed by the Rockefeller Foundation, the government of Kuwait, the Arabian–American Oil Co, and a few individuals).

By 1965, supplementary reading and school libraries had become a major focus of the FBP. It already had major projects of this sort in the United Arab Republic, Iran, and Pakistan. Its largest new supplementary-reading project included 500,000 copies of reprints of about twenty-five titles from FBP editions previously published in Arabic, selected by the Egyptian Ministry of Education. It was publishing books suitable for young people in Cairo, Beirut, and Baghdad, and 30,000 copies of these books in Arabic were provided for a school library plan in Morocco. USAID financed both of the projects in Cairo and Morocco. The FBP also surveyed the subject of supplementary-reading books in the Philippines, financed by a grant from the Ford Foundation, and produced a report, "Children's Books in Philippine Languages."

During 1965, the FBP "moved strongly" into the field of materials for newly literate readers and was hoping that this could be "a continuing major activity" in its future.[71] The largest new project was in Iran, in cooperation with the Ministry of Education. Tehran Branch manager Homayun San'atizadeh had become director of the first experiment in literacy "saturation" in the province of Ghazvin. The FBP had given him a leave of absence at the request of Iran's prime minister. The FBP also helped in establishing *Payk* (Courier), a magazine concerning newly literate people, and assisted in setting up a hundred sample village libraries. It also assisted in developing and producing materials for teaching literacy and in providing reading materials. The publication of *Payk* was considered to be "perhaps the most comprehensive and best coordinated" project from a new literates' magazine "in the world."[72]

Tehran continued providing its technical assistance to the printing plant project in Kabul. The distinctive feature of this undertaking, as seen from the FBP headquarters, was that Iranians, and not Americans, were providing the technical assistance. About twenty Iranians were in Kabul for six or eight months and an equal number of Afghans were being trained in Tehran at the Offset Printing House.[73]

Continuing its process of internationalization, the FBP greatly extended its global role, attending with all managing directors of FBP's operating offices and about a dozen members of the New York staff the triennial meeting of the International Publishers Association held in 1965 in Washington. The present and former FBP board chairmen were among the principal speakers. Following up on this meeting, the FBP sent a message to each of the 700 delegates, and special letters to the executives of national book associations, inviting cooperation and offering help. It also began to participate in international conferences on the subject of "Books for Human Development," involving American, British, German, and Canadian official and private publishers as well as executives of UNESCO.[74]

When on May 27, 1965, more than fifteen managing directors of the FBP gathered for their first full meeting since it was formed, they all reported that American books were more in demand than any other translations in their home countries. The managing director of the Lebanon office, Mohammad Najm, reported that "American–English books are now taking first place over French and English–English books." He further said: "In the Arab world, in the last 10 years, 70 percent of translations are of American books, 30 percent of others." The managing director of the Egyptian office also noted that "[t]he Russians have had a program for translating books into Arabic. It was limited and not too successful because it concentrated on controversial subjects." A quote from the managing director of Lebanon at this meeting reveals the symbolic position of the FBP at the time: "As Coca-Cola has raised the standards of the local refreshment industry, Franklin has raised the standards of publishing" (Shepard, 1965).

The year 1966 was distinguished by a broadening of FBP's international contacts, one aspect of which involved enlarging the International Advisory Board to include representatives from Brazil, Iran, Nigeria, the United Arab Republic, and the United Kingdom. Other notable global developments of this year included the appointment of new members to its board, which included Archibald S. Alexander, assistant director of the US Arms Control and Disarmament Agency, Rodman Job, former director of the Peace Corps in Nigeria, and Theodore Waller, president of Grolier Educational Corp. In this year, the FBP International Advisory Board was extended to include Asadollah Alam (1919–78), Minister of Royal Court, Iran. The FBP further arranged with l'Association nationale du livre français à l'étranger such that, with their help and financial support, twelve French books were translated into Arabic in Cairo and six into Persian in Tehran.[75]

The FBP had already increased its disbursements by over 100 percent over the last four years and in 1966 had disbursed the highest monies in its history. The 1966 annual report states: "Using disbursement of money as a rough general index, it is clear that the total of FBP activity during the year was higher than ever before. Total disbursement was $4,036,600 as compared with $3,550,600 in the previous year, which was the highest to that time."[76] The general expansion and acceleration of work was such that during this year, the FBP had published one-sixth of all the books published in its entire fourteen years of operation. The Cairo office was prominent in publishing children's books. Indonesia was more involved in university-level books in the social sciences. The Iraq office was active in vocational education. The East Pakistan office was interested in supplementary books for school libraries. The Latin American projects were in the field of medicine. A total of about 10,000,000 textbooks in Arabic, Persian, and Pashto were produced with FBP cooperation during the year.

The training division continued to carry out its projects during the year in Asia, Africa, and Latin America. In a new development, the British Book Development Council cooperated with the FBP in editorial training workshops in Nigeria, held in Ibadan and Nsukka. The textbook-writing training program extended to Africa. That year, the FBP also started a new project for teacher-training textbooks in Bengali for East Pakistan, financed by the fund under Public Law 480.[77]

In the school library project up to this time, the most extensive FBP programs were in the two wings of Pakistan, where about 445,000 copies of books in Urdu and Bengali had been supplied, and in the United Arab Republic, where 496,000 supplementary-reading books in Arabic had been provided for Egyptian schools. In 1966, the FBP was also installing fifty model schools in Afghanistan with collections in Persian, English, and Arabic, aided by a grant from the Asia Foundation and in cooperation with the Ministry of Education.[78]

As for Iran, however, one new development was the country's 1966 legislation requiring all municipalities to devote 1.5 percent of their annual budgets to libraries. The establishment of the Institute for the Intellectual Development of Children and Young Adults (IIDCYA), sponsored by Queen Farah Diba, had also extended the library work already begun by private groups, the Literacy Corps, and others with which the FBP cooperated. The publication of *Payk* continued in 1966 under the same sponsorship, and with FBP help, easy-reading books for the newly literate were published in 50,000-copy editions. The FBP, sponsored by USAID, selected and sent examples of new-literacy reading materials from US sources in sample collections to USAID education officers in twenty-three countries. The FBP was hoping that these English-language examples would provide the basis for local adaptations.

Financially, in 1966 the FBP received more than $4,200,000, of which 17 percent came from the US government, 18 percent from US private corporations, 6 percent from operational income, and 59 percent from foreign sources. That year, the Council on Books in Wartime, a non-profit organization established during the Second World War, was dissolved and its remaining assets (about $17,500) were given to the FBP. The American foundations (the Ford Foundation, W.K. Kellogg Foundation, Commonwealth Fund, Rockefeller Brothers Fund, Old Dominion Foundation, Alfred P. Sloan Foundation, Asia Foundation, Population Council, and Heineman Foundation) and numerous publishers (fifty-eight firms that year) continued to contribute financially. Moreover, corporations that were not directly in the book business started to financially support FBP efforts, including Arabian–American Oil Co., Canada Dry Corp., General Motors Corp., and Xerox Corp.[79] The ministries of education in Afghanistan, Iran, and Saudi Arabia; the Imperial Organization for Social Services (Iran); Iraq's Ministry of Culture; and the governments of Kuwait and Sudan were all financing FBP projects.[80]

By 1967, organizing seminars and training programs for book-industry personnel and textbook writers had become an important part of FBP activity. These seminars were increasingly held in Latin America and Africa. In Rio de Janeiro, the FBP sponsored the first Brazilian seminar for booksellers and distributors in 1967, which was funded by the Kellogg Foundation. A similar seminar for publishers was held in Mexico (the country's first seminar of this kind). In Ibadan, the FBP in collaboration with the Peace Corps organized and carried out a textbook-writing workshop for Nigerians.[81] In New York, the FBP conducted a ten-day seminar in book publishing procedures for a group of eighteen publishers of religious books from ten Asian, African, and Latin American countries. Lit-Lit, a division of the National Council of Churches, had sponsored the seminars.[82]

While in its first few years, the FBP was mainly focused on its Regular Translation Programs and geographically on the Middle East and Asia, by the late 1950s it had started to move toward the field of textbook writing, supplementary reading, and library development. The "success" of the Regular Programs of the FBP assisted it in making this new move, which was accompanied by the internationalization of its offices to include Africa and Latin America. During the early and mid-1960s, the FBP was in its most favorable period of activity, both financially and in terms of the range and international context of its operations. Financially the FBP was receiving funds from a variety of American foundations, from publishers, and from the United States and other governments. Internationally it was undertaking operations concerning the education and book industry of Third World countries and carrying out surveys on this subject on several continents. Late in the 1960s, however, this most favorable period of FBP operations came to an end as the organization was pushed to reshape its structure and limit its scope of operations due to international political developments and internal financial constraints.

Reintroduction as an International Educational Development Program (1968–75)

Both financially and structurally, 1968 was the start of a new period of organizational development for the FBP. The FBP began to face an unfavorable situation as the revenue under one of its major contracts with the US government was significantly reduced (to a total of $444,200 in comparison to the 1967 amount of $556,300 and 1966 amount of $735,100). The US government started its shift of focus away from technical and capital assistance, and the FBP was pushed to rely more on foundations, corporations, banks, and individual donors to carry out its reorganization and ensure the continuation of its work. US publishers as a group doubled their previous year's contributions. However, the FBP still had to adapt or cease some of its operations. In the Middle East and Asia, the "slow pace of economic recovery in Indonesia" and the "lingering aftermath of the Pakistan–India war" pushed the FBP to reduce its staff and curtail its programs.[83] In Africa, the FBP concluded its book industry development program supported by USAID and the Ford Foundation. As a result of the civil war in Nigeria, the FBP reduced its participation there to a Nigerian part-time consultant. With the closure of several local offices, in a shift from its initial structure and policy, the FBP started to conduct some of its operations in these countries from its New York headquarters.

The FBP's board of directors "reshaped" the organization in the direction of "greater flexibility" so that it could continue to operate within the context of the new international educational developments. The UNESCO Conference on Book Development in Africa, held in Accra in February 1968, was a landmark in UNESCO's interest in the area of book development. This conference recommended that countries establish their own book-development organizations. Another key event was the International Publishers Congress convened in Amsterdam in 1967, which focused on the ways in which the book industries of the developed countries could provide assistance to the industries in the developing countries. World Bank president Robert S. McNamara, in his address to the bank's 1968 annual meeting, had also emphasized the technological revolution in the field of education and had reported a threefold increase in World Bank lending for education development, to be invested in textbooks, in audiovisual materials, and the use of modern communications techniques for teaching purposes.[84]

Facing financial hardship and in line with the above-mentioned international educational developments that had resulted in growing commitment by governments, international organizations, and publishing industries to educational initiatives, the FBP reshaped its structure, policies, and methods in order to reintroduce itself as an international educational development program. This shift started in 1968 and was clearly defined in 1970 under the FBP's new president, Carroll G. Bowen.

The FBP no longer framed itself as a translator of American books into local languages but instead foregrounded its experience in organizing and administering translation programs for university textbooks, general and professional reference books, and young people's supplementary-reading books. Furthermore, the FBP framed its activities in a new manner in which their technical assistance (such as the training of book-industry personnel and advising of local publishers) and consultative services to education ministries were foregrounded. Therefore, in this reframing, the FBP was presented as an administrator and organizer of translation projects, conferences, and seminars for publishers and educators and of country and regional book-development surveys.[85]

Importantly, during this shift, the FBP became more closely and publicly affiliated with USAID; in 1968, the FBP signed a contract with it under which "many of the latter organization's book activities formerly handled internally" were to be handled by the FBP.[86] Another development in this new period occurred in the relation between the FBP and the US publishing industry. Previously, the US publishing industry was providing the FBP with executive and technical personnel as consultants for Special Projects, as members of the FBP's board of directors, and was providing their direct financial support through annual contributions. More specifically, US publishers facilitated FBP operations by selling the translation rights of their books at a nominal fee. In 1968, however, the FBP's role was changed to assist US publishers in their attempts at developing joint-venture operations in local countries or in import and distribution of their books in the countries where it had firsthand knowledge. The FBP was also to provide the US publishers with bibliographical information and market surveys of these countries. When compared to the 1950s, at which time the FBP's operations were the major conduit through which hundreds of American books were translated into the local languages of developing countries, there is no doubt that the new articulation was a substantial reshaping of the organization's operations.

The same reshaping can be seen with regard to the funds from corporations, foundations, and other non-profit organizations. In the 1950s and early 1960s, the FBP's function was to come into contact with the national ministries of education in each of the countries in which it had a local office and then to carry out its Special Projects using the funds assigned by the US foundations. Now the FBP had to expand its affiliations with corporations, foundations, and other non-profit organizations within the educational fields of their international programs of community building in Asia, Africa, and Latin America.

In light of this new framing, the FBP now focused on reporting and foregrounding its operations in its training programs. By the end of 1968, the FBP had arranged and carried out or supervised training in the United States of more than two hundred managerial-level personnel (editors, designers, illustrators, distributors, booksellers, printing press operators) from over thirty countries. Most of these training programs were sponsored by USAID, and the managerial-level personnel attended workshops of four to ten weeks' duration. The FBP was also responsible for the training of an equal number of short-term visitors to the United States. The FBP had further provided training in local countries through its overseas offices and associated organizations.[87]

On January 27, 1969, the *Sixth Annual Report of the US Advisory Commission on International Educational and Cultural Affairs* pointed to the FBP's potential in fulfilling US international educational objectives. The law that had created this commission required it to report to Congress annually; the Sixth Annual Report was in fulfillment of this. The report argued that US educational and cultural programs (1) were an effective and significant element in US long-term foreign relations; (2) were an effective and essential tool to inform national intellectual and political leaders, the press, and other information media on American character and policies; (3) had effectively contributed to removing hostility toward the United States and to offsetting pro-communist propaganda; and (4) had provided an invaluable means for keeping channels of communication open in both directions, at times when and in places where political tensions or hostility blocked official diplomatic relationships.

The report pointed to several examples of the effectiveness of the former US International Educational and Cultural Affairs programs by pointing out that in most countries with long-lasting exchange programs, an "impressive number of key people" at the time—at very high levels in political and public life, in press and information circles, and in education—were former grantees. US International Educational and Cultural Affairs had also been markedly "successful" in selecting leaders and potential leaders in developing countries. Moreover, they had established strong, fruitful, and continuing relationships through exchange programs with educational institutions, educational policymakers, professors, and teachers.[88]

As an appendix to this report, the committee included recommendations prepared for the Secretary of State on International Book and Library Programs. It urged that all US government agencies concerned with international book and library development should be instructed to assign a higher priority to these programs and to more effectively coordinate their activities in this area with each other and with the private sector. The first objective within the committee's recommendations was for the United States to benefit from the FBP for the purpose of assisting the development of international book publishing. In the committee's opinion, the government, the USIA, and USAID had never taken full advantage of the FBP's potential.[89]

In February 1969, the FBP prepared a pamphlet for the USIA entitled *Books for Developing Countries: A Guide for Enlisting Private-Industry Assistance*, pursuant to the national book policy statement approved by the US government in January 1967. This national book policy statement had emphasized the "importance of encouraging book publishing capability in the developing countries." The preparation and publication of the pamphlet by the FBP was in order to guide the USIA and other US government agencies in "ways to involve the private sector of American book publishing in implementing the national book policy overseas."[90]

The year 1969 was also a continued period of transition for the FBP as its need for restructuring its overall organization continued. The board of directors continued to debate the following questions: where, with whom, by what means, and how the FBP would perform. The program continued its major operations, but the international socio-political developments of the Cold War and internal FBP financial constraints resulted in the diminishing of some activities, and some reductions and retrenchments that year. Among the international political developments were the intense internal instability in both wings of Pakistan and the depressed economic conditions in Indonesia.[91] The FBP also closed its offices in Beirut, Baghdad, and Kuala Lumpur.

Following the closer affiliations between the FBP and USAID, in 1969 the FBP coordinated all activities relating to the selection and procurement of books for USAID and its overseas missions. It established a Book Procurement Improvement and Bibliographic Center for this purpose.[92] Another area in which the FBP started to expand its role was in operating as a national clearinghouse for translation rights. From early 1970, the FBP ran an International Copyrights Information Center (INCINC), which was established as a central, noncommercial agency through which publishers in developing countries would be directed to US publishers for translation rights.[93]

In 1969, the FBP continued its affiliation with textbook publication in Iran and Afghanistan, publishing over 41,000,000 copies in Iran and 3,000,000 textbooks for Afghanistan. This figure was double the FBP's output from the previous year in this field, making the total number of textbooks produced in Persian and Pashto approximately 130,000,000. The FBP also doubled its 1968 textbook translations in the United Arab Republic, adding ten additional editions (totaling 46,000 copies), making this a total of 150 editions in 2,347,600 copies. This operation had continued despite the absence of diplomatic relations between Egypt and the United States. Using funds made available by USAID, the FBP moved further into textbook writing in Indonesia through conducting a seminar for Indonesian writers that was intended to upgrade secondary school textbooks. The school library development plans were further carried out in both wings of Pakistan, and four teacher-training manual titles were published (33,000 copies) during 1969 in Bengali for teachers in East Pakistan, bringing total production of such manuals in Bengali to 117,800 copies.[94]

The reduction in US government funding of the FBP continued in 1970, dropping down to $217,289. Funding from banks, book publishers, and foundations also declined to $221,567. The Iranian Imperial Organization for Social Services ($5,521,127) and the Afghanistan Ministry of Education ($547,543) remained the primary sources of foreign funds. To encourage individuals to financially contribute, under the Tax Reform Act of 1969, cash contributions to the FBP by individuals in 1970 and later years were allowed as deductions for federal income tax purposes.

By 1970, the FBP had concluded its transitional process of reintroduction. Under Carroll G. Bowen's presidency, the FBP was reframed as a "development institution" principally concerned with the planning and delivery of educational materials. In 1970, Bowen framed its work for ensuing years as follows: "For what we are trying to do is to change a translation service into a development institution." Bowen further pointed out that "FBP's focus on educational materials has been an evolution, not a revolution. From a preoccupation in 1952 with the cultural export of what was valid and useful in American culture, we moved perceptibly in the direction of university textbooks, school books, and supplementary reading."[95] By education, the FBP meant the deliberate, systematic, and sustained effort to transmit or evoke knowledge, attitudes, values, skills, and sensibilities. The FBP included both formal and informal structures in its definition of educational structures. This not only encompassed schools, colleges, institutions, and universities but also included families, churches, libraries, museums, publishers, youth groups, radio, and TV networks.

As a reflection of the FBP's new direction and framing, it continued to limit its Regular Translation Programs while maintaining or developing its affiliation with USAID and as an intermediary between US and Third World publishers. The FBP's renewed focus on educational materials (at the expense of reducing or halting the Regular Programs) was pursued in offices such as Jakarta and Tehran. The Jakarta office completely turned down any request from publishers for the Regular Program, except for those titles for which funding could be found. At this time, its major work was to carry out Text Writers Training Projects in Tugu, funded by USAID. It conducted five of these in total, the last of which was scheduled for January 1971. The Jakarta office of the FBP was also translating six university titles to be distributed through university bookshops; USAID was responsible for providing free paper for their publication.[96]

In Iran, the FBP was involved in the publication of a Persian version of UNESCO's *Courier*. The Tehran Branch's editorial department supervised the translation, and its production department handled layout and proofreading. This continued for six issues. Further, the FBP had observed that, with the rise of TV, light reading was on the decline, so besides children's literature, it was continuing to move deeper into the field of university books. The ideal situation for the FBP was its Tehran editors maintaining regular contact with faculty members so as to be able to diagnose areas of textbook need in connection with existing or planned courses and then to decide to translate or adapt a certain American title. The board of directors of the FBP also for the first time started to include international representatives, with Abdolreza Ansari, Princess Ashraf's deputy for Social and Education Affairs, becoming a board member.[97]

With the reintroduction of the FBP as a development organization, its link with USAID was further solidified. The FBP monitored the process of book selection and book procurement by USAID missions, acting as the liaison between USAID and the jobbers. In 1970, the FBP received and transmitted approximately 500 orders from some forty-four missions to the jobbers, involving over 64,000 separate items. It also sped up the completion of orders through direct calls to publishers and follow-ups with the jobbers. Furthermore, in early 1970 INCINC was established, run by the FBP. INCINC prepared a model contract that informed publishers in other countries of the negotiating agreements for the publication of translated editions of US books. In 1970, the majority of requests to INCINC were from India.

In 1971, the FBP continued to manage the INCINC and to monitor the book procurement project for USAID. The FBP also initiated several fresh developments related to its new directions. It contacted Ministry of Education or USAID officials in South Korea, Indonesia, Thailand, South Vietnam, Nepal, Pakistan, Iran, and the United Arab Republic and offered the services of the FBP's new integrated program. A new Washington office was especially established to regularly represent the new direction of the FBP to the US government agencies that were donors of aid to the foreign education sector. This office frequently communicated with the five regional bureaus of USAID (as well as the Bureau for Technical Assistance and the Office of Private Overseas Program in the Agency), with the International Bank for Reconstruction and Development (IBRD), and with the Bureau for Educational and Cultural Affairs of the US State Department. It discussed the development of educational materials with the embassy staffs of the missions of Indonesia, India, Pakistan, Korea, Turkey, and Tanzania.[98]

In 1971, the greatest headway was made in Pakistan, where USAID and the government of Pakistan signed an agreement in late June, and USAID allocated about $1 million in US-owned rupees to a four-year project to provide low-cost textbooks in science, technology, and vocational studies at the high school and college levels, through English-language reprints and translation/adaptation of American textbooks. The FBP saw this as its first attempt at its new program approach to materials development for formal education, combined with publishing and distribution development.[99] The Jakarta office completed a ten-week textbook writers' training program funded by USAID on March 25, 1971. Several dozen Indonesian textbook writers participated in the seminars and listened to lectures from American and Indonesian consultants. Many of the writers completed their manuscripts during the term.[100]

The FBP continued both its Book Procurement Service for USAID and its role as the organizer of INCINC. In INCINC, in addition to the model contract, it also devised a rights request form to serve as a guide to foreign publishers on how to apply for publishing rights. In the Book Procurement Service, its collaboration resulted in an increase in volume of ordering, from an average of 4,660 items each month to 8,380 items a month, and a decrease in the time for filling orders.

The textbook projects in Egypt, Kabul, and Tehran continued in 1971. In Kabul, alongside the publication of twenty-three titles (a total of 1,974,288 copies during that year), the office distributed 1,804 titles of books in English and Persian given by the Asia Foundation to twenty-six school libraries in Kabul and the provinces. In Pakistan, 62,010 copies of books were donated to 826 libraries in high schools, intermediate colleges, and universities, making the total number of copies distributed by this office 254,370—to 1,729 libraries of educational institutions and 357 libraries of municipal corporations, municipal committees, and town committees.[101]

In another substantial move away from its initial policy, during 1971 the FBP started to directly emerge as a publisher and for the first time in its history published three books bearing the colophon of FBP/Tehran. Two of the books were on statistics, and the third was a scientific dictionary. The Tehran Branch was now aiming to build an image of itself as a publisher of reference works and university-level textbooks.

In 1971, the FBP was also called upon by the Central Committee of Celebration of the 2500th Year of the Foundation of the Imperial State of Iran to undertake a number of translations from Persian into several European languages, including Russian, French, Spanish, and English. It also prepared and produced an album of reproduced miniatures and illuminated pages from *Shāhnāmah bāysanqurī* in three languages.[102]

In 1972, for the second time in a few years, the FBP, which continued to face substantial financial hardships, "redefined" its specific objectives. As a result of the financial hardships, the FBP was considering the question of whether it should still remain "independent" or become an official governmental organization.[103] To reassess its role in international book publishing development and to investigate ways of acquiring alternative financial sources, the FBP established two committees in 1972. The first was the Committee to Study Merger, chaired by Datus C. Smith, Jr., former FBP president, which recommended that the FBP remain "independent" from government if it could possibly do so. The second committee was the FBP

Task Force, which was responsible for searching for an internal solution to FBP's financial problems. The Task Force recommended that the FBP expand its influence worldwide, make a new and concerted effort to make its purpose and objectives more widely understood, and somewhat extend its sponsorship in the non-book-world. The FBP came to pursue these recommendations.[104]

Still, the financial hardship resulted in the closing of offices. The FBP's office in Indonesia was shut down, and the FBP's affairs there were handled by a consultant. The FBP's contract with USAID in the Book Procurement Services was terminated as of June 30, 1972, after three years. During these three years, the FBP monitored book orders from the USAID Missions totaling $380,000. The FBP, however, continued to operate INCINC. During these two and a half years, the FBP had processed nearly 300 rights requests, mainly from India.[105] The FBP also organized a four-month tour funded by USAID for the purpose of assessing the operations of the Nepalese Ministry of Education's textbook manufacturing plants.[106]

In 1972, John H. Kyle and the Tehran Branch managing director held meetings with the Centre for Educational Development Overseas (CEDO) in London to discuss possible FBP–CEDO cooperation. The Tehran Branch created a Center for Educational Technology (CET) for which Kevin Smith, vice-president of Educational Development Corporation, Inc., performed a two-week-long survey in Iran. This center was an audiovisual facility for Iran's formal and nonformal educational materials.[107]

Another new development in 1972 was the relocation of the Washington office of the FBP to Islamabad, making it the second FBP office there. The reason was that, under a USAID contract and in cooperation with the Ministry of Education, the FBP had started to expedite the local production of authorized Urdu translations and English-language reprints of some 300 US college textbooks in science and technology. Anders Richter, the FBP's vice-president, became its director, another substantial deviation from the initial policy of not having any American managers in the local offices.[108]

In 1973, the FBP's financial hardships continued, and it operated on a break-even basis, in this case meaning that it spent not more than it took in from contractual work and from direct contributions. General supporting contributions were lower than the FBP had expected. That year, the Lahore office was closed and all FBP activities in Pakistan were assigned to the director of the Islamabad office. Also, in Dacca, three American advisors were sent to work closely with counterpart personnel on the Bangladesh School Textbook Board. Importantly, after ten years, the contract between the Afghanistan Ministry of Education and the FBP came to an end, and the Ministry's printing plant in Afghanistan, which was managed by the FBP, was turned back to the Ministry. The Kabul office continued its library development program and created fifty more new school libraries throughout the country, each with 500 volumes of books from the Tehran office. The Asia Foundation continued to fund this library development project.

The most apparent program development in 1973 was a contract with the People's Republic of Bangladesh to provide advisory and acquisition services for the Ministry of Education in making textbooks available to the students at all levels. This was the first contract with a foreign government in ten years, and it took a team of resident American advisors a year and a half to operationalize. As a portion of this contract, the New York office ordered and shipped $440,000 worth of US college textbooks for distribution to Bangladesh university libraries to replace books lost in the recent war.[109]

Other FBP initiatives in 1973 included the continued development of the CET as a department of the Tehran Branch, which was the FBP's first large-scale effort to provide an audiovisual and electronic communication dimension to its production of educational materials. The FBP was hoping to make it an example for other nations. That year, the FBP also developed plans for a more systematic approach to its library development projects. This new project employed a school-to-school structure, based on which a cooperating US school raised money to create a school library in a developing country; it started with books for Bangladesh schools. The Dacca office was responsible for coordinating the procurement of the books and the setting up of the libraries.[110]

In November 1973, the FBP signed a contract with the World Bank (International Bank for Reconstruction and Development) to make a study of all aspects of the bank's publishing program, with special attention to the distribution of the World Bank's publications in developing countries. The FBP submitted its report to the World Bank in May of 1974. The FBP also signed an agreement with UNESCO to conduct a survey of the economics of book publishing in developing countries.[111]

Financially, the year 1974 followed the relative rise of US government funds for the FBP that began in 1973—total US government funds reached $667,259. The private, foundation, and bank financial supports, however, declined to $92,562.[112] In this year, the FBP concluded its Pakistan low-cost textbook project, which had started in 1971 and was funded by USAID. With the conclusion of this project, the FBP's office in Pakistan was closed. The Kabul office was also on the verge of closing due to the termination of the FBP's contract with the Afghanistan Ministry of Education.

Therefore, by 1974 the three remaining active offices of the FBP were the Dacca, Tehran, and Cairo branches. Under the new contract between the FBP and the Bangladesh Ministry of Education, 30,313 American English-language university-level textbooks, selected by Bangladesh university professors, and 438 periodical subscriptions were procured and distributed to the six Bangladesh universities. This project was funded by USAID. The FBP also provided technical assistance in the planning, production, and distribution of 38 million Bengali school textbooks and produced a pilot issue of a classroom magazine.[113]

In Iran, the CET signed a contract with the Education Development Center of Newton, Massachusetts, under which the latter prepared a plan for the implementation of educational technology in Iran. The Tehran Branch then submitted this plan to the Iran's Plan Organization. The plan included sixteen projects, three of which involved National Iranian Radio and Television. In June 1974, this center in Tehran also published the first issue of a new quarterly, *Educational Technology*, in an edition of 2,000 copies.

The Tehran Branch further produced twenty-one titles intended for use by children and adults—and on the subject of reading, writing, arithmetic, and reading from the Quran—for Iran's literacy campaign. In total, it had produced around two million copies of books for the Literacy Corps and for the National Committee for World Literacy under the Ministry of Education. It had also printed 27,500 literacy campaign posters.[114]

Since 1971 the FBP consultant John H. Beardsley had worked on behalf of the Tehran Branch with the Ministry of Higher Education in the planning of an open university. This plan resulted in the establishment of the Azad University of Iran (*dānishgāh āzād-i īrān*), which offered its first courses for teacher training in autumn 1975. At that time, the FBP was also working with the Free University to meet its printing and publishing needs.[115]

Due to the fact that the FBP's Annual Report of 1975 is missing in the archives, not enough information is at hand on FBP activity in that year. However, a declassified telegram from the US embassy in Kabul to the US embassy in Tehran, dated January 1975, reveals an extended curriculum- and textbook-project agreement between the United States and the government of Afghanistan, which had to be carried out by the Tehran Branch. According to this document, this extension was signed by Ambassador Eliot on January 4, according to which document USAID agreed to have 773,000 of Afghanistan's textbooks printed by the Tehran Branch. The books were to be delivered to Kabul by March 1975 as a donation from the US government. This document records the official request from the US embassy in Afghanistan to the US embassy in Tehran to facilitate the delivery from Tehran to Kabul as a diplomatic shipment: "Customs formalities, export permissions, through shipment without transfer to other nationality trucks, etc. should be expedited via diplomatic shipment from embassy to embassy."[116]

In sum, by 1974, the FBP had "reintroduced" itself as a development program and had undergone "certain departures" from its traditional mode of operation. John H. Kyle, in his presidential address in 1974, notes that for its first two decades the FBP's work was primarily based on the objective of addressing elite and literate audiences, for which the Regular Program worked to produce American books in translation. By 1974, however, the FBP's task had transformed to "assisting in the planning, creation, production, and distribution of educational materials for the very poorest, most underdeveloped peoples."[117] As a result of this focus on nonformal education materials, the FBP had also extended its field of work to audiovisual education and all forms of educational technologies.

As for moving away from its initial policies and structures, a few instances include (1) the presence of more FBP technicians in the field offices, which the FBP tried to justify by highlighting "the complexity" of the new challenges it faced; (2) the move toward Special Projects at the cost of terminating its Regular Programs; (3) the FBP's operation as a publisher in some offices such as the Tehran Branch; and (4) a more solid and open affiliation with US governmental organizations such as USAID.

Years of Decline (1975–7)

The 1973–5 recession in the United States, in which high unemployment and high inflation existed simultaneously (also referred to as stagflation), dramatically affected the FBP's financial condition, as this corporation was substantially relying on US government and private-sector funding. This became so serious that, in 1975, the FBP's continued operation was considered doubtful. As a result of this, the board of directors began to consider liquidation and the assignment of the FBP's assets and ongoing projects to other organizations. Still, the FBP managed to reduce its staff and expenses by about half and continued for another two years.

By 1976, the FBP's local offices had been reduced to three—in Iran, Egypt, and Bangladesh. Its funds from the US government had again reduced significantly, to $359,159. In this year, the FBP announced that the Tehran Branch would become an independent Iranian non-profit corporation with the same purpose and objectives as in the past; it was to continue to work on a contractual basis, retaining the name of the FBP.[118]

During 1977, the FBP acquired a few contracts. It signed a $211,000 contract with the Philippine government to advise on various aspects of its elementary and high school textbook program, partly financed through a World Bank loan. Also during this year, Linda Scher, a new FBP program officer with a background at school magazine publisher Ginn & Co., went to Egypt for a month and worked with staff members on the planning of a school magazine, supported financially by the Ford Foundation. Published early in 1977, this magazine, at a length of sixteen pages, was distributed to sixty schools in Egypt for testing.[119]

The FBP's annual report of 1977 shows that the board of directors was still hopeful that the FBP would manage to continue in face of all financial hardships. However, the publication of an article in the *New York Times* in late 1977 resulted in the board of directors deciding on formally dissolving the FBP. On December 26, 1977, two reporters, John M. Crewdson and Joseph B. Treaster, in their article "Propaganda Network Built by the C.I.A.," pointed to certain ties between the FBP and the CIA. Investigating the worldwide propaganda campaign by the CIA, this report revealed that in the late 1960s when "the agency's communication empire was at its peak," the CIA had connections with more than 800 news and public information organizations and individuals at different levels of importance. This network was known officially by the people inside the CIA as the "Propaganda Assets Inventory." The first important attack on this "communication empire" occurred in 1967, when some CIA financial ties to academic, cultural, and publishing organizations were disclosed. A decade later, however, many still had remained hidden.

Crewdson and Treaster revealed that according to former CIA officials, the Committee for Free Asia "was founded by the CIA as the Eastern counterpart of the Free Europe Committee." Later, this committee changed its name to the Asia Foundation, one of the many foundations, which funded several FBP projects. Crewdson and Treaster claimed that the Asia Foundation "provided cover for at least one C.I.A. operative and carried out a variety of media-related ventures."

As for the affiliation between the CIA and the FBP, the article claimed that according to former and current agency officials, both the FBP and Walker & Co. (a publishing house founded in 1959 by Sam Walker, a Second World War veteran and wartime correspondent) received CIA subsidies. The article also claimed that a spokesman at the FBP confirmed that the program had received grants from the Asia Foundation and "from another small foundation for an African project, both of which were exposed in 1967 as being supported by C.I.A."[120]

In response to the above article, Datus C. Smith, former FBP president, wrote a memo to the FBP board noting that in 1967, when the allegation of CIA infiltration of cultural organizations first surfaced, he had checked all the lists of "phony" CIA foundations and that, while the FBP had made grant applications to almost all of them, only the Asia Foundation had accepted them. In this memo, dated December 28, 1977—just two days after the publication of the article in the *New York Times*—Datus C. Smith claimed that the FBP's only source of funds with any CIA connection during these twenty-five years had been $179,448 from the Asia Foundation.[121]

According to a CIA declassified "Memorandum for the Record," one of the FBP projects the Asia Foundation funded had enabled the FBP to enter into a contract with the government of Afghanistan to produce primary school textbooks.[122] The Asia Foundation advanced the sum in January 1964. The foundation's advance had to be covered by a formal letter of agreement with the FBP, according to which the profits accruing to the FBP in the discharge of a contract with the Royal Government of Afghanistan had to be turned over to the Asia Foundation until the full amount of the advance made by the Asia Foundation to the FBP was repaid. This document further clarifies why it was the FBP, with the Asia Foundation's financial support, which performed the services that normally would be performed by USAID. This was so because, for "political and procedural reasons," the project could not be carried out by USAID. The US embassy had advocated for the participation of the Asia Foundation in a cable dated October 24, 1963. In this cable, the US ambassador to Afghanistan had sent a strong endorsement of the proposal to the Assistant Secretary of State for Near East Affairs and requested that his endorsement be brought to the personal attention of the director of Central Intelligence.

The US ambassador's endorsement was based on three considerations. First, the project presented an opportunity for the US government to exert a "lasting" influence on the "educational system and students" of Afghanistan. Second, this could help the United States actually live up to its often expressed encouragement to the government of Afghanistan in the development of a "more Western oriented culture and government system." Third, and most "crucial," however, was that it appeared certain that "unless the request for assistance was met by Americans the project would go, by default, to the Soviet Union." According to this "Memorandum," the project was supported in all areas of interest to the Americans, including by the Covert Action staff, the Near Eastern division, and at the desk level in the State Department.[123] The Asia Foundation, however, was lacking funds, so it requested that the USAID provide supplemental funds as an increase over its then-current budget authorization for the fiscal year of 1964.

A few months after the publication of the *New York Times* article, in June 1978, the same daily published another article on the FBP, this time to announce the FBP's closing. However, this article, written by Herbert Mitgang, did not share the critical view expressed by Crewdson and Treaster. Instead, it endorsed the FBP, describing it as one of the great non-profit ventures in international publishing. The article, not pointing to the effects of the financial constraints as well as the reported CIA ties, instead asserted that the FBP was closing due to the fact that it had "completed" its mission of translating cultural and educational works and of helping a dozen developing countries get their own publishing houses off the ground. The writer further claimed that, while the FBP was registered with the Department of State's Advisory Committee on Voluntary Foreign Aid, it had managed to remain independent of government interference. In a response to the previous article published in the same daily, Mitgang wrote that, while the FBP had received funds from one CIA front—the Asia Foundation—the FBP had not been aware of the foundation's role (Mitgang, 1978).

In a report authored for the Library of Congress in 1986, on a selective listing of organizations that promoted books and reading and on administered literacy projects, the following account was given for the FBP's decline: "The major reason was rapidly decreasing support from the United States Information Agency, which had helped fund Franklin from its beginning, but Franklin also faced internal financial and management difficulties, particularly in certain field offices." According to this report, as government and foundation interest in its activities had sharply decreased, in October 1977 the FBP's board of directors had suspended all operations. In the following year, the board decided to close the corporation, and liquidation was completed in 1979 (Cole, 1986).

The FBP's remaining cash balance and receivables, amounting to $8,000, were given to the Center for the Book at the Library of Congress. According to Datus C. Smith, before this contribution, the FBP's assets in Egypt had been given to an Egyptian non-profit organization in order to continue the FBP's operations there, and the assets in Iran with a total value of $10 million were given to an Iranian non-profit organization, which continued operations until the 1979 revolution (Smith, 2000).

Chapter 5

FRANKLIN BOOK PROGRAMS IN IRAN: CONTEXT, ESTABLISHMENT, AND REGULAR TRANSLATION PROGRAMS

The Tehran Branch was the second office among the FBP local branches, next to its Cairo one. It was established in 1954, a few months after the CIA-sponsored coup against Prime Minister Mosaddeq on August 19, 1953. Soon, in the context of the close alliance and friendly political and cultural relations between the United States and the post-coup regime in Iran, the Tehran Branch became the most "successful" among the FBP branches, undertaking a variety of operations in both the FBP's Regular Translation Programs and also its Special Projects. The Tehran Branch's long and multifaceted history is detailed in the following two chapters; its historical context, national development, and Regular Translation Programs will be discussed in this chapter. This chapter begins with a discussion of the importance of Iran within the wider geopolitics of the Cold War era and historicizes the cultural rivalry between the United States and the Soviet Union in Iran. It then goes on to explore the establishment of the Tehran Branch as part of and a continuation of Iranian–US cultural and educational relations. The Tehran Branch's Special and Textbook Projects will be addressed in the next chapter.

Soviet–US Rivalry in Iran during the Cold War and the Role of the Iranian State

In 1941, Allied forces occupied Iran so that US and British forces could transport supplies for the Soviet Red Army, which was under attack by the Germans. This Anglo-Soviet invasion was also justified on the pretext that Reza Shah, the first monarch of the Pahlavi regime, while declaring neutrality, continued friendly relations with Germany. The Allied forces deposed Reza Shah in 1941 and installed his son, Mohammad Reza Shah, on the throne.

During the early years of occupation, especially up to the point of the Red Army winning the Battle of Stalingrad in 1943, the British and Soviets had close relations. The Soviets saw the occupation not as a way of building openly Marxist organizations but as a method of helping them in their war effort (Abdul Razak, 2018). Iran's Communist Party, the Tudeh Party, was established at this early stage of occupation in 1941, without British objection. During its first two years of operation, the Tudeh Party was mostly committed to the international fight against fascism, as declared in its first program in February 1942. With the Soviet victory at the Battle of Stalingrad, however, the alliance between the occupying forces in Iran started to weaken. The Tudeh Party became more aligned with the Soviet Union, and the British, who had used to see the party as composed of progressive left-wing elements, started to increasingly perceive it as a pro-Soviet entity (Abrahamian, 1982, p. 305).

By the end of the Second World War, the polarization of the world socio-economic order between the capitalist bloc, under US leadership, and the socialist bloc, under the leadership of the Soviet Union, heavily shaped the emerging international order. Allied forces had agreed with each other to withdraw from Iran six months after the end of the war. This deadline arrived in early 1946. However, the Soviet Union's late withdrawal of its forces from Iran and the moral and military support the Soviet Union showed for the short-lived Azerbaijan People's Government (in power between November 1945 and December 1946) and Kurdish Republic of Mahabad (in power between January and December 1946) in the northwest of Iran were seen by Iran and the United States as a Soviet expansionist policy. This late withdrawal of Soviet army forces from Iran led to an impasse known as the Azerbaijan Crisis. The Azerbaijan Crisis played a significant role in the development of the Cold War between the United States and the Soviet Union. Further, the United States' active role in pushing Soviet troops out of Iran showed that the Truman administration had developed a clear conception of its interests in the Middle East and especially Iran (Blake, 2009).[1]

Soviet forces began to leave Iran in March 1946, at which time the Iranian state sent in its army to regain full control over the two provinces. Iran's army defeated the two governments and restored Iran's centralized control over both regions. The Soviet presence in Iran and Soviet–Iran relations deteriorated. The Iranian government also became sensitive toward any cultural activity by the Soviets and communists in Iran. In 1949, the Tudeh Party was banned, and the Iranian state began to maintain "tight restrictions on Soviet cultural programs and events" (Mossaki & Ravandi-Fadai, 2018, p. 427).

For a few years, especially during the short-lived prime ministership of Mohammad Mosaddeq (1951–3), the Iranian government followed a "policy of Negative Equilibrium, which advocated Iran's maintenance of a neutral stand" toward both superpowers (Blake, 2009, p. 62). In the field of cultural relations, Mosaddeq's policy of negative equilibrium resulted in restrictions for both sides, such as the closing of all information and cultural centers outside of Tehran, including those belonging to the USIS.

From the early years of the Cold War, US policy in the Middle East was directed toward a series of objectives: (1) the containment of Soviet encroachment and influence and maintaining the balance of power in the region, (2) maintaining the flow of oil to Western Europe and the United States, and (3) access to the Suez Canal (Offiler, 2015). In August 1953, the CIA (in a joint operation with British MI6) sponsored a coup that toppled Mosaddeq and was followed by closer relations between the restored Shah and the United States. After the coup, the United States "began to openly identify with its oil interests in Iran," as US oil companies started to earn a major share in Iranian oil (Blake, 2009, p. 185). In a foreign policy shift, Iran changed its policy of negative equilibrium to become a pro-US ally in the Cold War international order. Following these new relations, in 1955 Iran joined the Baghdad Pact, a military alliance of the Cold War. This military pact was intended to contain the Soviet Union.

Under the leadership of Stalin's successors, Soviet foreign policies moved to tactics of cooperation, which briefly improved relations between Iran and the Soviet Union. In December 1954, the two countries signed an agreement to settle the frontier problem caused by the Soviet-built dam on the Araxes river (Dmytryshyn & Cox, 1987), and a three-year commercial agreement between the two countries was signed in 1956 (Golan, 1990).[2] However, even under this commercial agreement, any presence of Soviet advisors met with the Iranian state's continued wariness. With the establishment of SAVAK (*sāzimān-i ʿiṭilāʾāt va amniyat-i kishvar*; National Organization for Security and Intelligence) in 1957, this organization became responsible for monitoring anyone with Soviet links (Mossaki & Ravandi-Fadai, 2018).

The 1958 revolution in Iraq, Iran's western neighbor, with its agenda of liberating Iraq from its ties to Britain and the United States, resulted in Iraq's withdrawal from the Baghdad Pact. The Iranian state consequently signed a mutual defense agreement with the United States in 1959 to further fortify its relations with the country. This mutual defense agreement allowed for the creation of US military bases in Iran. The agreement also resulted in the deterioration of already limited relations between Iran and the Soviet Union (Golan, 1990).

From 1962 to 1979, Iranian–Soviet economic relations improved. However, as will be shown in the following section, the betterment of economic relations only boosted the two countries' cultural exchange programs in a restricted manner. After Egypt and India, Iran became the third-largest partner in trade with the Soviet Union. Among the Third World countries, Iran also became the second-largest recipient of Soviet economic assistance (Golan, 1990, p. 178). As a condition of some of these economic contracts, such as the contract for the Soviet construction of a steel mill in Isfahan, the Iranian state asked Soviet officials to modify and revise the content of Soviet radio content being broadcast against the monarchy in Iran.[3] Trade between the two states reached $1 billion by 1971. In 1976, Iran and the Soviet Union signed a five-year trade agreement with a value of $3 billion (Matin-Asgari, 2013, p. 33).

In spite of the above Iran–Soviet relations, the Pahlavi state continued to act as a pro-capitalist and anti-Soviet force in a couple of international and regional conflicts, as with Iran's support for the US invasion of Vietnam and Iran's military actions against groups supported by the Soviet Union, including in the Dhofar rebellions. US–Iran cultural and educational relations also further developed during these two decades (1953–79) with the continuation of operations in the Point Four program in Iran; the rise of US-centered student migration; and the development of cultural, educational, and publication ties such as the operations of the Tehran Branch of the FBP.

Soviet–Iran Cultural and Educational Relations

While this research does not intend to historicize Soviet-sponsored publications in Iran, nonetheless a glance at such Soviet efforts at knowledge production in the country, and the role of the Iranian state in monitoring and blocking them, is necessary in order to compare the scope and methods of the Soviets' cultural diplomacy in Iran with similar US endeavors. It also helps in the analysis of the active role that the pro-capitalist Iranian state played with regard to the promotion or prevention of knowledge production during the Cold War.

The Society for Cultural Relations between Iran and the Soviet Union (*anjuman ravābiṭ farhangī īrān bā 'tiḥād shawravī*) was an Iranian organization which curated cultural relations between the two states. Founded in 1943, the Society worked closely with the All-Union Society for Cultural Ties with Foreign Countries (*Vsesoyuznoe obschestvo kul'turnoi svyazi c zagranitsei*; VOKS), which "directed, supported, and supplied" materials for it (Mossaki & Ravandi-Fadai, 2018, p. 429). In this sense, VOKS's relation to the Society was similar to the British Council's relation to the Anglo-Persian Institute (established in Iran in 1942) and to the US State Department's relation to the Iran–America Society (established in 1946). The Society, however, was legally an Iranian organization headed by an Iranian director, although it had Soviet citizens (usually fluent in Persian) within its staff too. The Society marks the height of Soviet Union-sponsored cultural diplomacy in Iran (Pickett, 2015). The Soviet Union financially sponsored the Society's costs, such as rent, and also provided it with "guidance." The Society encouraged writers to travel to the Soviet Union and to reflect on their journey in writing, and it organized plays, concerts, and sporting events.

Between 1943 and 1946, the Soviet Union actively pursued cultural ties with Iran. During the occupation years and until the Azerbaijan Crisis of 1946, the Society opened branches in a few cities and rural areas. A VOKS office was established in Iran's Azerbaijan, headed by the Soviet consul in the city of Rezayieh. Among the Society's initiatives was the holding of the First Congress of Iranian Writers in 1946, which seventy-eight writers and poets attended. However, this active engagement declined substantially after the withdrawal of Soviet forces from Iran. With the end of the Azerbaijan Crisis, the ambitious adventures of the Soviet Union in Iran shifted radically toward "moderate expectations" (Mossaki & Ravandi-Fadai, 2018).

Between 1946 and 1953, the Society organized only a few cultural exchange initiatives. In 1950, it organized the first Festival of Soviet Cinema (Mossaki & Ravandi-Fadai, 2018). Following the 1953 coup, and as the Iranian state took a pro-US foreign policy, the Society's operations were minimized (Pickett, 2015, p. 808). In early 1957, after a period of difficult relations between the two countries, a group of Soviet musicians came to Iran for a few performances. In addition to cinema and music, sport was also exploited to build cultural relations; wrestling, weightlifting, chess, and later soccer were the most popular joint athletic events organized in the 1950s and 1960s (Mossaki & Ravandi-Fadai, 2018).

The Soviet embassy in Tehran, wary of Iranian State's preventing the circulation of classics of Marxism-Leninism and political literature, distributed the magazines *Soviet Union* (*Sovetskii Soyuz*) and *New Time* (*Novoe vremya*) in English and French translations within Iran. Both magazines were devoid of a clear communist propaganda intent. It was only by the early 1960s that educational cooperation developed between scholarly institutions of the two countries in various disciplines, primarily Iranian studies, on which the Soviets, who also owned numerous Persian medieval manuscripts, had developed much scholarship over the century. The Institute of the People of Asia (IPA) of the Academy of Sciences of the USSR (*Institut narodov Azii*) began to work with Tehran and Isfahan universities, the National Library of Iran, the Book Society of Iran, and the Iranian Society for the Study of Ancient Iran to disseminate Soviet scholarship on Iran and Oriental languages, and facsimile publications of Persian classical manuscripts. Mossaki and Ravandi-Fadai argue: "While Soviet Iranian studies was closely and unapologetically linked with state policy, by focusing on classical Persian literature, Soviet scholarship was able to present a less politicized face" (Mossaki & Ravandi-Fadai, 2018, p. 439).

Moreover, the Soviet Union was even "surprisingly unresponsive" in the many opportunities to exploit cultural relations so as to counter American and British influence. Mossaki and Ravandi-Fadai argue that for the Soviets, the primary concern was to have a peaceful southern border, in search of which they would not engage in propaganda activities against the Shah. In sum, the Soviets were mostly driven by pragmatism rather than by ideology in their relations with their southern neighbor.

As such, the educational and cultural activities of the Society and the attempts of the Soviet Union to mobilize knowledge within Iran were limited. Still, the Iranian state was wary of any such attempts. SAVAK closely monitored the Society and any Soviet cultural program. The study of the SAVAK archives shows the extent of efforts and also the means employed by the Soviets for distribution of their cultural products in Iran and how Iranian intelligence actively operated to limit or block such attempts.

For instance, in a confidential SAVAK report dated June 14, 1963, the agency reported that Radio Moscow was attaching gifts—including textbooks and scientific books, postal cards of Russian landscapes, and Russian stamps—to the letters it was sending as a response to personal correspondence from its Iranian audience. The document noted that SAVAK had seized all of these gifts, pointing out further that Radio Moscow, noticing that its gifts were not being delivered, had recently begun using Soviet embassy personnel, the Society, and the Soviet embassy's Chamber of Commerce to bring in and distribute these gifts.[4] SAVAK also had informants inside the Tudeh Party and its former members to investigate possible clandestine activities by the Soviet Communist Party.[5]

The SAVAK archives also reveal that the improvement in Iranian–Soviet economic ties and relations in the early 1960s, which resulted in several economic and commercial contracts (as noted above), did not mean that the Iranian state put aside its constraints on communist- or Soviet-sponsored cultural influences. SAVAK's reports on the Soviet Azerbaijan Fair in Iran (*namāyishgāh 'āzarbāyjān shawravī*) exemplify how the Iranian state was monitoring any attempts by the Soviet state to distribute its sponsored publications.

The Soviet Azerbaijan Fair was held between May 17, 1965, and June 7, 1965.[6] Sensitive of possible Soviet propaganda activities during the fair, SAVAK detailed the fair's programs, reported on the content of lectures, and listed the people who attended. On May 26, 1964, the head of the Third Office (*mudīr kul idārah sivum*)[7] of SAVAK sent a letter to the head of SAVAK in Markazī province (*riyāsat sāvākāt 'ustān markazī*), asking for a detailed report on the fair to be sent to his office, including the number of people who were attending, the social and economic class of these visitors, the propaganda activities of the Soviets, the effects that the visit had on the people of each class (and how each class of visitors was reflecting on the Soviet Union and its industrial progress), whether current and former Tudeh Party members were among the visitors, whether the officials and political representatives of other states were commenting on the fair, and Iranian–Soviet relations in general.[8] In the next few days, the head of SAVAK's office in Markazī province reported back on the questions,[9] a second document dispatched from SAVAK's office in Markazī province discussed the Iranians who visited the fair,[10] and SAVAK listed the journals that were distributed during the fair and comments made by Iranian visitors.[11] Soon Mohammad Reza Shah was briefed on the Soviet Azerbaijan Fair in person.[12]

SAVAK was cautious about relations between the Soviets and the Iranian press. In a report dated April 30, 1966, 1965/6 is mentioned as the year that the Soviets achieved more than everything they had achieved in the previous twenty-five years in terms of publishing their views in dailies in Iran. According to this report, in the previous twenty-five years it was only the Tudeh Party newspapers that would write in favor of the Soviets; neutral newspapers would do so rarely, and liberal ones never. SAVAK, however, was concerned, following the signing of the contract between the two states for the Soviet construction of the Isfahan steel mill (in 1964), that the Soviets had clandestinely negotiated with daily newspapers and succeeded in incorporating the views of the Telegraph Agency of the USSR (TASS), the official Soviet news agency, in Iranian dailies.[13] The Soviet cultural and press activities in Iran are further detailed and analyzed in another SAVAK document (no date), which pointed out that the Soviet Union used two methods to "penetrate" (*nufūz*) the Iranian press: financial assistance and various acts of "blandishments" (*taḥbīb*). The methods of the Soviet embassy in Tehran toward financing the publication of articles were either direct payment for the publication or the publishing of an article along with an advertisement. The same SAVAK report listed the following offers to press editors as examples of the "blandishments": inviting them to Soviet embassy parties; invitations to visit the Soviet Union; and the provision of special access to Soviet hospitals, banks, and airlines. The Soviet Union also attempted to import printing machines into Iran and so sell them cheaply on long-term payment installment plans.[14]

Soviet-printed journals were usually mailed to the organizations affiliated with the Soviet embassy, in languages including Persian, English, Russian, and Armenian. Books in Persian and English, limited in their titles but abundant in copies, were intended for distribution among ordinary people. The Soviet-sponsored journals in Russian and Armenian consisted of more titles, but only a few copies of each. The books in Persian were usually translations of books by Russian writers that were published in the Soviet Union and entered Iran as quality products sold cheaply. Most of these books were fiction.[15] The communists' bravery in the face of hardships, their resistance in confronting fascism, and their comparison of Russia under the Tsars and under the Soviets were subjects commonly narrated in the novels and short story collections. The other kind of books printed by the Soviets in Persian was on the scientific and industrial progress of the Soviet Union, especially in the field of astronomy. The official bookshops in Iran, however, did not sell communist books, as they were illegal—so books containing clear communist propaganda were only distributed through the postal system.

In the field of children's literature, SAVAK reported that the Soviets had recently (i.e., in 1966) published an illustrated book in English and imported 25,000 copies into Iran. The report asserted that this book was on animals and their lives; although not having any communist subtext, SAVAK still worried that, if distributed among children in kindergartens and private primary schools in Tehran, it might result in pleasant memories of the Soviets in the children's minds.[16] Children's books in Persian were also imported to Iran. As a contemporary example, the report pointed to an illustrated pamphlet with the name *The Tale of the Fisherman and the Fish* (*ḥikāyat māhīgīr va māhī*). This fairy tale in verse, written in 1833 by Alexander Pushkin, narrates the tale of a fisherman who catches a golden fish; the golden fish promises to fulfill any of the fisherman's desires if he frees it. The tale reveals how this "promise" obsesses the fisherman's wife and pushes her toward becoming more and more greedy—resulting in a tragedy. SAVAK's report interpreted the storyline of this pamphlet as anti-capitalist and anti-monarchy, as a story that would affect children's attitudes toward the queen, guardians, and nobility within society and one that would result in an apprehension of the concept of class from a communist perspective.[17]

SAVAK's attention to the possible involvement of Soviet embassies in publication activities in Iran was not limited to the Soviet embassy in Tehran, where the Iranian government had already confined the Soviet's diplomatic activities. It also extended to Soviet embassies in Baghdad and Kuwait.[18] On December 17, 1966, Iran's Foreign Ministry summoned the Soviet embassy's press attaché in Tehran to object to the publication of an article on the Vietnam War and the dispatching of propaganda journals from the Soviet Union to individuals in Iran, and it reaffirmed that the Soviet embassy's journals and news bulletins should not contain any ideological content.[19] SAVAK was also sensitive to and monitored any distribution of books published by Progress Publishers, a Soviet publisher founded in 1931.[20]

SAVAK was also clear that the improvement of economic and political relations between Iran and the Soviet Union should not extend to improved educational relations. In a letter from the head of the Eighth Office (*'idārah kul hashtum*)[21] to the head of the Third Office, dated December 5, 1968, SAVAK criticized the buying of educational tools and technologies from communist countries for Iran's polytechnic educational institutions, arguing that "compared to the educational products of the developed countries, the Communist educational tools were not worth buying." SAVAK also pointed out that the Soviets had proposed several educational contracts to Iran's Ministry of Education and also to Iran's Organization for Planning and Development yet asserted that none of these proposals should be accepted. The report asserted that the Soviets should "never" get the chance to "embed" (*jāsāzī*) their ideas in the Iranian youth and university students.[22]

Through an archival study of the SAVAK documents, the above section demonstrated how the Iranian state was closely monitoring, reporting, and effectively and actively blocking any Soviet cultural and educational activities. Now, I will move to discuss US–Iran cultural and educational relations in the same historical period and how the Iranian state not only did not have the same concerns when it came to the United States, but collaborated closely with various US knowledge and educational production activities in Iran.

US–Iran Cultural and Educational Relations

According to Datus C. Smith, the first president of the FBP, the most "successful" of all FBP offices was the Tehran Branch (Smith, 2000). However, to understand the reasons behind this "success," we need to analyze the importance of the Middle East in the US policy of containment during the Cold War, which was discussed earlier in this chapter, and to historicize US–Iran educational relations from 1950 when the Point Four program started its activities in Iran.

US government-sponsored overseas education modernization programs began in 1950 as part of the Point Four program, which continued into the 1960s through USAID (Garlitz, 2012b). President Harry Truman signed the Act for International Development on June 5, 1950. Two months later, Franklin S. Harris was dispatched to negotiate the terms with the government of Iran for an agreement to provide technical assistance. Iran was one of the first countries to receive such attention. This agreement was "the first time that the U.S. government made international education part of its Iran strategy" (Shannon, 2017, p. 21). On October 19, 1950, a memorandum of understanding was signed between Ambassador Henry Grady and Iran's Prime Minister Ali Razmara, providing for US technical cooperation in a rural improvement program. The memorandum between Point Four and the Iranian government was the first Point Four international agreement, which testifies both to the importance of Iran for the Technical Assistance Program and the "disturbed economic and political situation" of Iran at the time (Hendershot, 1975, p. 11).

In 1975, Clarence Hendershot, who served as the US education director in Iran (1961–5), published a book called *Politics, Polemics and Pedagogies*, on the US Technical Assistance Program in Iran. As someone who served in the "thick of these educational" activities, Hendershot attempted in this book to cover and analyze the sixteen-year time span (1951–67) of the program. In his preface to the book, Hendershot lists several "basic considerations and facts," which should be kept in mind in any study of the US Technical Assistance Program in Iran, one of which is that the program was intended to eliminate the threat of communism from "within and without." Hendershot asserted: "The host government was sharply aware of grave Communist threats from within and without. The donor was equally concerned that these threats be eliminated within and contained from without" (Hendershot, 1975, p. xvi).

According to Hendershot, the rise of the nationalist prime minister Mosaddeq to power on April 28, 1951, intensified the "urgency" that the US Technical Assistance Program felt for undergoing an "educational emergency program" in Iran (Hendershot, 1975, p. 11). When Mosaddeq resigned on July 16, 1951, as a result of his conflict with the Shah over the right of appointing the Minister of War and the Chief of Staff, the political conditions for the Point Four program became even worse. Mosaddeq's resignation and the subsequent appointment of Ahmad Qavam by the Shah led to the mass demonstrations of July 16, 1952, known as the 30 Tīr Uprising, which pushed the frightened Shah to dismiss Ahmad Qavam, submit to Mosaddeq's demands, and reappoint him as the prime minister on July 21, 1952. Reflecting on the events of the 30 Tīr Uprising, Hendershot describes it as a "trying period" for Americans, as walls were plastered with "Yankee go home" signs. As a result of this intensified anti-American sentiment, "[t]he Mission felt strong pressure to make a show of activity as early as possible. Orders were issued to implement projects without delay" (Hendershot, 1975, p. 11). The Education Division of Point Four in Iran called

> for the opening at once of a demonstration elementary school in Tehran even though it was mid-term, and in the provinces to proceed urgently with a range of activities, but with first priority given to the training of the elementary school teachers for an immediate impact on the improvement of the Iranian school system.
>
> (Hendershot, 1975, p. 21)

Later, the chief of the Education Division, Hoyt J.B. Turner, in a personal letter written to Hendershot, revealed insights into why the "training of teachers" was such a priority for their emergency teaching program:

> Eighty percent of the teachers were communists. This is why a large part of our total efforts were directed toward In-service Education. We felt that if we could meet face to face with these teachers that we could eventually change their attitude which proved to be correct.
>
> (quoted in Hendershot, 1975, p. 21)

In addition to teacher training, another activity that Point Four developed rapidly in Iran during the same school year (1952/3) was the provision of books, magazines, pamphlets, and visual aids to support the curriculum in the "demonstration" schools. These activities were centered in a publication section of Point Four. From the outset, the lack of adequate numbers of books for pupils and the complete absence of any other reading materials in the schools were identified, and a program was undertaken in cooperation with Iran's Ministry of Education to revise the textbooks so as to "modernize" the content, to prepare teachers' guides, and to write pamphlets for supplemental reading. Point Four also began to manage a library in Tehran and to provide library services for the provinces; hundreds of copies of books were distributed there.

According to the director of Point Four in Iran, Mosaddeq once observed that "Point Four is like the Iranian tarantula; it jumped up and down and frightened people, but had never been known to bite anyone" (quoted in Hendershot, 1975, p. 21). While this quote, attributed to Mosaddeq, apparently meant to push Point Four toward more active technical assistance in Iran, paradoxically what made the socio-political conditions most favorable for US educational assistance was the coup against Mosaddeq himself. The coup was planned and sponsored by the CIA and MI6 and implemented on August 19, 1953, in face of these agencies' increasing fear of Iran's possible turn toward communism and the Soviet Union. Mosaddeq's insistence on the nationalization of the oil industry in Iran had further made him an enemy in the eyes of the British and the United States.

The restoration of the Shah to power and the change in government after the coup resulted in closer relations between the Iranian government and the United States Information Service (USIS), which had suffered from several decisions made by Mosaddeq, such as the closing of all information and cultural centers outside of Tehran (including those belonging to the USIS).[23] Just two months after the coup, on October 2, 1953, an official document on USIS activities in Iran stated:

> The changed political situation has created the need and provides an opportunity for our office to do a full scale job within Iran. The Zahedi[24] government is recognized throughout the country as being one brought in and supported by the U.S. Whether this is true or not is immaterial. We have placed squarely upon our shoulders the responsibility for it; therefore, it is of the greatest importance that no stone be left unturned to make this regime successful.[25]

With the toppling of Mosaddeq and the consequent Iranian state suppression of nationalist and leftist activists inside the country, the US educational assistance programs in Iran could no longer be described as a "lazy tarantula." All the educational initiatives that had been started in the unfavorable socio-political conditions of the short-lived Mosaddeq government developed dramatically after the coup. Moreover, after the coup Point Four was no longer alone in pursuing these initiatives, as the Tehran Branch of the FBP was founded in 1954. The Tehran Branch became a major factor in the success of several Point Four operations, most notably in the improvement in the quality and quantity of textbooks for elementary schools that was conducted under the Tehran Branch's administrative leadership (Hendershot, 1975).

The post-coup close relations between Iran and the United States drastically changed the educational and cultural relations between the two countries. Mathew K. Shannon analyzes the history of US–Iran educational relations during the Cold War in the context of the larger US strategy of containment. Shannon observes:

> Education, a form of soft power with the ability to transform nations and, perhaps, to win hearts and minds, became a means by which the US could cultivate friendly relations with nations at risk of falling under Soviet influence.
>
> (Shannon, 2017, p. 2)

Between the 1950s and the end of the Pahlavi regime, the US and Iranian governments continued to rely on international education to fortify relations. By the end of the 1950s, it was much easier to travel from Iran to the United States than to the Soviet Union. There was no direct path for Iranians to go to Soviet universities until the mid-1960s; even the Soviet–Iran rapprochement of the mid-1960s only relatively improved such relations. The educational assistance that was initiated during the Truman administration in the 1950s continued to guide educational programming up until the late 1970s. By the 1970s, these educational initiatives had become "larger in scope," with "more sophisticated aims." The US-centered flow of students from Iran was strengthened by the rise of international education combined with bilateral security agreements, regional defense pacts, and other forms of cooperation. The focus of these educational relations was mostly on military training, technical education, and cultural exchange (Shannon, 2017, p. 95).

One of the ways of facilitating the US-centered student migration was through the granting of awards. The State Department's International Educational Exchange Program was responsible for awarding grants to foreign leaders, scholars, and students. The most prestigious of these exchange program awards was the Fulbright Program, directed by a US president-appointed Board of Foreign Scholarships in Washington. Iran was the first Middle Eastern country to sign a Fulbright agreement in 1949. By the late 1960s, the State Department reported that "in a few countries, of which Iran is perhaps the best example, it can be said that we are 'scraping the bottom of the barrel' because most of the meaningful leaders […] have already been given grants under this program" (quoted in Shannon, 2017, p. 28). American Friends of the Middle East (AFME) was another US organization active in the educational realm of the cultural Cold War. AFME prioritized those students whose studies informed the question of development and placed leading students in prestigious US universities (Shannon, 2017). Its field office opened in Tehran in August 1953.[26]

US universities were early enthusiastic supporters of the US government-sponsored overseas educational aid programs. Several US universities were actively involved in the modernization of Iranian education during the 1950s and 1960s. Between 1951 and 1955, Brigham Young University (BYU) worked with Iran's Ministry of Education in reorganizing its curriculum and also sent specialists to aid with instructing elementary and secondary school teachers. Utah State Agricultural College (USAC) worked closely with the agricultural faculty of the University of Tehran, Karaj College, to modernize it along the lines of US agricultural colleges, and it continued its affiliation with Iran's agricultural educational programs to disseminate knowledge of farming to rural areas (between 1951 and 1964). The University of Pennsylvania (UPenn) also sent advisors to Shiraz to transform Pahlavi University in line with the US higher education system (during 1962–7)

(Garlitz, 2012b). It is in the context of the US Cold War educational and cultural relations with the Iranian state—which predated or coexisted with the Tehran Branch—that the Tehran Branch was established.

Tehran Branch: Establishment and National Development

During its quarter century of operation (1954–77), the Tehran Branch translated around 850 titles into Persian; most of the authors were American, with a few British and French, and fifty books were original titles by Iranians.[27] More than fifty publishers worked with the Tehran Branch, including well-known houses such as Amīr Kabīr, Andīshah, Bungāh Tarjumah va Nashr Kitāb, and Ibn Sīnā (Smith, 2000). Abbas Amanat, a prominent historian of modern Iran, describes the FBP's role in Iran as follows: "In the area of culture, perhaps no American initiative was as influential as Franklin Publication House." He adds that in due course, this initiative became "a model for other Iranian publishers" (Amanat, 2017, p. 647). The Tehran Branch's first manager, Homayun Sanʿatizadeh, was a key figure both in the establishment of the branch and in most of its early developments and achievements. FBP records and memoirs, and reflections by its staff, have pointed to his formative role. Sanʿatizadeh played an essential part in building a network of intellectuals, translators, and editors who worked for the Tehran Branch and also in negotiating various contracts and arrangements between the Tehran Branch and the royal family, politicians, and education officials in Iran. Sanʿatizadeh is also credited by several historians of Iran's modern publishing as being the most influential individual in modernizing the industry in Iran.

Homayun Sanʿatizadeh was the son of Abdulhussain Sanʿatizadeh Kermani (1895–1973), a writer-merchant and part-time bookseller who was the forerunner in science fiction and utopian fiction in modern Persian literature. His mother, Qamar Taj, was from the Dowlatabadi family, notable for its role as advocate of the public schooling system in Iran. Sanʿatizadeh's uncle and aunt were respectively the educationalist Yahya Dowlatabadi (1862–1939) and the women's rights activist Sediqeh Dowlatabadi (1882–1961).

Sanʿatizadeh began his primary schooling in the Zoroastrian School in Tehran (presently called Jamshid Jam), where the influential bibliographer and iconic figure in the field of Iranian studies, Iraj Afshar (1925–2011), also attended. The two became lifelong friends. Sanʿatizadeh finished his primary school in Kerman, a province in the southeast of Iran. He later left Kerman to attend Alborz College in Tehran. Alborz College, formerly American College, was established in 1873 as an American Presbyterian missionary institution, but its properties had been bought by the Iranian government in 1940 (Armajani, 1985).[28] At Alborz College, Sanʿatizadeh learned English under the encouragement of Samuel Martin Jordan (1871–1952), an American Presbyterian missionary in Iran.

Following the occupation of Tehran in 1941 by the Allied forces, Sanʿatizadeh left school and went back to Kerman, where he assisted his grandfather in managing the affairs of the orphanage he had established. As stated by Sanʿatizadeh in his interview with Alinejad, the social and economic crises of Kerman, a province struggling with famine and devastating social inequality, pushed Sanʻatizadeh toward leftist dispositions (Alinejad, 2016). He later moved to Isfahan where he finished his high school education, but he never pursued higher education. Instead, Sanʻatizadeh began to work in a bazaar for a local firm and soon used his knowledge of English to translate the commercial correspondence for the company. According to his sister Mahdokht Sanʻati, Sanʻatizadeh also used his knowledge of English and his communication skills to develop a few small commercial arrangements with the British forces in Iran during the occupation. Sanʻatizadeh further expanded on the social network of his novelist father to establish close relations with Mohammad Ali Jamalzadeh (1892–1997), a prominent writer and pioneer in modern Persian fiction, and with Hassan Taqizadeh (1878–1970), a distinguished senior politician, constitutionalist, and scholar (Sanʻati, 2014). In 1942, Sanʻatizadeh joined the Tudeh Party, becoming secretary of its Central Committee. According to Mahdokht Sanʻati, his brother even held some of the executive meetings of the Tudeh Party (*dabīrān ḥizb*) in his room at their mother's place in Isfahan. In 1946, Sanʻatizadeh left the Tudeh Party.

In 1947, Sanʻatizadeh opened his own firm, reproducing posters and selling flyers. His gallery became a social hub for men of culture and politics, such as Parviz Natel Khanlari (1914–90), scholar of Persian literature and at the time the first director of the University of Tehran's newly established Tehran University Press.[29] Manuchehr Anwar (1928–present), a former news anchor at BBC Radio who later became the first supervisor of the Tehran Branch editing bureau, recalls that Sanʻatizadeh was first introduced to him in 1953 by Nader Naderpour (1929–2000), a prominent Persian modern poet, as a man who had an "open house" party every Friday. According to Anwar, several prominent Persian poets of the time, such as Naderpour and Sohrab Sepehri (1928–80), the well-known and influential modern poet and painter, were present at Sanʻatizadeh's weekly parties (Alinejad, 2016).

According to Sanʻatizadeh, he was first introduced to the FBP during a poster exhibition he had curated of impressionist artworks, on the second floor of the Sanʻatizadeh Museum located on College Avenue in Tehran. He had invited US embassy officials, and the cultural attaché of the embassy came with two Americans from the FBP board of directors. As noted in Chapter 3, when the FBP officials traveled to the Middle East for the first time, the US missions were asked to treat them "as private businessmen."[30] The two representatives of the FBP board of directors, one of whom was Datus C. Smith, the president of the FBP, negotiated with Sanʻatizadeh to appoint him as FBP's local manager in Iran (Sanʻatizadeh, 1995). In line with the general policy of the FBP with regard to choosing local managers, Sanʻatizadeh was not a publisher, nor did he have detailed knowledge of the industry—but he was well connected and energetic. Concerning Sanʻatizadeh, Smith said:

> His intellectual creativity and instinctive understanding of book publishing joined with his courage and entrepreneurial wisdom in bringing almost immediate success to the project.
>
> (Smith, 2000)

The Tehran Branch commenced operations on March 6, 1954 (Amuzigar, 1977) with a monthly budget of $2,000 and two clerks working under the management of San'atizadeh (Yadegar, 1979).[31] It was first located on Naderi Avenue in Tehran, beside the Naderi Hotel. In 1956, it moved to the College intersection. The Tehran Branch's initial objective, following the FBP's early policy, was not to publish books itself. It prepared Persian translations of titles from the list from FBP headquarters and negotiated their publication with local publishers. The Tehran Branch prepared print-ready titles and handed them over to other publishers for printing and publication. In exchange, the Tehran Branch received 15 percent of the cover price as royalty (Alinejad, 2011). On the first page of FBP-sponsored books, the sentence "with the collaboration of mu'sisah intishārāt firānklīn [Franklin Book Programs]" was printed.

Through Regular Translation Programs and through Special Projects—such as the sponsorship of workshops for textbook writers, sponsorship of workshops for the publishers, the *Persian Encyclopedia* project, and various collaborations with Iran's Ministry of Education—San'atizadeh developed a wide range of social and intellectual networks for the Tehran Branch. He used any opportunity to build relations with the royal family, senate members, and key translators, intellectuals, and publishers of the time. The list of contributors to the Tehran Branch included Mohammad Reza Shah, Queen Farah Diba, and the Shah's sister Ashraf Pahlavi. Taqizadeh, the head of the senate, was a local advisor to the Tehran Branch. The list of translators in the Regular Translation Programs of the Tehran Branch included the royal family (Queen Farah Diba and Princess Ashraf Pahlavi), senate members (such as Amir Hossein Zafar, Mohammad Hejazi, and S.R. Shafaq), high-ranking officials (Shoja al-Din Shafa, Ebrahim Khwajeh Noori, and Parviz Natel Khanlari), and prominent men of literature, professors, and intellectuals (such as Mohammad Ali Jamalzadeh, Jalal Al Ahmad, Simin Danishwar, Ahmad Birashk, Parviz Dariush, Mohammad Ali Eslami Nadushan, Saeed Nafisi, Mohammad Qadi, A.H. Aryanpour, and Bahmad Sholevar). In a few years, San'atizadeh became one of the most influential managers in the publishing industry in both Iran and regionally.

The active role of San'atizadeh in the early 1960s as a messenger from the Shah to the leaders of the National Front sheds light on his politics at the time. The National Front was a liberal nationalist political organization founded by Mosaddeq in 1949, which was suppressed after the coup. In the early 1960s, San'atizadeh held several meetings with a few members of the National Front, hoping to encourage them to accept working within the current regime's political structure. According to confidential minutes of a conversation between William Green Miller (1931–2019; a US diplomat in Iran) and Hosein Mahdavi (a member of the Central Committee of the National Front), which took place in Miller's residence on December 11, 1963, Mahdavi told Miller that San'atizadeh had come to his place with the intention of informing Dariush Homayoun and Mahdavi of a personal conversation he had with the Shah, in which the latter agreed to the inclusion of younger talents in the government. San'atizadeh had told them that this did not mean that the Shah was ready to limit his power, but instead that it was an opportunity for National Front members to work within the current regime and its structure. According to these minutes, following this meeting with the Shah, Sanʿatizadeh had approached Homayoun and Mahdavi to encourage them to join the government at high ranks. Mahdavi points to another meeting Sanʿatizadeh had with Allahyar Salih (1897–1981), leader of the National Front from 1960 to 1964, with a similar message. Mahdavi analyzes this move as a new effort on the part of the Shah's regime to create a division between moderate and radical members of the National Front.[32]

In 1965, Sanʿatizadeh was appointed as the first head of the National Committee for the International Campaign against Illiteracy (*kumītah millī paykār jahānī bā bīsavādī*). This committee was established following a literacy ceremony held by UNESCO in Iran (Alinejad, 2011). A top-secret document from the US embassy records the conversation between Sanʿatizadeh and Martin F. Hertz, Counselor for Political Affairs at the US embassy, which took place at the Hertz residence on October 10, 1965. This meeting happened just a few days after Sanʿatizadeh's appointment as the head of the National Committee. In this conversation, Hertz asked for Sanʿatizadeh's opinion on the contract between Iran and the Soviet Union for the construction of the Isfahan steel mill, on the literacy programs in Iran, on Dariush Homayoun, and on whether Sanʿatizadeh could introduce any future leaders among the Iranian youth to the US embassy. According to this document, Sanʿatizadeh pointed out that, in a personal meeting with the Shah, he had raised the issue of Soviet involvement with the steel mill project and the improvement of Iran–Soviet relations. Sanʿatizadeh's analysis, according to this report, was that the Shah thought that the new Soviet leadership, as compared to the pursuit of Stalin-era expansionism, was more interested in its internal affairs. Sanʿatizadeh also explained to Hertz that the student demonstration in the United States against the Shah, and the publishing of articles written by the National Front members in prestigious US dailies,[33] had hurt the Shah, who was starting to look more compassionately toward the Soviets. Sanʿatizadeh further pointed out that the Campaign against Illiteracy had satisfied the Shah, as he was looking to further exploit his position as a leader in the struggle against illiteracy and probably hold upcoming international conferences as well.

In this meeting, Hertz further inquired about Dariush Homayoun,[34] his biography, and whether Homayoun would accept working with the Shah's regime at its highest levels. Sanʿatizadeh, who revealed biographical information on Homayoun, related that Asadollah Alam, Minister of the Royal Court, had also recently asked him about Homayoun. Sanʿatizadeh asserted that Homayoun would not be bought by the regime but might collaborate on certain projects with the regime as he himself was doing. Hertz asked Sanʿatizadeh to let him know of any possible future leader that the embassy could invest in, as part of the embassy's program of identifying Iranian youth who might be recruited as key future leaders in Iran.[35] Sanʿatizadeh introduced a few people, including Ali Asghar Mohajer who later succeeded him in his role as Tehran Branch manager.[36]

Sanʿatizadeh took a leave of absence from his position as the manager of the Tehran Branch to focus full-time on his position as the head of the National Committee for the International Campaign Against Illiteracy. The campaign was launched in Qazvin, a city in the northwest of Iran in which half the population were Turkish- and half Persian-speakers. For a year and a half, San'atizadeh was the head of the Campaign Against Illiteracy in Qazvin and was responsible for administrating literacy programs in Persian for 80,000 people. The campaign expanded to rural areas around the country in 1967. While the aim was to increase literate adults by 4.5 million, according to the official statistics in 1970 no more than one million adults had taken the classes and only 450,000 had completed the advanced class (Alinejad, 2011).

The importance of San'atizadeh in Iran's educational sphere in the late 1960s, and for the FBP operations in Iran and regionally, can be seen from records of a luncheon that the FBP held on February 17, 1967, at the Princeton Club of New York. The FBP invited the US corporations and banks with substantial interests in Iran. The purpose of this luncheon was to serve as an "opportunity" for the New York business community to hear "brief remarks about the economic and educational revolution in Iran." Datus C. Smith had written letters of invitation less than three weeks before and introduced San'atizadeh as follows:

> [He] has the liveliest and best informed mind of any Middle Easterner I know. He has been the director of our work in Iran from the beginning and is credited by many people with the creative thinking behind a number of important developments in the economic as well as the educational sphere.

Reflecting on the FBP's thirteen years of operation in Iran, Smith further remarked that "[u]nder Mr. Sanati's direction Franklin's work in Tehran has made it one of the moving forces in Iran's socio-economic development." This luncheon was hosted by Mr. Edward Booher, chairman of the FBP's board of directors, who emphasized the role of the book "as a basic tool of development" in an effort to foreground to industry the role of publishing and communications in the developing countries.[37]

The invitation was sent to several US corporations and banks with interests in Iran or the Middle East in general. Pan American World Airways, Bristol Myers, Colgate-Palmolive, PepsiCo International and Canada Dry were selling their products or services in the country. Pfizer International was constructing a pharmaceutical manufacturing plant in Tehran. The Lummus Company was building a $20 million petrochemical complex for the Abadan Petrochemical Co. Ltd., which was jointly owned by the National Petrochemical Co. of Iran (owned by the National Iranian Oil Company) and B.F. Goodrich Co. The Lummus Company was responsible for engineering, procurement of materials, and construction of the entire complex. Mobil Oil Co. had a 7 percent interest in Iranian Oil Participants, Ltd. Standard Oil Company of New Jersey also had the same number of shares in this venture as Mobil Oil Co. Allied Chemical International had a $150 million joint venture with the National Petroleum Company of Iran for the extraction of natural gas in Bandar Shapur. It also had a nylon plant in Tehran financed by private investors through the Industrial and Mining Development Bank of Iran. P.G.W. Strub, the manager of Special Projects of Allied Chemical International in the Middle East, was "well acquainted" with Mr. Kheradjou, the managing director of the Industrial and Mining Development Bank of Iran, who was also a member of the FBP and "a strong supporter" of FBP's activities in Iran. The Financial Institutions Growth Fund was invited, as the president of this company wished to introduce Mr. James Roosevelt, son of Franklin D. Roosevelt, to San'atizadeh. The Financial Institutions Growth Fund and the Fund of Funds were at the time involved in substantial negotiations with the Shah of Iran and, based on the FBP documents, were looking to build connections with San'atizadeh on the issue of these economic negotiations.

A few days after the event, the FBP enclosed a brief release on the session along with a brochure describing the FBP's activities in the various countries of Asia, Africa, and Latin America and sent them to the corporations that had attended, hoping that the release would be published in their internal bulletins (such as Standard Oil Company's *The Lamp*, Chase Manhattan Banks's *Chase Manhattan News*, and the Lummus Company's *The Lummus Sphere*). According to this release, San'atizadeh discussed "the process of industrialization in developing countries, in the context of the relation between education and consumption" in his address at the Princeton Club. This FBP release was written in the hope that an understanding of the FBP's role in the countries where it operated would serve to have the FBP recognized by industry as "a partner in development."[38]

San'atizadeh left the Tehran Branch in 1969. He claimed that one of the reasons behind his resignation was a financial dispute he had with the FBP headquarters. According to him, the Tehran Branch had given a loan of $300,000 to the New York office, which the headquarters had not repaid (Alinejad, 2016). The second and last manager of the Tehran Branch was Ali Asghar Mohajer (1922–96), a graduate of law who formerly worked for the Ministry of Finance and, before the 1953 coup, was affiliated with the socialist and nationalist Iran Party. Mohajer had joined the Tehran Branch in 1956 (Mohajer, 1962).[39] As will be discussed in Chapter 6, San'atizadeh and several staff members pointed to Mohajer's mismanagement as the reason for the Tehran Branch's gradual demise. However, Mohajer never wrote a reflection on his days in the Tehran Branch.

Publishing Industry in Iran

The history of print in Iran dates back to the Safavid dynasty (1500–1736), when the first printing plant was installed in Julfa, Isfahan. During the Qajar dynasty (1796–1925), several lithograph and movable-type printing houses were installed in Tehran, Tabriz, and a limited number of other cities. But the printing of books remained for the most part economically unprofitable and was thus dependent on government support and the financial support of official patrons, in addition to the activities of a few anti-despotism networks of activists. In 1898, a private enterprise with the name of the National Firm for Book Production (*shirkat millī ṭab' kitāb*) was established, in which were affiliated Mohammad Qazwini (1874–1949), distinguished scholar of Persian culture,[40] and Mohammad Ali Foroughi (1877–1942), a scholar and senior politician (Azarang, 2002).

The printing industry further developed during the reign of the first Pahlavi monarch (1925–41) with the establishment of the University of Tehran (1934) and several modern schools, the development of literacy programs, and the more active role of government in publishing books and journals. During this time, Iran's Ministry of Education edited and published several textbooks with fairly good editing, layout, and production qualities. Private publishers in early twentieth-century Iran, however, remained mostly bookseller-publishers, occasionally publishing new titles (Azarang, 2002) mainly to be sold by their own bookshop or within a limited number of bookshops.

Several factors contributed to developments in the publishing industry during the reign of the second Pahlavi monarch (1945–79): the development of schools, universities, and educational and cultural institutions; the growth of the intellectual environment and reading public; library development; the establishment of organizations for textbook writing; the establishment of new disciplines and departments related to book printing in universities and other educational institutions; and the establishment of book fairs and book communities (Azarang, 2002). The Tehran University Press (founded in 1946) expanded its operations during this period and became one of the largest publishing institutions in the country, publishing university textbooks. The National University of Iran (established in 1959) and Aryamehr University of Technology (established in 1966) both founded their own publishing houses. Bungāh Tarjumah va Nashr Kitāb (Royal Institute for Translation and Publication), a not-for-profit organization, was founded in 1953 under the auspices of Mohammad Reza Shah. It was a leading publishing house, which began the first systematic translation of Western classics into Persian, as well as a series of translations of children's books, and mass publications of critical editions of Persian classics (Amuzigar, 1977). Two other government-sponsored not-for-profit publishing houses were the Society for the National Heritage of Iran (*anjuman-i ʾāṣār-i millī*; established in 1921) and the Iranian Culture Foundation (*bunyād-i farhang-i irān*; established in 1963). Both specialized in publishing critical editions of medieval mystical, literary, artistic, and Islamic texts. The Institute for the Intellectual Development of Children and Young Adults (*kanun-i parvarish-i fikrī kūdakān va nawjavānān*), founded in 1965 and patronized by Queen Farah Diba, specialized in the publication of children's books as well as the production of audiovisuals for teens. Several government ministries and organizations also established publishing within their own sectors, such as the Iranian Planning and Budget Organization, the National Geography Organization of Iran, the National Iranian Oil Company, the Statistical Center of Iran, the Ministry of Sciences, and the Ministry of Interior Affairs. The most prominent private publishers during this second Pahlavi reign were Amīr Kabīr, Nīl, and Khavrazmī—all three of which collaborated with the Tehran Branch on several titles as publishers of its sponsored translations.[41]

While, as listed above, several private, not-for-profit, and government-sponsored publishing houses were operating during the second Pahlavi reign, there is historical consensus that the FBP's Tehran Branch was the founder and promoter of modern book publishing in Iran (Azarang, 2002; Bayat, 1995; Alinejad, 2016).

The Tehran Branch was an "intervention" in the natural and gradual development of the Iranian publishing industry. The Tehran Branch introduced modern editing, cover design, indexing, and page layout to Iran's publishing industry (Bayat, 1995).

The following were major characteristics of the printing, publishing, and sale of books in Iran before the intervention by the Tehran Branch (Sanʿatizadeh, 2004):

1. Bookstores and publishers were not separate entities. Private publishers were mostly bookstores, which occasionally published titles and sold in their own bookshops.
2. Bookstores were not familiar with modern methods of marketing books. Most of them had counters that blocked the access of potential buyers to the books.
3. Bookstore-publishers exchanged books with each other based on bartering.
4. Bookselling and publishing was still a family occupation, one inherited by the new generation.
5. Finally, bookseller-publishers were not familiar enough with the content of the books and their possible readership to assist them with promotion strategies.

Datus C. Smith describes Iran's publishing industry prior to the establishment of the Tehran Branch in the following terms:

> Before Franklin had stimulated reforms, book selling was almost entirely by publishers, as a means of disposing of their own books and some few secured through exchange with other publishers. Occasionally they would take some books on consignment from authors trying to publish their own books. The educational function of booksellers in informing the general public of all books available was virtually unknown.
>
> (Smith, 2000)

Sirous Alinejad, a journalist and biographer of Sanʿatizadeh, argues that prior to the Tehran Branch the working relations in the publishing industry in Iran were not modernized; there were no defined or established rules regulating the relation between an author/translator and the publisher. The contract between publisher and translator/author was usually a verbal one, not based on any written legal contract. The legal system in Iran also did not cover the issue of copyright until 1969, the year when the first copyright law was ratified (Alinejad, 2016).[42]

The Tehran Branch was also the first publishing house in Iran that established an atelier to supervise the layout and printing process (Alinejad, 2016). This atelier office, under the supervision of the graphic designer Hormoz Wahid (1928–99), was responsible for selecting the font, typesetting, and layout, for the spell-checking and correction of the Tehran Branch's sponsored books, and for the supervision of the print and bookbinding process (Alinejad, 2016). The Tehran Branch also published the *Persian Encyclopedia*, which was a turning point in the standards of reference book publishing in Iran.

Further, the Tehran Branch was a major contributor to the professionalization of editing and proofreading in Iran. The editing techniques in Iran were modeled on those of the West and were systematically introduced into the country's publishing industry in the 1950s by Bungāh Tarjumah va Nashr Kitāb, the Tehran Branch, and Tehran University Press (Emami, 1997). According to Manuchehr Anwar, in his interview with Sirous Alinejad, while Bungāh Tarjumah va Nashr Kitāb was established a year before the Tehran Branch, the editorial committee of the former in its early years was responsible solely for selecting books for publication and did not have any systematic and professional editing guidelines (Alinejad, 2016, p. 174).[43] Sirous Parham and Manuchehr Anwar, both pioneers in introducing modern editing to the Persian publication industry, worked as editors for the Tehran Branch. The Tehran Branch was also among the first publishing houses that established a uniform orthographical rule. Later, the professionalization of editing was further developed by the next generation of editors in the Tehran Branch (Alinejad, 2016).

The role of editors in the Tehran Branch extended to proofreading the translations and checking them against the original English for possible errors and omissions. Editors would also work on improving the translator's style, "especially by replacing Arabic words and constructs with Persian equivalents" (Emami, 1997). Translators were evaluated based on a sample translation of a few pages of the assigned book. The Tehran Branch would then buy translation rights and begin to edit the work. Later, private-sector publishers such as Amīr Kabīr, under the management of Abdulrahim Jaʿfari, followed the Tehran Branch in establishing editing bureaus in their publishing houses. The methods and models adopted by the publishing houses in the 1950s are still widely in use in Iran (Emami, 1997).

The staff of the Tehran Branch, in its editing bureau and layout atelier, included numerous influential writers, translators, scholars, and artists of the time. Karim Emami, chief editor of the editing bureau, pointed out that a few of the editors and staff of the Tehran Branch were former political prisoners and therefore unable to obtain work at governmental offices. However, these ex-prisoner intellectuals and translators were still able to find work at the Tehran Branch, or, as Emami frames it, the Tehran Branch was "compassionate" toward them and provided such work. SAVAK also tolerated the cooperation of such ex-political prisoners with the Tehran Branch, as it helped the agency to monitor their activities, given that their work was in a place where their relations were public and so could constantly be checked on (Emami, 2001).

The editing bureau of the Tehran Branch was formed under the supervision of Manuchehr Anwar, the former BBC radio presenter who became chief editor (*sarvīrāstār*). He was followed by Najaf Daryabandari (1929–2020), a former Tudeh Party member and prominent literary writer and translator. Other chief editors of the Tehran Branch include:

- Hamid Enayat (1932–82),[44] a former Tudeh Party member before the coup. After the coup, Enayat joined the League of Iranian Socialists, a socialist nationalist party founded in 1960. In that same year, Enayat served as the secretary of the Confederation of Iranian Students (CIS) in Europe.

- Mahmoud Enayat (1932–2012), a former Iran Party member and journalist.
- Karim Emami (1930–2005), a former journalist of the Tehran-based English-language daily *Kayhan International* (1962–8). Emami joined the Tehran Branch in 1968 as an English-language editor and cultural director; he was later promoted to the position of chief editor and served in this position between 1968 and 1974. In 1974, Emami left the Tehran Branch and joined National Iranian Radio and Television, where he established Sorush Press.[45]
- Hasan Marandi (1930–2004), psychologist and scholar.

According to Emami, the chief editors were responsible for choosing the titles for translation, consulting with the Tehran Branch manager when necessary (Emami, 2001).

Other than the chief editor, the editing bureau consisted of senior editors (*vīrāstār 'arshad*), editors (*vīrāstār*), and assistant editors (*kumak vīrāstār/vīrāstyār*). Under the general supervision of the chief editor, senior editors were each responsible for editing certain categories of books: Mahmood Behzad (1913–2007), biologist, was editor of scientific books; Ahmad Sami'i Gilani (b. 1920), translator, was editor of literary works; Mahshid Amir Shahi (b. 1937), novelist and journalist, was editor of fictional works; Shams al-din Adib Sultani (b. 1931), linguist and translator, was senior editor of psychology and philosophy books; Naser Pakdaman, translator and scholar, was senior editor of economics and sociology texts; Abolhassan Najafi (1929–2016), literary translator, was senior editor of literary works, especially translations from the French; Ahmad Mir'alaei (1942–95), prominent literary translator,[46] and Amir Jalal al-Din A'lam (b. 1941), literary translator, were editors of general and also literary works; Mahdokht San'ati (b. 1933)[47] was editor of children's and teen books;[48] and Mohammad Reza Hakimi (1935–2021) was editor of books on Islamic studies (Emami, 2001). Gholam Ali Hadad Adel (b. 1945), a conservative politician in the contemporary Islamic regime and currently the president of the Academy of Persian Language and Literature, also worked as an editor in the Tehran Branch for a year.

The Tehran Branch, as mentioned earlier, in addition to sponsoring translations, also sponsored a few original titles in Persian—among which were the first two volumes of Yahya Arianpour's *History of Modern Persian Literature: From Saba to Nima* (*az ṣabā tā nīmā, tārīkh-i ṣad-u panjāh sālah adab fārsī*) (1971). Ahmad Sami'i Gilani, senior editor at the Tehran Branch, proofread and edited these two volumes. According to Najaf Daryabandari in his interview with Mozafari Savuji, it was the Tehran Branch that for the first time, in Iran's publishing history, suggested a book on a specific subject to an author. The first title to come from such a suggestion was authored by the popular historian Mohammad Ebrahim Bastani Parizi (1925–2014) (Mozafari Savuji, 2010). Mohammad Ali Eslami Nadushan (1925–2022), prominent literary critic,[49] was the senior editor who supervised this initiative. The renowned translator Goli Emami also began her career as a secretary at the Tehran Branch, where she helped catalog the in-house library and translated her first books, such as *Pippi Longstocking* by Astrid Lindgren (1945, translated by Emami to Persian in 1970).[50]

Those working for the Tehran Branch remained influential in later publishing developments within Iran, even after the 1979 revolution, and post-Revolution academic publishers employed former Tehran Branch staff. An example can be found in the Center for Academic Publications (*markaz nashr dānishgāhi*), an important publishing house founded in 1981, which under the management of Nasrollah Porjavadi, scholar of Persian literature and Sufism, recruited several of the former staff of the editing bureau of the Tehran Branch, such as Abolhassan Najafi and Maʿsumi Hamedani (Alinejad, 2016).

Regular Translation Program

The Tehran Branch, as with other branches, started its operations with the Regular Translation Program and only moved to Special Projects in the late 1950s when it had solidified its relations with the royal family, political leaders, the local publishing industry, and intellectuals through the sponsorship of dozens of translations. In this section, I will briefly discuss the history of translation in modern Iran and then move to a historicization of the Tehran Branch's translation methods, the titles that it translated, and an overall analysis of these titles. I will also provide some details about the reception of these translations, and the Tehran Branch's efforts to include its sponsored translations in Iran library development projects. It should be noted that the production and publication of the *Persian Encyclopedia*, the first modern encyclopedia in Iran, will be discussed in the next chapter.

From the early nineteenth century, with the growing presence of the British East India Company in India, Persian became a subject of scholarly interest for the British.[51] Persian was the official governmental language during the Mughal rule of India (1526–1857); therefore, with the British colonization of India, translations from Persian to English and from English to Persian increased. Some Iranian students sent by the Qajar court to England also undertook translations from English to Persian. Mirza Saleh Shirazi (1790–1845),[52] one of the first Iranian journalists, and Mirza Reza Mohandes (1787–1883), translator and architect, were among the second group of Iranian students sent by the Qajar court to England in 1815 to study European science and technology; both translated a few works from English into Persian (Emami, 1998).

Translation of European books to Persian increased substantially during the nineteenth century, but most books were translated from either French or German. During the reign of Nasir al-Din Shah (1848–96), a state-sponsored translation organization was established. Iran's Guarded Domains Printing and Translation House (*dār al-ṭibāʿ va dār al-tarjumah mamālik-i maḥrūsah īrān*), which was later renamed the Governmental Ministry of Printing and Translation (*vizārat-i intibāʿ va dār al-tarjumah dawlatī*), worked under the directorship of Mohammad Hassan Iʿtimad al-Saltaneh (1843–96), a Qajar senior politician and author. This government institution published several translations, mostly non-fiction (history and geography) titles from the French (Emami, 1998).

Until the end of the Second World War, French was the dominant European language in Iran's intellectual environment. French was the European language taught at the secondary schools and used in the translation of non-fiction books and textbooks. With the occupation of Tehran by the Allied forces in 1941, learning English and soon thereafter translations from the English became common. After the 1953 coup and the suppression of the nationalist and communist political movements, and following the rise of US-centered student migration, many Iranian intellectuals were pushed away from political involvement and toward literary and translation activities, especially from English. With the return of American- and British-educated Iranians and the establishment of the Tehran Branch (1954) and also the establishment of Bungāh Tarjumah va Nashr Kitāb (1953), the dominant language of translation shifted from French to English (Emami, 1998).

In line with the general policy of the FBP, most of the titles that the Tehran Branch sponsored did not contain overt political propaganda. Yet they appeared with the endorsement of distinguished local leaders, which assured them of a reception they would never otherwise have had.[53] The Tehran Branch from its early years used its Regular Translation Program to build a network of local translators, local advisors, intellectuals, and publishers. It further used the Regular Translation Program to connect with the royal family and gain its trust, which later crucially assisted the Tehran Branch in moving toward its Special Projects— that is, educational publishing.

The first publisher that worked with the Tehran Branch was Ibn Sīnā, under the management of Ibrahim Ramezani (1918–?). It published the series of books on the sciences by B.M. Parker.[54] Many publishers (Datus C. Smith gives the number as "more than fifty") cooperated with the Tehran Branch in publishing its sponsored titles. Most of the publishing was done by publishers in Tehran, but also in Tabriz, with a few in Shiraz and Isfahan. The firms with the largest number of books sponsored by the Tehran Branch on their list were Amīr Kabīr, Andīshah, Bungāh Tarjumah va Nashr Kitāb, Ibn Sīnā, Iqbāl, Jībī, Omīd-Yazdānī, Ṣafī'alīshāh, and Sukhan (Smith, 2000).

In its first year (1954/5), the Tehran Branch sponsored the translation of five books: Cora Mason's *Socrates, the Man Who Dared to Ask* (published by Ma'rifat: 1,500 copies); Helen Shacter's *How Personalities Grow* (published by Ibn Sīnā: 2,000 copies); Bertha Morris Parker's *Animals We Know* (published by Ibn Sīnā and Dānish: 5,000 copies); Thornton Wilder's *The Bridge of San Luis Rey* (published by Zavvār: 2,000 copies); and William Saroyan's *The Human Comedy* (published by Ibn Sīnā and Dānish: 2,000 copies).

During the following year, the Tehran Branch moved toward sponsoring titles in the area of economic theory and the social sciences. In 1955/6, the Tehran Branch sponsored the translation of twenty-eight new titles and the second printing of Helen Shacter's *How Personalities Grow*. In this same year, it also sponsored the publication of its first original title in Persian, B. Pazargard's *Political Opinions of Western Philosophers* (*naẓarāt siyāsī falāsifiyah qarb*), published by Iqbāl. Notable in this year's publications were George Soule's *Ideas of the Great Economists* (published by Ibn Sīnā); Cressy Morrison's *Man Does Not Stand Alone* (published by Iqbāl and Amīr Kabīr); Egon Larsen's *Men Who Changed the World* (published by Amīr Kabīr), and Princess Ashraf Pahlavi's translation of Benjamin Spock's

Baby and Child Care, Vol. 1 (published by Ibn Sīnā and Amīr Kabīr), of which 10,000 copies were printed. This title, as described by the FBP, was not in one of the usual FBP categories, but its translation by the Shah's twin sister could benefit the FBP as a whole.[55] In his interview with Alinejad, Sanʿatizadeh, the Tehran Branch manager, reveals that this book was ghost-translated by someone else but published under the name of Princess Ashraf Pahlavi, to build a connection with her and the royal family generally. Later, this connection was exploited by Sanʿatizadeh when he asked Ashraf Pahlavi to sponsor half of the cost of the *Persian Encyclopedia* project (Alinejad, 2016, p. 75).[56] As will be pointed out later, Princess Ashraf also played a crucial role in helping the FBP begin its first Special Educational Project in Iran.

In 1956/7, forty-nine new titles were released. Three of its previous sponsored titles—namely Hendrik Willem van Loon's *The Story of Mankind* (published by Ibn Sīnā), Cressy Morrison's *Man Does Not Stand Alone* (published by Iqbāl & Amīr Kabīr), and O. Spurgeon English's *A Guide to Successful Fatherhood* (published by Ṣafīʿalīshāh)—were also reprinted. Other notable titles during this year were Majid Khadduri's *War and Peace in Islam* (published by Iqbāl) and Rezazadeh Shafaq's *US Writings on Iran* (also published by Iqbāl). In this third year of operation, the Tehran Branch expanded its publications to include books on public administration and industrial management. It continued sponsoring titles to build connections with the royal family, such as the Persian adaptation of Sarah K. Bolton's *Lives of Poor Boys Who Became Famous*, which included a chapter by Mohammad Reza Shah on the life of his father (published by Amīr Kabīr and Iqbāl: 20,000 copies), and also the second volume of Princess Ashraf's translation of Spock's *Baby and Child Care*.

In 1957/8, the Tehran Branch published thirty-six new titles; notable are Will Durant's *The Story of Philosophy* (Dānish), Mark Twain's *The Adventures of Tom Sawyer* (Ṭahūrī), Majid Khadduri's *Law in the Middle East* (Iqbāl), a biography of Benjamin Franklin by Ali Akbar Kasmai (Ibn Sīnā), Carleton Coon's *Caravan: The Story of the Middle East* (Zavvār), and the first and second volumes of George H. Sabine's *A History of Political Theory* (Amīr Kabīr). According to the FBP, Sabine's book was categorized under books providing the intellectual basis for anti-communism.[57]

In 1958/9, thirty-three new titles were published—including volumes one and two of Will Durant's *Our Oriental Heritage* (published by Iqbāl) and two volumes of a handbook for boys by the Boy Scouts of America (published by Ibn Sīnā). The Tehran Branch further addressed religious content in line with showing US scholarly interest in Islam, with for example Harry W. Hazard's *Atlas of Islamic History* (published by Ibn Sīnā) and Joseph Gaer's *The Wisdom of the Living Religions* (published by Ibn Sīnā). In 1959/60, thirty-one new titles came out. Norman Buchanan and Howard S. Ellis's *Approaches to Economic Development* (published by Ibn Sīnā), Samuel Eliot Morison's *Christopher Columbus, Mariner* (published by Amīr Kabīr), and Saxe Commins and Robert N. Linscott's *The World's Great Thinkers: The Political Philosophers* (published by Sukhan) are a few examples.

By 1960, the Tehran Branch was publishing in a variety of subject areas, ranging from economic and educational theory and development, to the life and biography of US leaders and presidents. In 1960/1, seventy-six new titles and four reprints were published. Kate V. Wofford's *Modern Education in the Small Rural School* (published by Shafaq), Lorena A. Hickok's *The Story of Franklin D. Roosevelt* (published by Nīl and Amīr Kabīr), Vincent Sheean's *Thomas Jefferson* (published by Nīl and Amīr Kabīr), Sterling North's *George Washington* (published by Nīl and Amīr Kabīr), Katharine Scherman's *Catherine the Great* (published by Nīl and Amīr Kabīr), and Noel Streatfeild's *Queen Victoria* (published by Nīl and Amīr Kabīr) were among them. Generally, 2,000 copies of each book were published. However, in the case of books on biology and science, the print run could reach as high as 5,000.

It should be noted that, as with other branches, the Tehran Branch also actively pursued any opportunity to ensure that its sponsored books were used for school library development projects. For instance, in the summer of 1959, a Special Project for high school libraries in Iran was inaugurated. Through the active participation of Sanʿatizadeh, the project was funded by Iran's Ministry of Education, the Ford Foundation, the Iranian Book Publishers Association, and the National Teachers College; 400 high school libraries were created. In each library, about a hundred titles sponsored by the Tehran Branch were included in the nucleus of books supplied jointly by the Ministry and the publishers.[58]

In a manner similar to Cairo Branch's sponsored titles, the Tehran Branch's sponsored titles were reviewed favorably by distinguished scholars. Journals such as *Rāhnamā-yi Kitāb*, *Sukhan*, *Yaqmā*, *Andīshah va Hunar*, and *Ruznāmah Mihr-i Īrān* published reviews on the Tehran Branch's translations. For instance, Hafiz Farmanfarma'iyan's review of Sabine's *History of Political Theory* (translated by B. Pazargad, 1958) appeared in the first issue of *Rāhnamā-yi Kitāb* (1958); Ahmad Birashk's review of Gamow's *Biography of the Earth* (translated by M. Behzad, 1958) appeared in the second issue of *Rāhnamā-yi Kitāb* (1958); and Manuchehr Sotoudeh reviewed Hazard's *Atlas of Islamic History* (translated by M. Erfan, 1959), which was published in the fourth issue of *Rāhnamā-yi Kitāb* (1958). More than a dozen of the reviews published on the Tehran Branch's sponsored books were later collected and published in a volume by the Pocket Books Company (see *Mūʾasisah intishārāt firānklīn*, n.d.). Another initiative of the Tehran Branch was the establishment of *Book of the Day* (*kitāb ʾimrūz*), a journal dedicated to book review. *Book of the Day* published eight issues during 1971–4. According to Karim Emami, Tehran Branch editor-in-chief, *Book of the Day* was a result of the intellectual environment of the editorial bureau of Tehran Branch, in which the team discussed the content of the journal, conducted interviews for the journal, and produced reviews of books, many of which were among the Tehran Branch's sponsored titles.

Many of the FBP sponsored translations on the subject of education theory were reprinted several times and ended up being used for teacher-training programs in Iran. The rising reliance on such translated books for addressing educational modernization in Iran was the subject of a few criticisms by dissident thinkers.

Teacher and children's story writer Samad Behrangi (1939–67) was an outspoken opponent of the uncritical appreciation of US books on education. Informed by his experience as a primary school teacher in rural areas in the West of Iran, where the mother tongue of students was mainly Azeri Turkish and the schooling system was suffering from a substantial lack of financial resources and physical facilities, Behrangi argued that the growing trend of translation and teaching of US educational books did not have any meaningful relation to the lived realities of the majority of Iranian students (Behrangi, [1965] 1969).

Through several revealing anecdotes, Behrangi narrated the life of a teacher in Iran who was taught John Dewey's books in the teacher-training programs and then was appointed to a rural area. There, the teacher had to deal with realities such as a lack of basic means of transportation, a lack of energy resources, and an absence of even basic sex education, all in a context in which students were facing economic hardships and food shortages on a daily basis. Behrangi argued that rather than translating US books, books on education and pedagogy should be written by Iranian educationalists and based on in-depth study of the reality of life for students, with attention to students' ethnic and geographic differences. He contended that the translation of US books should only be a means to inform the teachers of certain practices and ideas and not to present them with a role model (*sarmashq*) to follow. Even when it came to the translations, Behrangi contended that the priority should not be on translating US books but that it would be of more relevance to translate books related to educational challenges from neighboring countries (such as Pakistan, Afghanistan, and Turkey), as they were facing tensions and problems similar to Iran.

The translation and uncritical appreciation of US educational books, according to Behrangi, were a result and an indication of the fact that the Iranian educational system and educational elites were neglecting to define and address Iran's "pedagogical and cultural challenges and problems" (Behrangi, [1965] 1969, p. 12). In pointing to Iran's real educational challenges, Behrangi stresses that alongside an in-depth analysis of students' needs and challenges based on fieldwork, it is important to have a detailed understanding of the real life of teachers in Iran and the budgetary limits of schools, as well as all the facility shortages in different rural areas. Behrangi therefore suggests that books on education should be rooted in close contact with the realities of education in Iran and should reflect those realities (Behrangi, [1965] 1969, p. 21).[59]

In the late 1970s, Azarang, an editorial staff member of the Tehran Branch, started to provide a descriptive bibliographical list of the Tehran Branch's sponsored titles published between 1954 and 1974. Once it was completed, this descriptive bibliography was approved by Karim Emami, chief editor of the Tehran Branch editing bureau. However, according to Azarang, during the anti-Shah demonstration of 1979, certain individuals who considered Tehran Branch publications as contributing to the legitimacy of the Pahlavi regime attacked the bureau and threw this bibliographical manuscript out into the street (Azarang, 2002). Although this approved bibliographical list was destroyed, FBP records contain a list of all the books that the FBP sponsored in different languages.

With the termination of FBP operations, this second list was given to the Library of Congress, along with its archival set of publications. According to this list, the archival collection set numbered about 3,000 titles and comprised 1,151 translations into Arabic, 850 into Persian, 331 into Bengali, and smaller totals in other languages.[60] The approximate division of subject matter was as follows: for literature, 19 percent;[61] children's books, 18 percent; history, 17 percent; science (including medicine), 15 percent; psychology and education, 12 percent; Persian and Islamic studies, 9 percent; philosophy, 7 percent; and art at 3 percent (Smith, 2000).

Chapter 6

FRANKLIN BOOK PROGRAMS IN IRAN: SPECIAL EDUCATIONAL PROJECTS, REACTIONS TO THE TEHRAN BRANCH, AND DEMISE

In addition to the Regular Translation Programs, the Tehran Branch was also involved in sponsoring Special Projects: first, production of the *Persian Encyclopedia*, which started in 1956, followed by sponsoring the establishment of the Offset Printing House, in 1958—at that time, the largest printing house in the Middle East—and the Pocket Books Company (*sāzimān kitābhā-yi jībī*), beginning in 1960. The Pocket Books Company published small-format books at lower prices. This company also manufactured racks to sell books in unconventional settings, such as supermarkets (Smith, 2000). The Tehran Branch further organized and administered the sending of the managers of several other publishing houses to participate in workshops in the United States, England, and France (1963). As well as this, they provided loans to and technical advice for the establishment of the Pars Paper Company, beginning in 1968.[1]

The Special Projects of the Tehran Branch in addition included several contracts and arrangements with the ministries of education in Iran and Afghanistan. Under contract with Afghanistan's Ministry of Education, the Tehran Branch published Afghanistan textbooks (between 1957 and 1964). In the late 1950s, state-sponsored literacy campaigns were undertaken in Iran. As a result of these campaigns, the literacy rate rose steadily throughout the 1960s and 1970s, reaching nearly 75 percent by 1979 (Amanat, 2017).[2] During this period, the Tehran Branch became the foremost publishing organization in the country, with a variety of projects organized, administered, and executed under arrangements and contracts with the Iran's Ministry of Education. In 1960, the Tehran Branch sponsored and sent several Iranian writers to the United States, England, France, and Germany to study textbook writing. The Tehran Branch also joined with Iran's Ministry of Education to found the Educational Publications Center (active 1963–77). This cooperation resulted in the publication of the *Payk* magazine series; these student magazines were used as a model by the FBP to encourage its other local branches in Pakistan and Bangladesh to pursue publications of the same kind.

With the expansion of the Tehran Branch's operations to educational publishing, reactions against it intensified. Jalal Al Ahmad was an influential intellectual who began to write a series of articles and essays criticizing the role that the Tehran

Branch was playing in Iran. Disillusioned with the organization, Al Ahmad wrote harsh personal attacks against Sanʿatizadeh and also criticized the hegemonic role that the Tehran Branch was playing in Iran's cultural and educational spheres. After an archival and historical investigation into the Tehran Branch's Special Projects in Iran and Afghanistan, this chapter discusses Al Ahmad's criticism of the branch's hegemonic cultural production role in Iran. The chapter will end with a study of the demise of the Tehran Branch in 1977 and how the post-revolutionary regime appropriated the remaining properties of the Tehran Branch machinery for its agenda of Islamicizing the culture.

Production and Publication of the Persian Encyclopedia

As discussed earlier, one of the projects of the FBP was the production of a translation-adaptation of the *Columbia–Viking Desk Encyclopedia* in the languages of its local offices. The FBP's sponsored encyclopedias were five in number—in Persian, Arabic, Urdu, Bengali, and Indonesian. The *Persian Encyclopedia* project started in 1956. Sanʿatizadeh estimated that this project would cost $300,000. The FBP headquarters instructed Sanʿatizadeh to discuss this project with "philanthropic organizations" (*muʾassisāt khayrīyah*) in the United States, including the Ford Foundation. Sanʿatizadeh had a meeting with the board of directors of the latter. The Middle Eastern branch of the Ford Foundation, located in Beirut, sent a representative to Tehran to study the proposed project and agreed to pay $150,000 of the publication costs, on condition that the second half would be paid on the Iranian side. According to Sanʿatizadeh, he first negotiated with Iranian private enterprises, but to no avail. Then, he proposed the project to the Shah's twin sister, Ashraf Pahlavi, who accepted personal sponsorship of the second half of the costs.[3]

Sanʿatizadeh appointed Gholamhosayn Mosaheb (1910–79), a graduate of the University of Cambridge and a mathematician and university professor, as the editor-in-chief for this encyclopedia. Mahmood Mosaheb (1912–99), translator, and Ahmad Aram (1902–98), textbook writer and translator, were his colleagues in this project. The Tehran Branch further sponsored Mosaheb's attendance at encyclopedia-writing workshops in the United States, England, and France (Alinejad, 2016). More than forty people collaborated in the *Persian Encyclopedia* project either as writers of original entries or as translators.

The *Persian Encyclopedia* project was first located in the Tehran Branch's office but later moved to a separate office on Naderi Avenue where a library of encyclopedias eventually developed. Sanʿatizadeh claimed that while the Ford Foundation paid its share, Ashraf Pahlavi never contributed what she had promised. In his interview with Alinejad, Sanʿatizadeh further claimed that he paid her share personally but included Ashraf Pahlavi's name anyway as the donor in the financial records of the Tehran Branch (Alinejad, 2016).[4]

In 1966, the first volume of the *Persian Encyclopedia* was published by the Pocket Books Company. The *Persian Encyclopedia* was published in three volumes, each

31 x 21 cm in size, in a three-column format following that of the *Columbia–Viking Desk Encyclopedia* model (Ashuri, 1994). The publication of the second volume was delayed because, following the change of Tehran Branch management from Sanʿatizadeh to Ali Asghar Mohajer, Mosaheb, who worked as the editor-in-chief of the *Persian Encyclopedia* project for ten years, also left the project. Reza Aqsa (1907–?), a translator, succeeded Mosaheb, and the second volume was published with the Pocket Books Company seal by Amīr Kabīr publishers in 1978. The third volume was in its final stages when the 1979 revolution delayed its publication until 1999.

The *Persian Encyclopedia* was "the first general encyclopedia in Persian compiled along modern lines." It included about 30,000 entries translated from the *Columbia–Viking Desk Encyclopedia*, complemented by about 10,000 original entries on Iran (Ashuri, 1994).⁵ The *Persian Encyclopedia* had a lasting influence on later publications of the same genre. Dariush Ashuri, a prominent translator, contends that the innovations that the *Persian Encyclopedia* introduced to Persian typesetting were the following: "The special attention to word spacing"; "the use of numerals and scientific symbols"; and its "comprehensive system of abbreviations." Further, this encyclopedia adopted "strict rules for linking Persian characters, precise use of punctuation, and the International Phonetic Alphabet, albeit with some arbitrary variations." Ashuri praises the overall accuracy and consistency of the *Persian Encyclopedia* in terms of showing the precise pronunciation of words. He also points out that under Mosaheb's direction, a special committee, which included Ahmad Aram, Mostafa Moqarrabi (1914–98), Safi Asfia' (1913–2008), and a group of literary and scientific scholars, introduced a substantial number of neologisms and scientific terms into the Persian language, predominantly in the areas of geography, physics, and mathematics. Ashuri concludes:

> *Dāyirat al-maʿārif* may be criticized for the preponderance of foreign entries, especially biographies, that are of little use to the average Persian reader. The quality of the Persian articles in the compilation is uneven. The abundance of abbreviations relative to the size of the encyclopedia complicates the reader's task. Nonetheless, *Dāyirat al-maʿārif* can be considered the forerunner of modern encyclopedic compilations in Persian and is quite useful as a desk reference.
>
> (Ashuri, 1994)

The Tehran Branch also published the *List of Persian Articles* (*fihrist-i maqālāt-i fārsī*). This bibliography, which was pioneering in its kind, contains a subject index of Persian-language articles and research reports published in periodicals and anthologies (in Iran and outside of the country) on the subject of Iranian studies (Monzawi & Monzawi, 2000). The Tehran Branch also published the second editions of the first two volumes of the *List of Persian Articles* (covering respectively up to 1959 and 1959–66, and published respectively in 1969 and 1976) and the first edition of the third volume (covering 1967–71 and published in 1976).

Development of the Printing Plant (Offset Printing House)

By 1957, the Tehran Branch was already in contract with both the Iranian and Afghanistan ministries of education concerning the publication of their textbooks, the details of which will be discussed later. As a result of these publication contracts, the Tehran Branch was facing criticism that it was using the entire workload capacity of the printing plants in Iran for its projects. The Tehran Branch, therefore, suggested the need to establish a modern printing house in Iran, and under its supervision the Offset Printing House was established. According to Jaʿfari, the manager of Amīr Kabīr publishers, Sanʿatizadeh began to negotiate a loan with the FBP headquarters in 1957 (Jaʿfari, 2009). Sanʿatizadeh also worked toward registering a stock company in Iran; this company was registered under the name of 25th Shahrivar Company (*shirkat-i 25 shahrīvar*) (Alinejad, 2016). In 1959, the FBP's board of directors authorized an FBP loan of $150,000 to 25th Shahrivar Company to purchase printing machinery from abroad. The loan was secured from the profits of FBP's earlier textbook production projects.[6]

Sanʿatizadeh first installed four offset printing machines at a location on Qavam al-Saltaneh Avenue in Tehran and later rented a much larger space on Goethe Avenue. The start-up capital for the company was three million tomans, one-third of which had already been paid through the FBP loan and the sale of shares to the Imperial Organization for Social Services (Alinejad, 2011); the other two-thirds had to be paid in due time by the shareholders. According to Sadr, the Tehran Branch was not itself a shareholder, and 70 percent of the shares were for the Imperial Organization for Social Services (Alinejad, 2016), which was the foundation sponsoring Iran's textbook project. As for the other shareholders, there are two different accounts. According to Jaʿfari, the other shareholders were the publishers Amīr Kabīr and Ibn Sīnā, as well as the bibliographer Iraj Afshar (Jaʿfari, 2009). An annual report from the FBP, however, notes that the shareholders were eleven book publishers and four individuals (given as the president of the senate in Iran [i.e., Seyyed Hassan Taqizadeh], the leader of the opposition in the senate, a Supreme Court justice, and the Shah).[7]

Seyyed Hassan Taqizadeh, distinguished politician and constitutionalist, who at this time was the head of the Iranian senate,[8] was appointed as head of the Offset House board of directors. Sanʿatizadeh resumed his position at this time as the CEO of the company for four years (Alinejad, 2016). In the early 1970s, the Offest Printing Company was relocated to Surkhe Hesar in Tehran. Javad Mohseni, who had used to work in the offset publication sector of the Iran National Bank, was appointed as the supervisor of the printing house.

Offset Printing House began operating with the publication of both Iranian and Afghan textbooks. In a few years, this printing house became the largest in Iran and printed a diverse range of materials. Its most "useful" operation, as described by the president of FBP, was the production of "a million copies of the new textbook" under contract with the Iranian and Afghan ministries of education. The most "impressive achievement" of this printing house, however, was the reproduction in full color of the manuscript of the *shāhnāmah bāysanqurī*, a project sponsored by the Iranian government for the occasion of the 2500th Year of the Foundation of the Imperial State, in 1971.[9]

The Offset Printing House was also crucial for a few of the FBP and Tehran Branch's regional contracts and projects. While the Tehran Branch continued its technical assistance to Afghanistan's Ministry of Education printing plant, twenty Afghans were being trained in Tehran at the House.[10] The Offset Printing House was also involved in the FBP's other overseas projects dealing with color printing, assisting the FBP in dealing with its color-printing problems in other countries in which it operated. Datus C. Smith, the president of the FBP, noted:

> "Joint runs" were made for three of the colors, and then a separate printing for the black plate, with the text supplied in its own language, for each office. Because of the different directions in which the languages read, it was necessary for Tehran to do one run for Persian, Arabic, and Urdu, and then "flop the negative" for the left-to-right languages of Bengali, Malay, and Indonesian.
>
> (Smith, 2000)

Mass Distribution of Books in Iran (*kitābhā-yi jībī Project*)

In 1960, the Tehran Branch established the Pocket Books Company under the management of Dariush Homayoun, a journalist and intellectual who in 1977 became Iran's Minister of Information and Tourism. Majid Roshangar, a journalist and editor, succeeded Homayoun in 1961. The Pocket Books Company aimed to use the paper usually wasted in the process of book production to publish affordable pocket-sized books, a size not known to Iran's book market at that time. The idea was that the book price should be reduced to a cinema ticket price, which meant 20 rials for books of less than 300 pages and 30 rials for books of more than 300 pages.

The objective of the Pocket Books Company, from the FBP's perspective, was to build a national distribution similar to that of mass paperbacks in the United States, which was lacking in the Iranian publishing market. The country's publishing sales and distribution were primarily in Tehran; publications from other cities did not effectively reach the other parts of the country. Books published in Tehran did not achieve actual national distribution either. The FBP sponsored the Pocket Books Company to make books available at points not reached by traditional bookselling and at attractive prices to average readers (Smith, 2000).

Contrary to the general early policy of the FBP, in this project the Tehran Branch operated as a stand-alone publisher itself and would negotiate with the local publishers to buy the rights for reprinting books that they had previously published, in the new pocket size. The Tehran Branch paid a royalty to the publisher and published a given title in quantities two to three times higher than usual, and distributed them widely, using new venues for book presentation such as supermarkets, bus stops, food markets, and bicycle shops. The Pocket Books Company published hundreds of books in pocket size, each in print runs of five to ten thousand copies. A few years later, the company added a 21 x 11.5 cm size, which it published in runs of three to ten thousand copies. The size was chosen to easily enable to reader to carry the books (*Mū'asisah intishārāt firānklīn*, n.d.). The Pocket Books Company also opened several bookstores in Tehran (Alinejad, 2016). By 1963, about 4,800 wireracks had been placed at strategic points in the country (in the metropolis, provincial cities, market towns, and some villages), which were serviced at regular intervals.[11]

However, the early financial success of the Pocket Book project soon ended. In 1969, the Pocket Books Company became an independent legal entity registered as a stock company. Still, it continued to rely on members of the Tehran Branch editing bureau, such as Jahangir Afkari, Ahmad Samiʿi Gilani (in literature), Naser Pakdaman (in sociology and economics), and Hamid Enayat (in philosophy and sociology). According to Roshangar, the manager of the Pocket Books Company from 1961, while the Tehran Branch was constrained to publishing translations of US books, the Pocket Books Company did not have this limitation, and thus it was able to publish translations from other languages such as German, French, English, and Arabic (Roshangar, 2010).

However, the decline of the Pocket Book project, which had started a few years before, continued. By 1971, the Pocket Book project had ceased to produce any standard-size low-priced pocket books. The mass market had deteriorated, and the size of editions reduced from 10,000 in its early days to 3,000. The Pocket Books Company closed seventy-four of its inactive sales outlets in Tehran and collected their books. Starting from 1971, it also stopped the delivery of books to local bookshops; it became the bookshops' duty to pick them up. A third new policy was that no books were taken back once sold to the bookshops or sales agents.[12]

Datus C. Smith reflected on the objectives for establishing the Pocket Books Company and its gradual decline, stating:

> The Jībī organization had substantial success in all ways except commercial profit. Soon everyone else wanted to publish books in that way, so Jībī's competition was severe. The hoped-for revolution in book distribution was achieved, though the Jībī investors themselves did not get the profit they deserved.
>
> (Smith, 2000)

Other reasons have also been given for the commercial failure and decline of the Pocket Books Company. First, after a decade of operation, the book market was saturated with these types of books, and with the rise of publishing costs, the project lost its profitability. Second, with the rise of television broadcasting in the 1960s, pocket books were soon marginalized (Azarang, 2002). The Pocket Books Company continued operations until 1976. In that year, as part of the final dissolution of the Tehran Branch, the company was sold to Amīr Kabīr publishers.

Workshops for Publishers

In December 1961, the manager of the Tehran Branch organized a seminar for booksellers in Tehran, financed by UNESCO. This seminar was mostly devoted to the problems of the book trade and proposals for their solution. Following this seminar, a US training program for Iranian bookseller-publishers was planned and then carried out in November and December 1962. This workshop addressed many aspects of the trade, such as manuscript production; editorial work on manuscripts; book design, layout and illustration; printing and binding; and distribution and promotion. In 1963, Joseph Margolies went to Tehran to advise eight Iranian book publishers in their joint venture to set up a model bookshop; Margolies further instructed on a four-day course for fifty-four booksellers (Hemphill, 1964).

Also in 1963, the FBP headquarters sponsored several local publishers for participation in workshops on sales, distribution, and printing of books held in the United States, France, and England. The Iranian group was composed of Javad Eqbal (Iqbāl publications), Hasan Maʿrefat (Maʿrefat publications), Ibrahim Ramezani (Ibn Sīnā publications), Majid Roshangar (a staff member of the Tehran Branch and later the manager of the Pocket Books Company), Naser Moshfiq (Ṣafīʿalīshāh publications), Abdulali Karang (manager of the FBP's Tabriz Branch), Jahangir Shamsavari (affiliation unknown), Mahmood Azimi (Dihkhudā Bookshop), and Abdulrahim Jaʿfari (Amīr Kabīr publishers).

In a letter dated March 6, 1963, Ali Asghar Mohajer reported to Byron Buck in the FBP office in New York about the publishers' workshops sponsored by the FBP. The group of publishers, on their way from the United States to England, had traveled across the Atlantic by ship. According to this report, the publishers were scheduled to meet booksellers in London as well as in the suburbs and were set to visit Windsor Castle and the Oxford University libraries. The most fruitful part of the program, Mohajer contended, had been the visits to publishing houses, particularly the visit to the Penguin publishing house. In London, they stayed in hotels, but in Windsor, "a public relations officer from the Oil Companies" hosted the group of publishers. After London, the group went to Paris. Mohajer reported that the publishers benefited a great deal from the visit in France, as they found that the way the French publishers ran their businesses was very similar to their own methods.[13] In Paris, one of the publishers the group visited was Éditions Gallimard (Jaʿfari, 2009).

Development of the Paper Production Company
(Pars Paper Company)

From its early days, the FBP had recognized the need to import paper into Iran so that the Tehran Branch could conduct its regional and national Regular Translation and Special Educational projects. As mentioned earlier, the FBP established its second branch in Iran in 1959, in Tabriz in the northwest of the country, and this was in order to facilitate the importing of this paper—which was specifically needed in the late 1950s to produce the new FBP-sponsored textbooks.

As a non-profit corporation working in the educational field, the FBP was eligible to receive grants under Public Law 480. According to Smith:

> The FBP received large amounts (eventually about $4 million worth) of finnmarks which were disbursed in Helsinki. The funds were used for purchase of Finnish book paper which FBP then imported into Iran.
>
> (Smith, 2000)

In the beginning, the import route was out of the Baltic to the Atlantic and Mediterranean, through the Suez Canal and up the Persian Gulf to Khorramshahr. But upon the closing of the canal as the result of the Suez Crisis (1956–7), the only remaining route seemed to be around Africa, which took months longer. Smith states:

> But an imaginative member of the Tehran staff asked, "Why not the shortest possible route, through the Soviet Union?" With some difficulty that was arranged, with the paper coming in sealed cars to the Persian border. There was great complexity of paperwork getting the shipment out of the USSR and into Persia, so a Franklin office was established in Tabriz for that clearing operation.
>
> (Smith, 2000)

A decade later, the idea for the FBP to support the establishment of and provide technical aid to the Pars Paper Company was initiated by San'atizadeh, as a new solution to the Tehran Branch's paper shortage. In 1968, the FBP provided the newly established Pars Paper Company with technical advice on producing paper from bagasse, the fibrous residue left over after the sugar is extracted from sugarcane. Following the establishment of a sugar factory in Khuzistan, a province in the southwest of Iran, the objective of the Pars Paper Company became making paper from bagasse. The capital investment for the Pars Paper Company came from both the Iranian government and the private sector. San'atizadeh, who had very high expectations for the future developments of the company, terminated his cooperation as the manager of the Tehran Branch and became the CEO of this paper company in 1968. The company, however, was not successful in realizing its production objectives.

Afghanistan Textbook Project

Afghanistan, a southern neighbor to the Soviet Union, was another country of crucial geopolitical and strategic contestation between the capitalist and socialist blocs during the Cold War, culminating in the Soviet–Afghanistan War from 1979 to 1989. Education and knowledge production were important yet still understudied sites of conflict between the United States and the Soviet Union in Afghanistan. Based on World Bank figures, by 1940, Afghanistan had 324 elementary and secondary schools and the total enrollment was approximately 60,000. In 1956, enrollment numbers increased to about 121,000 in 762 elementary and secondary schools. In 1973/4, the national literacy rate was about 11 percent, and the education of most of those who were literate was limited to early years of school, as only 6 percent of males and 1 percent of females had finished sixth grade (Mobin Shorish, 1997).

In the 1950s, the United States became worried that there was a lack of US cultural and educational influence in Afghanistan. Therefore, it employed its publication networks, notably the Tehran Branch of the FBP, to fill this gap. The FBP from its early days actively attempted to make sure that its sponsored books found their way to the educational systems of the countries concerned, one of which was Afghanistan. The FBP's objective was to facilitate the circulation of its sponsored books to any regional countries with a potential readership in the languages it was publishing in. Therefore, similar to the Cairo office (which was responsible for circulating its Arabic translations to other regional Arab countries), the FBP hoped that the Tehran Branch would circulate its sponsored Persian translations to Afghanistan.

By 1956, with the efforts of the Tehran manager, San'atizadeh, Afghanistan's Ministry of Education ordered 1,000 to 2,500 copies each of more than a dozen Persian FBP books, which were airlifted from Tehran. The Iranian Publishers Association, which was also established by the efforts of the same manager, persuaded Iranian Airways to reduce air-freight rates for books to Afghanistan. "Thus, with the help and at the cost of the Afghanistan government itself, substantial numbers of American books are going into this highly strategic country which up to the present time has been almost impervious to American cultural influences," the FBP proudly stated.[14] The Afghanistan Ministry of Education continued to place such orders for FBP-sponsored books produced in Iran. For instance, in 1956, this ministry placed an order for 400 to 600 copies each of several of FBP's Persian books suitable for university use and for a combined 2,500 copies of eighteen juvenile titles.[15]

The FBP's active attempt to export its sponsored books to the Afghan educational system expanded when, through the agency of its Tehran office and under a contract with the Afghanistan Ministry of Education, the FBP actually began to print Afghanistan school textbooks. The Afghanistan textbook project was the third such project after those based in Tehran (1955)[16] and Cairo (1956). By January 1957, the FBP had received a written invitation from Afghanistan's government to undertake "one of the largest textbook projects ever planned in Asia." Afghanistan's textbooks project commenced in the fall of 1957, when the Afghanistan Ministry of Education asked FBP to supply new design and artwork and carry out the physical production of textbooks for Afghanistan.[17] The textbooks were to be produced in Iran, as Afghanistan did not have adequate facilities at the time. According to Datus C. Smith:

The FBP office in Kabul, indeed the whole Afghan operation, resulted from approaches by the Afghan government to Franklin in New York. But the Americans recognized at once that the real possibility of success would be through their Persian colleagues.

(Smith, 2000)

Abdulrahim Ja'fari, the manager of Amīr Kabīr publishers, quotes San'atizadeh to the effect that the Afghanistan textbook project started with an instruction from the FBP headquarters to San'atizadeh, asking him to travel to Afghanistan to negotiate the establishment of a FBP branch there (Ja'fari, 2009). However, San'atizadeh, contrary to the reminiscences of Datus C. Smith and Ja'fari, mentions that the reason for his first trip to Afghanistan was to promote the Tehran Branch's sponsored translations in Afghanistan (Alinejad, 2016).

In Afghanistan, San'atizadeh contacted a few bookstores and Afghanistan's Ministry of Education, but to no avail. Then, Robert MacMakin, a US Point Four agent in Afghanistan, suggested to San'atizadeh that he could introduce him to high-ranking officials of the Ministry, as they were to be MacMakin's guests in a private gathering at his residence. According to San'atizadeh, a year and a half after this private meeting, he received a telegraph from Afghanistan's Ministry of Education asking if the Tehran Branch was interested in publishing the Afghanistan textbooks (Alinejad, 2016). San'atizadeh further points out that at the time there was competition between the United States and the Soviet Union for publishing Afghan textbooks. Afghanistan's Ministry of Education had first approached the Soviet Union for the publishing work, but while the texts were written and approved by the Ministry, the Soviet publisher had added certain images (such as of oppressed peasants) to the texts. Consequently, Afghanistan's Ministry of Education terminated its contract with the Soviets and began working with the Tehran Branch. In his interview with Alinejad, Ali Sadr further points to a certain Dr. Javid—whom he introduces as a PhD student at the University of Tehran and son-in-law of Mohammed Zahir Shah (1914–2007), king of Afghanistan—as another contact who helped facilitate this agreement (Alinejad, 2016). According to San'atizadeh, a man by the name of Mr. Ma'rouf was the Afghan Ministry of Education's representative, charged with ensuring that the Tehran Branch's role was limited to printing and that it did not change the content or layout of the textbooks as provided and approved by the Ministry (Alinejad, 2016). This representative lived in Tehran for a year, editing and proofreading the textbooks under print (Smith, 2000).

The Tehran Branch published Afghanistan's textbooks from 1957 until 1964. Throughout those years, the project was funded by the Afghan government. The paper for the printing of the Afghanistan textbooks was imported from Norway for shipment to Iran and financed by the Public Law 480 US government funds. Between the fall of 1957 and the end of 1959, sixty-one titles were delivered—a total of 1,460,000 copies. By the end of 1959, Afghanistan's Ministry of Education was negotiating for a new installment of textbooks, this time entirely for secondary schools. By the end of 1960, the Tehran Branch had published 1,491,000 copies of sixty-two titles for Afghanistan. By 1963, the total number of prints increased to ninety editions of textbooks for Afghanistan totaling 1,813,400 copies.[18] San'atizadeh reveals that the Tehran Branch's contract price was four times more than the project's costs, resulting in substantial financial revenue. He points out that the Tehran Branch made a profit of between $700,000 and $1,000,000 each year from the Afghanistan textbook project, which lasted until 1964—at which time the Kabul Branch of the FBP was established to take over the printing.

Technical Aid to the Printing Plant of Afghanistan's Ministry of Education

One of the objectives of the FBP was to gradually establish a branch in Kabul. While the FBP's role in printing textbooks for Afghanistan began in 1957 through the agency of the Tehran Branch, the FBP did not have a local office until 1964, when the Kabul Branch was established. The Tehran Branch played a crucial role in the establishment of the Kabul office. In 1963, under the contract with Afghanistan's Ministry of Education and aided by a loan of $100,000 from the Asia Foundation, the FBP accepted the tasks of overseeing the remodeling and re-equipping of the Afghanistan Ministry's printing plant, of training its personnel, and of producing its textbooks in both Persian and Pashto.[19]

The FBP commissioned the Tehran Branch to fulfill this operation. The Tehran Branch took over the Afghanistan Ministry of Education's printing plant in Kabul in order to re-equip it and train printing specialists (twenty Afghans and twenty Iranians).[20] The declassified CIA "Memorandum for the Record" helps us to understand the source from which the funding for this project came, and provides details on why the US embassy in Afghanistan endorsed this project. As discussed in Chapter 4, the loan of $100,000 for this project was from the Asia Foundation, a CIA front organization—money that enabled the FBP to enter into a contract with Afghanistan's government for the production of primary school textbooks. The US embassy strongly endorsed the project, as the ambassador considered it an opportunity for the US government to exert a "lasting" influence on the "educational system, and students" of Afghanistan.[21] According to Ali Sadr (the financial deputy of the Tehran Branch and a representative of the Tehran Branch in Kabul for this technical assistantship), Mohammed Zahir Shah, the king of Afghanistan (r. 1933–73), who sought Soviet assistance for road construction, was under pressure from the Soviet Union not to continue the publication of Afghan textbooks in Iran. Therefore, the FBP asked the Tehran Branch to send staff (including Ali Sadr) and to train locals to publish in Afghanistan (Alinejad, 2016).

In 1964, with technical assistance from the Tehran office, the Kabul Branch managed and reorganized the Afghanistan Ministry of Education's printing plant and published twenty-eight textbooks in a total of 717,000 copies in Persian and Pashto.[22] The Tehran Branch continued its technical assistance to the printing plant project in Kabul in 1965. The "distinctive" feature of this undertaking, as seen by the FBP headquarters, was that Iranians and not Americans were providing the technical assistance. About twenty Iranians were in Kabul for six or eight months, and an equal number of Afghans were trained in Tehran at the Offset Printing House.[23] Robert MacMakin, a US Point Four member in Afghanistan, was the FBP's printing advisor with the Afghanistan delegation. According to Sadr, MacMakin's salary of $10,000 a year was paid from the same fund mentioned earlier (Alinejad, 2016).

The Tehran Branch fulfilled its technical assistantship, resulting in the establishment of the FBP's Kabul Branch. With the founding of this office, the Tehran Branch's role in publishing textbooks for Afghanistan (from 1957 to 1964) ended, and from 1965 until 1975, the Kabul Branch continued the project. In 1969 alone, the Kabul Branch published 3,000,000 textbooks for Afghanistan. In 1975, the contract between the Afghanistan Ministry of Education and the FBP came to an end, and the printing plant in Afghanistan was handed back to the Ministry. During that decade, the production capability of the plant increased from a quarter of a million textbooks a year to five million textbooks a year.

While a thorough investigation of the textbooks printed by the FBP for Afghanistan is not the subject of this study, it is worth noting that these textbooks, produced during the 1960s and 1970s, have been criticized for the superiority these texts give to Pashtuns, their mode of dress and code of conduct (Mobin Shorish, 1997). It is argued that these texts also implied the "superiority of the West, even the former colonial masters." In addition, these textbooks are criticized for the patriarchal, "pyramidal" social structure they depict, in which male Sunni Pashtuns are at the top of the social structure, below them are other male Sunnis, and Shi'as sit as the inferior social group. Women were also completely unmentioned in these textbooks (except from rare references to Pashtun women). The content of the textbooks for children also often transferred knowledge about Europe and only rarely about Asia, Afghanistan's neighbors, or minority communities within the country (Mobin Shorish, 1997).[24]

The role of the Tehran Branch in textbook publications was not limited to Afghanistan. In the late 1950s, Iran's Ministry of Education undertook to reform Iranian textbooks for primary schools, and the Tehran Branch encouraged and sponsored such reforms and also played an active role in actualizing this policy. The Tehran Branch played a significant role both in the publication of textbooks for Iran's primary schools and in coordinating workshops for Iran's textbook writers in the United States and Europe.

Iran Textbook Project

With the establishment of Dar al-Funun (1851), the first modern institution of higher education in Iran, the quest for modern textbooks also began in earnest. The first textbooks used in this institution were translations of books brought over or written by the European teachers at Dar al-Funun. These textbooks were translated by the Iranian assistants of the Europeans and printed by Dar al-Funun's press solely for the purposes of the students at this institution. In keeping with the general educational curriculum of this polytechnic institution, the focus of these textbooks was on mathematics and the exact sciences (Birashk & EIr, 1997).

Three decades later, Mirza Hasan Rushdiyeh (1851–1944), a pioneer Iranian educationalist, established the first modern primary schools in Irwan (1883) and then in Tabriz (1888). Under the patronage of the constitutionalist Mirza Ali Khan Amin al-Dawleh (1843–1904), Qajar politician and grand vizier of Mozaffar al-din Shah (r. 1896–1907), in 1897, Rushdiyeh then established the first modern primary school in Tehran. Rushdiyeh also wrote twenty-seven textbooks.

In 1898 the Society of Education (*anjuman-i ma'ārif*)[25] was founded, also under the patronage of the above-mentioned Mirza Ali Khan Amin al-Dawleh. While the Society of Education did not define its objectives in an official document, its activities were mainly oriented toward establishing and developing European-style schools for educating administrative personnel.[26] The Society of Education helped found an independent publication firm called the Book Printing Company (*shirkat ṭab' kitāb*) (Anwar, 1985). This publishing house produced several history books and a few school textbooks on arithmetic, geometry, astronomy, health science, geography, social studies, and literature (Birashk & EIr, 1997).[27] Due to the dismissal of the grand vizier and the internal conflicts between the members of the Society of Education, this association was short-lived and dissolved in 1900, after less than three years of operation. With the establishment of the first national parliament in Iran following the Constitutional Revolution, educational reform became a major policy concern. A few laws were passed in 1907, 1910, and 1911 which established national priorities pertaining to education. The 1907 Education Law formally established the Ministry of Education. This ministry became the state institution directly responsible for implementing education policy (Marashi, 2008). At the same time, between 1897 and 1907, forty-nine modern primary schools (sponsored by the government, private fundings, or joint collaborations) were established in the country (Al Dawud, 1997).

As more schools were founded, other textbooks were written by the founders, teachers, and managers of these schools. For instance, the constitutionalist clergyman and poet Yahya Dowlatabadi (1862–1939) wrote *A Scientific Book on Morality, Pillars and Aspects of the Religion* (*kitāb-i 'ilmī dar akhlāq va 'uṣūl va furū' dīn*) and also *The Pedigree Tree on Morality, Pillars and Aspects of Religion* (*shajarih ṭayyibih dar akhlāq va 'uṣūl va furū' dīn*). Mirza Mahmood Khan Miftah al-Mulk, who worked in Iran's office of foreign relations, wrote *Teaching Persian Alphabets and Reading to Children* (*ta'līm al-Aṭfāl dar alifbā va qirā'at fārsī*). Mirza Reza Khan Mohandis al Mulk wrote a textbook on geography, and the statesman and nationalist Mohammad Ali Foroughi (1877–1942) wrote *A Brief History of Iran* (*tārīkh mukhtaṣar īrān*) (Mo'tamedi, 2003).

In 1911, the Fundamental Law of the Ministry of Education (*qānūn asāsī vizārat ma'ārif*) was ratified, according to which all schools, including primary urban (*makātib 'ibtidā'ī baladiyah*), primary rural (*makātib 'ibtidā'ī dihkadah*), secondary (*madāris mutivasiṭah*), and higher schools (*madāris 'ālī*) had to submit to the Ministry's centralized control and supervision, and the curriculum for each school grade was defined. The Iranian government started to establish primary and secondary schools in the country, and the Teacher Training Institution (*dār al-muʿalimīn*) was established (Moʿtamedi, 2003). Between 1918 and 1920, enrollment in primary schools increased from 24,000 to 28,600 (Al Dawud, 1997).

In 1922, the Law of the Supreme Council of Education (*qānūn shawrāy-i ʿālī maʿārif*) was ratified. This law defined a state-appointed committee entitled the Supreme Council of Education and recommended that textbook writers follow the curriculum issued by this council. With the advent of the Pahlavi regime in 1925, the state employed the educational system to construct an official Iranian/Persian nationalism. In doing so, "the Pahlavi state presented itself as the embodiment of national culture, the bearer of a common authenticity shared by state and society" (Marashi, 2008, p. 88). Therefore, the production of textbooks became very important—first, in a practical sense, because it enabled the Pahlavi state to standardize the education of its citizens; and second, in a symbolic manner, as "textbooks became conspicuous markers of modernity just as they were conspicuous markers of nationalism" (Marashi, 2008, p. 98). In 1929, the law asked for primary school textbooks to be reviewed by the Ministry of Education. However, this decree was implemented only gradually. On October 19, 1938, the Council of the Ministers ratified a resolution (*taṣvibnamah*) assigning responsibility for writing secondary school textbooks to the Ministry. This resolution also noted that textbooks should not only follow specified literary and scientific content but also should promote the "Iranian ancestral national characteristics" (*khiṣāl millī va milākāt rāsikhih bāshad kih az ʿahd bāstān sirishtih-yi Irāniyān būdah ast*). The Ministry appointed a committee of teachers and university professors that selected two to three authors for each textbook. In the next three years, eighty textbooks for secondary schools were published, sponsored by the Ministry; these were known as the Ministry's Textbooks (*kitābhā-yi vizāratī*). However, as the authors were mostly university professors and were not acquainted with the needs of students at the primary and secondary levels, many of these textbooks were ineffective (Birashk & EIr, 1997).

With the occupation of Tehran in 1941, textbook writing was again privatized, and the Ministry of Education, lacking financial resources, accepted this development. For two decades, private enterprise and a coalition of intellectuals and teachers wrote textbooks. However, this policy of the privatization of textbook writing was later criticized for (1) the inconsistency of the terminologies used in the textbooks; (2) the high price of the textbooks; (3) the ability of teachers to choose their own textbooks, resulting in changes in textbooks used as a consequence of the rotation of teachers; and (4) disorder in the publication and distribution of textbooks, which resulted in inadequate and untimely circulation (Moʿtamedi, 2003). In August 1943, the Iranian parliament passed the Universal Education Act (*qānūn ʾāmūzish va parvarish ʿumūmī*), which extended compulsory primary education to the entire country. A decade after this, the Tehran Branch was established.

In 1954, the Tehran Branch started to operate the FBP's Regular Translation Programs. In less than two years, the Tehran Branch extended its operations to move toward educational publications. In 1956, the Imperial Organization for

Social Services, founded in 1947 and headed up and patronized by the Shah's sister Ashraf Pahlavi, sponsored the publication of seventeen textbooks by the Tehran Branch for the first four grades of primary school. According to Jaʿfari, the manager of Amīr Kabīr publishers, Sanʿatizadeh was the active force behind this arrangement. Sanʿatizadeh asked for a personal meeting with the Shah, took a few Iranian and US textbooks to the Shah for him to compare, and made the case that the Tehran Branch could produce textbooks similar to the American ones, if the government sponsored it. Following this meeting, the Shah ordered the Imperial Organization for Social Services to subsidize the publications and then distribute them for free among the first four grades of the primary schools (Jaʿfari, 2009). Sanʿatizadeh also confirms the above account. Ali Sadr adds that in fulfilling this project, the Tehran Branch earned twice what it had cost (Alinejad, 2016). The Tehran Branch's responsibility was to re-illustrate, re-design, and supervise production, with no attempt at changes to the text. The new textbooks were delivered in the fall of 1957.

Subsequently, Iran's Ministry of Education asked the Tehran Branch to produce new geography and history books for grades five and six. This time, the role of the Tehran Branch was not limited to design and re-illustration; instead it had to prepare the draft content for the textbook. The geography textbook for the fifth grade was prepared as a translation-adaptation of E.J. Werner's *The Golden Geography: A Child's Introduction to the World* (1952). Mohammad Hassan Ganji (1912–2012), Iranian meteorologist and academician, supervised the adaptations, and the Tehran Branch undertook the manuscript preparation, illustration, and production of the textbooks. Iran's Ministry of Education had to approve the manuscript. Unlike with the first four grades, the publication of textbooks for grades five and six was still competitive, so to avoid commercial competition with local publishers, the Tehran Branch was to bind stock and turn it over to a newly formed cooperative of fourteen book publishers and sixty-eight booksellers known as the Book Distribution Company (*shirkat pakhsh kitāb*), for publication and distribution. By September 1959, the Tehran Branch had produced twenty-one editions of Iranian textbooks—a total of 6,626,000 copies.[28]

The publication of the geography textbook for grades five and six opened new operational areas for the FBP in the field of educational publishing in Iran. This geography book was superior to previous textbooks in terms of production techniques and content arrangement, and lower in price.[29] In the late 1950s, Iran's Ministry of Education moved toward a complete overhaul of textbooks. Hassan Taqizadeh, president of the senate and local advisor to the Tehran Branch, was appointed as the head of a committee to lay out principles for a complete textbook reform program. The Shah himself asked the Tehran Branch to take on the task of producing new textbooks for all primary and secondary grades (Alinejad, 2016).[30]

Consequently, in response to the request from the Iranian Ministry of Education, the Tehran Branch assisted the Ministry in "improving the content of the books" as part of their textbook reform. The costs of textbook revision were financed (1) for the primary school textbooks, in part by a grant from the Iranian

Ministry of Education and in part by the surplus from the Tehran Branch's earlier production of Iranian textbooks; and (2) for the secondary textbooks, by a grant of Iranian rials to the value of $140,000 under US Public Law 480.[31]

The crux of the problem, seen from the FBP's point of view, was a lack of qualified editors—individuals experienced in coordinating the team of authors, art editors, copy editors, and production personnel and out of it all producing a textbook geared to children of a certain grade. William E. Spaulding, president of Houghton Mifflin and chairman of the FBP board, argued that such editors and textbook writers could not be found in Iran and proposed that a group of Iranians come to the United States for a training program in American textbook editorial procedures.

The FBP undertook this training program with a grant of $85,000 from the Ford Foundation. An arrangement was made for a group of fifteen Iranian textbook editors to go to the United States in 1960 to take a special course at the Teachers College, Columbia University. The American Textbook Publishers Institute and the US Office of Education also cooperated with this FBP-administered training workshop. Mahmoud Sana'i (1919–85), professor of psychology at the University of Tehran and former cultural attaché in London, was the leader of the Iranian textbook editors. The FBP also appointed Byron Buck, former textbook editor with the Macmillan Co., to direct this training project. Buck went to Tehran for six weeks in the fall for preliminary work with the editors before they went to the United States.[32]

Byron Buck wrote a special report as an appendix to the FBP's 1960 Annual Report, dated September 23, 1960, on FBP's textbook-writer training program for Iran. According to his report, this workshop was part of Iran's textbook reform, in which the FBP was assisting the Iranian Ministry of Education. The report eulogizes the textbook reform, stating:

> As a result of the textbook reform now under way in Iran, the nation's schoolchildren will soon be using attractive, well-made, and pedagogically up-to-date textbooks and paying considerably less for them than they have paid for their textbooks in the past.[33]

Buck reports that the FBP first held preliminary meetings to discuss these training workshops. In these preliminary meetings, the representatives of Columbia University Teachers College (CUTC), Harvard University, the American Textbook Publishers Institute, the Institute of International Education (IIE), the Ford Foundation, the US Office of Education, and several US textbook publishing firms were in attendance. Next, Byron Buck from the FBP and Norton Beach of the Teachers College prepared the final syllabus.

A group of fifteen Iranian educators and book production personnel spent February–June 1960 in a seminar on textbook preparation—a seminar that brought them to the United States, France, and England. The cost of international travel and the group's three-month study was covered mostly by a grant from the Ford Foundation. Also, le Syndicat national des éditeurs (the French Book Trade

Association), working with the French Ministry of Cultural Affairs, arranged for a two-week program for the Iranian group in Paris, in which they would visit publishing houses and educational institutions and meet with French textbook editors. The British Council also arranged a one-month program for the group in England.

The three-month seminar in the United States was held at Columbia University's Teachers College, and personnel of the textbook industry and faculty members of the College participated. The seminar covered all stages of textbook production, from "idea to bound book," and was supplemented by visits to textbook publishing houses, individual sessions with textbook authors and editors, school visits, attendance at the 1960 meeting of the Association for Supervision and Curriculum Development in Washington, DC, and a three-day workshop arranged by the Office of Education. The first two weeks of the seminar were on the objectives, methods, and problems of education in the United States. During the following seven weeks, the group concentrated on textbook editing, with each individual participant concentrating on his subject of specialization. Specialists from New York and Boston textbook firms conducted lectures on the steps of textbook preparation. Some of the discussions were held in the US publishing houses. Teachers College specialists also conducted smaller lecture discussions for group members interested in the arts, science, mathematics, and social studies.

As part of the visit to the 1959 Convention of the Association for Supervision and Curriculum Development in Washington, DC, the Iranian group attended an exhibition in which every current elementary and secondary US textbook was on display. Following this attendance, the US Office of Education presented a three-day workshop in preparation of educational materials conducted in the Office's Educational Materials Laboratory (EML). In the final two weeks, Karim Fatemi, Assistant Minister of Education in Iran and the head of the division of the Ministry concerned with curriculum and textbooks, also participated in the workshops. Byron Buck further reports that

> [o]ne important part of this whole project is the extensive reference library provided for the new editors by Franklin Book Programs in Tehran. To date Franklin Book Programs has purchased a large number of text and reference books from American publishers and shipped them to Tehran. Supplemented by text and reference books from England, France, Switzerland, and Germany this library will be at the constant and exclusive disposal of the new editors and the individuals they select to write the new textbooks.

The textbooks in this library were intended to serve as models of design, organization, and pedagogic writing—and the possibility existed, of course, that a few of them would be selected for the translation-adaptation process.[34]

The Iranian textbook writers and editors who attended this seminar were a broad cross-section of Iran's educational and intellectual life, including Mahmoud Sanaʻi (1919–85), Ahmad Aram, Mahmood Behzad, Reza Aqsa, Mostafa Moqarrabi, Abolghasem Qorbani (1911–2001), Hafez Farmanfarmaʼiyan

(1927–2015), Houshang Pirnazar (1924–2007), and Fathollah Mojtabaei (b. 1927). Also, Mohammad-Zaman Zamani (1924–2016), Parviz Kalantari (1931–2016), Hormoz Wahid, Leili Ayman Ahi (1929–2018), Thamin Baghtcheban (1925–2008), and Shahnaz Sarlati participated in workshops on design, covers, and layout (Humāyūn ṣanʿatīzādah, n.d.). Upon their return, this group became the core cell of Franklin's Organization for Production and Writing of Textbooks (*sāzimān tahiyah va ta'līf kitāb-hā firānklīn*), which directed the preparation of completely new textbooks for the entire curriculum, both primary and secondary. The FBP's assistance in the textbook reform continued through manuscript preparation and illustration; the editors trained under the FBP program created manuscripts and submitted them to the Ministry of Education for approval (Hemphill, 1964). The first set of books produced under the supervision of Franklin's Organization for Production and Writing of Textbooks were distributed in 1961 (Bayat, 1995).

Two years later, in 1963, the Iranian Council of Ministers ratified a code by which the monopoly over the writing and production of textbooks for both the primary and secondary levels was given to the Ministry of Education.[35] The rising price of textbooks (as a result of increased royalties demanded by the authors, and the profiteering attitude of publishers) and the publishers' inability to answer to the demands by the deadlines set out were mentioned as the reasons for this reimposition of government monopoly (Birashk & EIr, 1997).[36] This resolution also resulted in the establishment of the Organization for Textbooks (*sāzimān kitāb-hā darsī*). The Organization for Textbooks, whose head had to be recommended by the Minister of Education and approved by the Council of Ministers, had to produce and write textbooks for primary and secondary levels under the supervision of the Ministry of Education. This resolution further ratified that, until the time when the Ministry's printing press became capable of meeting the printing load, the Ministry was to sign printing contracts approved by the Ministry of Education with a stock company comprised of publisher and printing houses. The Company for Writing and Publishing the Textbooks (*shirkat sahāmī tabʿ va nashr kutub dursī*) was established in this process.

On November 5, 1964, the first session of the Organization for Textbooks board of directors was held with the participation of the Iranian literary scholar Parviz Natel Khanlari,[37] Ziyaei, translator Reza Aqsa, science writer Mahmood Behzad, and the mathematician Mohammad Taqi Fatemi (1904–95). Behzad was appointed as the first chief of this organization, as suggested by the Minister of Education and approved by the Council of Ministers. In 1965, the educational system in Iran was modified again in terms of its structure and curriculum. The primary level was split into five grades, the middle level was introduced with three grades, and the secondary level became four years in length. The Organization for Textbooks, in addition to primary, middle, and secondary textbooks, was responsible for the writing and production of textbooks for teacher-training centers—that is, the Teacher Training Center for Teachers of Primary School (*danishsarāy-i muqadamātī*) and Teacher Training Center for Teachers of Middle School (*danishsarāy-i rāhnamāʾī*).

With the establishment of the Organization for Textbooks, Franklin's Organization for Production and Writing of Textbooks was dissolved after two years of operation. However, this did not result in the termination of the Tehran Branch's collaboration with Iran's Ministry in the field of textbooks. The Tehran Branch continued to operate as a mediator between the Organization for Textbooks, the Imperial Organization for Social Services, and the Offset Printing House. It also coordinated the supply of paper and administered the publication process. This collaboration remained one of the main sources of income for the Tehran Branch until the mid-1970s (Bayat, 1995).[38] By the educational year 1978/9, the Organization for Textbooks was responsible for 636 textbook titles, with a total of 70 million copies printed (Moʻtamedi, 2003).

The collaborations between the Tehran Branch and Iran's Ministry of Education were not limited to the Branch's active role in Iran's textbook reform. In 1964, the Tehran Branch also joined Iran's Ministry of Education in establishing the Center for Producing Reading Materials for New-literates (*markaz tahiyah khvāndanīhā-yi nawsavādān*). The objective of this center was to prepare, produce, and distribute wholesome, inexpensive supplementary-reading materials for children, teenagers, and youth. The center began to produce the *Payk* magazines, which evolved to become the most widely distributed of the educational materials of its kind in Iran's history.

Publication of Children's Literature and Payk Magazines

Before the Constitutional Revolution of 1905–11, the usual curriculum for primary schools was drawn from the Quran, medieval Persian classics such as Saʻdi's thirteenth-century *The Flower Garden* (*gulistān*), or from folk and popular fables. In 1876, Meftah al-Molk translated the first book for children, *Guidance for Children* (*taʾdīb al-aṭfāl*), a collection of twenty-one stories, via an Arabic translation of French originals. Talebof's *Book of Ahmad* (*kitāb aḥmad*), published in 1893, is another notable work, one modeled on Jean-Jacques Rousseau's *Émile* (1762) and tailored toward children's needs in late nineteenth-century Iran. With the educational reforms of early twentieth-century Iran, attempts at producing and publishing reading materials for children were intensified; for example, Mirza Jabbar Askardzadeh Bagcheban (1885–1966), who in 1924 founded the first modern kindergarten, also published a few books for children (EIr, 1991).

During the occupation of Tehran by the Allied forces (1941–6), as part of their program of "public relations and technical assistance," the British sponsored the publication of a few magazines for children by a group of local Iranians. *Kids* (*nawnahālān*), first published in 1942, was a supplement to the publication *Horn* (*shiypūr*). This supplement was published by the British Council for the next four years during the Allied occupation of Tehran, under the direction of ʻAbd Allah Faryar. Nūr-i Jahān was a publisher located in Tehran with a specific focus on children's literature and was affiliated with American Protestant missionaries. Nūr-i Jahān published some illustrated books and eight biographies of distinguished

Western politicians, including Abraham Lincoln and Benjamin Franklin. Children's journals, however, were not limited to those of the British and the American Protestant missionaries. In 1945, a few Iranians also founded children's journals, with Yamin Sharifi establishing a magazine called *Entertainment for Children* (*bāziy-i kūdakān*) while Ruhi Arbab began publication of the magazine *Children* (*kūdak*) (EIr, 1991). In 1948, Iran's Ministry of Education founded the journal *Pupil* (*dānishāmūz*),[39] and the Youth Organization of Iran's Red Lion and Sun Society (*sāzimān javānān jamʿīyat shīr va khawrshīd surkh-i īrān*) started publication of a children's magazine for its members. At the same time, the Iranian student organization affiliated with the Tudeh Party also began publishing a weekly magazine under the title of *Pupil* (*dānishāmūz*), the same as the Ministry of Education's journal. The Tudeh journal's intended audience were upper primary school and secondary school students, and it even held a contest offering prizes to young writers.[40] With the suppression of leftist organizations after the 1953 coup, this journal was shut down (EIr, 1991).

In 1954, with financing from the Common Fund of Persia and the United States (*ṣandūq mushtarak īrān va āmrīkā*), which was administered under the Point Four program, Iran's Ministry of Education began producing reading materials for schools. Four volumes of *Reading Materials and Entertainment* (*khvāndanīhā va sargarmīhā*) were published between 1956 and 1957 under the editorship of notable linguist and historian Ehsan Yarshater (1920–2018), specifically for children in the fourth, fifth, and sixth grades (EIr, 1991).

The publication of books for children increased rapidly in the 1950s with the establishment of two publishers: the Tehran Branch and Bungāh Tarjumah va Nashr Kitāb. In line with the FBP's policy of publishing books for children, the Tehran Branch began undertaking several sponsorships of children's books and supported the work of affiliated publishers in this area. Bungāh Tarjumah va Nashr Kitāb published three series: a children's series (*majmūʿah kūdakān*) for ages five to seven; a teen series (*majmūʿah naw javānān*) for ages eight to twelve, and a youth series (*majmūʿah javānān*) for ages thirteen to fifteen. As its fourth series, Bungāh Tarjumah va Nashr Kitāb published a translation of *Portraits of the Nations* (*chihrah milal*), sponsored by the Tehran Branch and intended for readers aged between nine and twelve (EIr, 1991). Next, in collaboration with the Tehran Branch, Sukhan began its children's book series and published two books: *Spinning Gourd* (*kadūy-i qilqilih zan*), a folk narration rewritten by Manuchehr Anwar, and *Ḥasanī*, another folk story rewritten by Farideh Farjam (Moezi Moghadam, 2010b).

A decade later, the Institute for the Intellectual Development of Children and Young Adults (IIDCYA) was founded on December 15, 1966, as the first specialized children's book publisher in Iran. The IIDCYA was a not-for-profit organization accountable to the patron Queen Farah. It was intended to provide a specialized educational space for children and teens, and a specialized library and also non-textbook literature for children. Its goal was to "produce and offer support and services for children in better settings than the grim and austere school classrooms" (Moezi Moghadam, 2010a). The IIDCYA's manager was Lily

Amirarjomand (b. 1939). Her career in the publishing industry started with working on children's books at Bungāh Tarjumah va Nashr Kitāb. In the early 1960s, she joined the Tehran Branch as a volunteer "to distribute boxes of books donated by the Franklin director among schools in the southern quarters of Tehran" (Moezi Moghadam, 2010b). The IIDCYA's publication section also hired Nur al-Din Zarrinkelk and Parviz Kalantari,[41] who had both used to work for the Tehran Branch. The Tehran Branch suggested another of its staff members, Firuz Shirvanlu, to Lily Amirarjomand (Sahba, 2017), and Shirvanlu joined the IIDCYA in 1967 as supervisor of its publication section.[42] The IIDCYA's publications began in 1967 with the following two children books: *The Little Mermaid* (*dukhtarak daryā'ī*), written by Hans Christian Andersen and translated by Queen Farah Diba, and *Uninvited Guests* (*mihmānhāy-i nākhvāndah*), a folk story rewritten by Farideh Farjam.[43] With the establishment of the IIDCYA, the Tehran Branch agreed to end its involvement in the publication of books for children and let the IIDCYA publish the books that the Tehran Branch had finalized, including the above-mentioned *Uninvited Guests* (*mihmānhāy-i nākhvāndah*).[44] The close relations between the Tehran Branch and the IIDCYA continued. For instance, in May of 1974, Lily Amirarjomand, the managing director of the IIDCYA, lectured to American library, education, and publishing groups about the work of her institute. The FBP honored her with a reception and dinner at the Princeton Club. Ali Asghar Mohajer, the managing director of the Tehran office, was also a board member of the IIDCYA.[45]

Publication and distribution of the Payk *series—a historical sketch*

In 1964, the Tehran Branch joined Iran's Ministry of Education to establish the Center for Producing Reading Materials for New-literates (*markaz tahiyah khvāndanīhā-yi nawsavādān*). Three years later, this center was renamed the Educational Publications Center (EPC) (*markaz 'intishārāt āmūzishī*). The EPC was founded to prepare, produce, and distribute wholesome, inexpensive supplementary-reading materials for children, teenagers, and youth. Another objective was to instruct teachers in teaching methods. It further aimed to teach Persian to students as the "national" language (Yadegar, 1979, p. 65). The EPC also began publishing the *Payk* magazine series. *Payk*s were illustrated magazines that were distributed every two weeks at a low price in all elementary and high schools in the country, even in the remotest locales (EIr, 1991). The pioneering work of publishing *Payk* was financially assisted by Mrs. Ellen Clayton Garwood. John Spaulding, vice-president of *Scholastic Magazines*, was the special consultant who went to Iran for the project of launching *Payk* magazine.[46] Spaulding worked on the project in Iran with Ali Asghar Mohajer, at the time head of the Tehran Branch editing bureau, for three weeks to set out the plans for the magazine (Filstrup, 1976, p. 441). The manager of all the *Payk* magazines was Iraj Jahanshahi (1927–91), educator and writer.

While *Payk* signaled the first widely distributed, systematic publication of educational supplementary-reading materials inside Iran, still no study to date has detailed its history or analyzed its content. A detailed discussion and analysis of these school magazines needs to be undertaken in a separate and thorough investigation. I have attempted to open this discussion here, through a brief study of a collection of more than 500 issues of *Payk*, as well as the FBP records. The collection I have studied consisted mostly of five editions for students. Therefore, a detailed study of the two magazines *Payk for Teachers and Parents* (*payk muʿallim va khānivādih*) and *Education and Training* (*āmūzish va parvarish*) is not included.

EPC publications: The EPC started publishing in 1964 with *Payk for Primary School Students* (*payk dānishāmūz*), and *Payk for Teachers and Parents* (*payk muʿallim va khānivādih*). *Payk for Primary School Students* was first published on December 22, 1964, in twelve pages in two colors for distribution specifically in the villages of Qazvin. A total of 1,500 copies of each issue were received by the children.[47] The opening page of this first issue was an article on the life of the Prophet Mohammad. In its second year of publication, *Payk for Primary School Students* became a sixteen-page journal. In the third and fourth years, it was published in twenty-four pages. However, from its fourth year, this version of *Payk* was established as a full-color biweekly, with fifteen issues a year in thirty-two pages. It was initially intended for students in the third, fourth, and fifth grades of primary school. With the change in Iran's educational system in 1971, which resulted in the establishment of middle schools, *Payk for Primary School Students* became aimed at students of the fourth and fifth years of primary school.[48] Its editor-in-chief was Esmaʿil Saʿadat (b. 1925), an educator and literary translator. *Payk for Primary School Students* contained poetry, stories, science materials, religious teaching, and monarchical historiography and commemoration of official ceremonies. It also published puzzles and games and invited the readers to send anecdotes, letters, and paintings to be included in its issues.

Payk for Teachers and Parents started with only eight pages but developed into a biweekly of thirty-six pages. It was published in fifteen issues a year, its goal being to coordinate the educational efforts in schools and at home "in training the body and soul of the children."[49] The objective of *Payk for Teachers and Parents* was to guide teachers and parents in general, but specifically teachers of primary and middle schools, and parents whose children were in these school years. The editor-in-chief of this version of *Payk* was Mahmoud Mahmoudi; later it was Mahdi Qasemiyah. *Payk for Teachers and Parents* contained articles on educational and training subjects and teaching methods, and book reviews and articles on scientific and social subjects to help teachers answer students' questions related to the content published in their version of *Payk*. It also published poetry, cartoons, and short stories.

In October 1967, the EPC started publication of a third version of the magazine. *Payk for Children* (*payk naw āmūz*) was intended for the students of the second and third years of primary school. It was a biweekly published fifteen times each year between the months of October and May. Each issue had fifteen pages and was printed by the Offset Printing House. Starting from 1974 (the eighth year of its publication), the journal began publishing twelve 32-page issues a year. Each issue generally contained two to three children's stories, one short essay on games and plays appropriate for children, one piece introducing future possible professions for children (such as becoming a postal worker, police officer, soldier, pilot, and so on), one short essay on technologies (such as trains or airplanes), a section on biology and zoology, and a section devoted to letters and paintings received from the children. Most of the issues also contain official historiographies of the Pahlavi monarchy, accompanied by pictures of the Shah, the queen, and the prince, as well as sections on Shi'a religious teachings. The back cover of all the issues of *Payk for Children* was a reprint of one of Erich Ohser's famous *Father and Son* cartoons.

At the end of the first issue of this journal, a guideline for parents was published that provided an introduction to the magazine and discussed how the journal should be used so that it fit into the children's study schedule. This guideline noted that this magazine was the first of its kind in Iran, and the purposes of the magazine were listed as follows: (1) to provide "appropriate" materials for the children to read; (2) as a means for children to spend their spare time reading "safe and effective" (*sālim va samarbakhsh*) materials, which would keep them away from the possibly false learnings surrounding them (*bad āmuzīhā-yi iḥtimālī muḥīṭ*); (3) to encourage and promote reading habits; (4) to develop children's knowledge; (5) to help children gradually learn how to read and write correctly; (6) to encourage children to write letters, stories, and draw paintings and then to send them to the magazine; and (7) as a tool for children's educational development.

According to this guideline for parents, the journal in its structure and content was informed by the educational and training experiences of Iran and "developed" countries. *Payk for Children* employed a simple language suitable for its intended audience.[50] The teachers were also encouraged to discuss the magazine materials in their classes. The note clarified that the publication of the magazine was not for commercial purposes, as its actual production costs were much greater than its selling price of two rials; the note reads: "Our purpose is to spiritually invest in the hearts and minds of the youth [*sarmāyah guḍārī ma'navī dar dil va damāgh nasl-i javān*], and to improve their present and future lives."[51]

In June 1969, the aims and plans of the EPC continued and expanded. A new magazine called *Payk for Kindergarten* (*payk kūdak*) was added to the previous three *Payk* magazines. *Payk for Kindergarten*, a full-color sixteen-page biweekly, was first published in October 1969. It was intended to be read by teachers and parents for children in kindergartens and in the first grade of primary school. Its editor-in-chief was Ferdous Vaziri (1929–80). Each issue contained children's poems, children's stories and fairy tales, narratives to develop primary scientific knowledge, narratives to develop children's social conduct, and a few paintings and illustrations for children to interact with and complete. Each issue further included images to assist children in learning how to read and write. *Payk for Kindergarten*, as with the other *Payk*s, invited its readers to engage with the magazine by sending letters and paintings and published a selection of such letters and paintings sent to its office by children. The last two pages of each issue provided guidance for parents to help them better use the materials for educational purposes at home.

In 1969, the EPC in meetings with the authorities of Iran's Ministry of Information further explored new ways to encourage children to read the *Payk*s.

As a result of these meetings, the Outstanding Child (*kūdak mumtāz*) contest was organized in cooperation with the children's program of Radio Iran. For this competition, the top student in each class had to get in contact with the children's program of Radio Iran; they would be called for a written exam in Tehran. The top students in the written exam would then be asked to participate in an oral exam. *Payk* magazine joined the children's program of Radio Iran from the second year of this competition in 1969, and became responsible for producing the questions for the written and oral exams. The questions were chosen from the textbooks as well as the content of the *Payk* magazines. The crown prince would then award the prize on the day of his birthday. While in the first two years this competition was limited to primary schools in Tehran, it became a national competition from its third year.

Moreover, the EPC came to an arrangement with the Ministry of Culture and Arts to prepare, publish, and distribute a biographical book on the life of the first Pahlavi monarch, entitled *Alasht, the Birthplace of Reza Shah the Great* ('*ilāsht, zādgāh-i a'lā ḥazrat riẓā shāh kabīr*).[52] The EPC also undertook to prepare and publish a pamphlet describing the Shiraz Arts Festival[53] in collaboration with the Ministry of Culture and Arts, to be distributed among the students of grades five and six.[54]

In 1969, the EPC took over the publication of the monthly journal *Education and Training* (*āmūzish va parvarish*), the official organ of Iran's Ministry of Education. In December 1969, *Payk for Primary School Students* published an article reflecting on the five years of *Payk* publication. It reported that at the time (i.e., December 1969) each issue of *Payk* had more than 600,000 readers throughout the country. By this time, the total pages of each of the *Payk* magazine series were as follows: *Payk for Primary School Students*—thirty-two pages; *Payk for Children*—sixteen pages; *Payk for Kindergarten*—sixteen pages; and *Payk for Teachers and Parents*—thirty-six pages.[55]

By 1970, the FBP was seeking to use the Tehran Branch's publication of *Payk*s in Iran as a model to be emulated in the production of similar media in its other local branches. In this year, representatives from the Tehran Branch visited the Lahore Branch to discuss an Urdu magazine on the pattern of *Payk* for Pakistan's primary schools. The Tehran Branch's manager and Lahore's managing director then met USAID personnel and Pakistan's Minister of Education to discuss this publication. The two managers also toured primary schools around the Lahore area to present them with examples of the *Payk*s. The FBP hoped to see such a project being realized in Pakistan, as the school headmasters and students there were eager for such a magazine. Two Iranian experts also went to the Dacca Branch (Bangladesh) and conducted a survey on the feasibility of a school magazine project there. The Dacca office negotiated with the local departments; however, there was no response.[56]

In October 1970, the EPC started publication of the fifth *Payk*, entitled *Payk for Youth* (*payk javānān*). In the first year, *Payk for Youth* was published in six issues of forty-eight pages each. In the following years it was published in twelve issues. *Payk for Youth* was intended for high school students and was priced at five rials (later the price went up to six rials). The technical and artistic design was carried out under

Hormoz Wahid, the supervisor of the Tehran Branch layout atelier. While the writers and editorial board of the previous four *Payk*s were mostly the same group of people, the editorial board of *Payk for Youth* differed and included senior editors and editors of the Tehran Branch—such as Karim Emami, Najaf Daryabandari, Mahmood Mosaheb, and Ali Asghar Mohajer. Later, in 1975, Ahmad Golshiri (1946–2022), a literary translator, became editor-in-chief of this magazine. *Payk for Youth* included stories and articles on national and international sports, cinema, politics, art history, fashion, sciences, and technology. In the fourth year of its publication, the journal stopped publishing articles on fashion and Greek philosophy and instead included articles on zoology and scientific discoveries. The editorial notes that the journal had decided to do so based on the criticisms it received from its readers.[57] *Payk for Youth* also introduced books, mostly those that were sponsored by the Tehran Branch and published by various publishing houses such as Jībī or Amīr Kabīr. At the end of each issue were physics and mathematics questions and answers for high school students.

In October 1971, middle schools were established in Iran. Starting from the educational year 1972/3, a new *Payk* for middle school students, *Payk for Teens* (*payk naw javānān*), started publication. It was a biweekly published in fifteen issues each educational year. Its manager was Iraj Jahanshahi, and it was under the editorship of its board of writers, a board that was similar to that of *Payk for Primary School Students* in its members.

The collaboration between the Tehran Branch and the EPC, which had begun in 1964, continued to 1977. In 1977, Soroush Press (*'intishārāt surūsh*), which was the publishing house of the national Iranian radio and television agency, replaced the Tehran Branch and collaborated with a newly established organization, Educational Research and Renovation (*sāziman pazhūhish va nawsāzī āmūzishī*), to continue the publication of the *Payk*s. The termination of the collaboration between the EPC and the Tehran Branch was given in a note of October 1977. This note stated that the Tehran Branch had been formerly responsible for the production and printing (*tahīyah va chāp*) of this magazine; however, the Tehran Branch's shortcomings and misconduct (*kūtāhī va sahl 'ingārī*) during the previous two years had resulted in termination of the arrangement.[58] The note does not provide any further details.

Circulation and readership of the *Payk*s: The collaboration between the Tehran Branch and Iran's Ministry of Education resulted in the widest circulation and readership of a supplementary student magazine in the educational history of the country. By 1967, the circulation of the *Payk*s had increased from about 50,000 to roughly 250,000, and they were distributed throughout most of Iran.[59] In 1968, *Payk*s increased total circulation from 250,000 in the previous year to 300,000. By this time, *Payk*s had found their way into "virtually every village in the country."[60] By 1969, the readership was estimated at 500,000.[61]

During the 1969/70 educational year, the EPC prepared, produced, and distributed (1) fifteen issues of *Payk for Kindergarten* at 100,000 to 105,000 copies per issue; (2) fifteen issues of *Payk for Children* at 200,000 to 220,000 copies per issue; (3) fifteen issues of *Payk for Primary School Students* at 300,000 copies per issue; and (4) fifteen issues of *Payk for Teachers and Parents* at 30,000 copies per issue. Further, the EPC prepared and produced eight issues of the monthly journal *Education and Training* for distribution among literacy corpsmen, students of teacher-training colleges, teachers, and other educators in Iran.

During the 1969/70 educational year, over 11,000,000 copies of *Payk* magazines and the monthly journal *Education and Training* were published. A report from Ali Asghar Mohajer, the manager of the Tehran Branch, included in that year's FBP Annual Report, informed readers:

> It can be safely stated that the majority of the kindergarten children and primary school students, as well as many secondary school students, teachers, and parents in all the cities in the country and in many of the villages have been among the keen readers of these educational publications. It should also be added that in some schools situated in less fortunate sections of towns, five students on the average have been reading each copy of Payk.

The manager of the Tehran Branch further reported that "the [*Payk*] magazines also tried to consolidate Persian in areas where this language is not spoken by all the inhabitants." During the academic year of 1970/1, the EPC received an average of 450 letters per day from children, youth, teachers, parents, and those concerned with education. The children's program of Radio Iran (*rādiyū īrān*) and the children-and-youth programs of national Iranian television also continued to make use of content from the *Payk* magazines in their broadcasting.[62]

The number of copies of each of the *Payk*s printed during the 1971/2 academic year was (1) *Payk for Kindergarten*: fifteen issues per year, 130,000 copies per issue; (2) *Payk for Children*: fifteen issues per year, 245,000 copies per issue; (3) *Payk for Primary School Students*: fifteen issues per year, 310,000 copies per issue; (4) *Payk for Teachers and Parents*: fifteen issues per year, 30,000 copies per issue; (5) *Payk for Teens* (in its first year of publication): six issues, 53,000 copies per issue; and (6) the monthly *Education and Training*: eight issues per year, 12,000 copies per issue.[63]

On December 1972, on the occasion of the eighth year of its publication, *Payk for Primary Students* published a report by the *Payk* editorial staff on all its publications up to that time, which included: *Payk for Primary School Students* (published since 1964); *Payk for Kindergarten* (published since 1969); *Payk for Children* (published since 1967); *Payk for Teens* (published since 1972); *Payk for Youth* (published since 1970); *Payk for Teachers and Parents* (published since 1964); and the monthly *Education and Training* (published for fifty-three years in Iran, but which joined the *Payk* series in 1969). Besides the *Payk* magazine series, *Payk* had also published six books for children and fourteen books for the literacy programs, including *To Read and Write* (*bikhvānīm va binivisīm*), and *To Read and Become Literate* (*bikhvānīm va bā savād shavīm*). The *Payk* editorial office reported that by December 1972, it had published 12,357 pages in total and claimed a readership of at least five million people throughout Iran for any issue of each of its series, and as many as 1,300,000 copies were sold of each issue. The report does not give an exact number for correspondence received from its readers but mentions one hundred thousand letters.[64]

By 1973, the combined printings of the six school magazines ran to nearly 1.2 million copies every two weeks, with an estimated readership of five per copy. Therefore, the FBP was reporting a total readership of seven million for all of the publications per issue.[65] By 1974, the *Payk*s (five children's editions plus one teachers and parents' edition) and the monthly *Education and Training* were distributed in a total of 18,287,000 copies.[66]

Method of distribution: By 1972, an extensive and wide-ranging method of *Payk* distribution had been organized. The *Payk* magazines were sent to all the education and training offices (*'idārāt āmūzish va parvarish*) in the country. These government offices were to distribute them among the schools under their administration. The General Office for Nomad Education (*'idārah kul āmūzish 'ashāyir*) was responsible for distributing the *Payk* magazines among the nomad students and their teachers. The IIDCYA also distributed the *Payk* magazines across all the children's and teen libraries it organized, as well as the rural libraries.

The General Office for Cultural Relations in the Ministry of Culture and Arts (*'idārah kul ravābiṭ farhangī vizārat farhang va hunar*) was responsible for distributing the *Payk* magazines in all the Culture Houses (*khānah farhang*) inside Iran, and also to the Iranian consulates, cultural centers, and embassies throughout the world. By doing so, they exposed many Iranians and Persian-speaking students, especially in neighboring countries such as Pakistan and Afghanistan, to the *Payk*s.[67]

Financial: It is important to note that the *Payk*s did not contain any advertisements and were sold at a much lower price than the cost of their production. This was mentioned several times in the *Payk* magazines themselves. The Tehran Branch subsidized their publication. In May 1971, *Payk for Primary School Students* thanked the Tehran Branch for its generosity in publishing these journals at such a high quality yet a low price, without governmental funding.[68] Additionally, in response to a letter to the *Payk for Youth* about its price, this *Payk* answered:

> The sales of this journal during the last year and this year only covers a portion of the costs of production, print, and distribution of this journal. If it was not for the financial sponsorship of an institution which would accept bearing the loss, the production of this magazine in this quality and with this price would have been impossible.[69]

The FBP's Tehran Branch paid the production and printing costs of the *Payk* series, as well as the salaries of *Payk* editorial members and staff (Alinejad, 2016).

An overview of the pedagogical themes and subjects included in the Payk *series*

As noted earlier, a thorough historical and textual study of the content of the *Payk* series is much needed. That said, the role of the Tehran Branch in the financial sponsorship, production, and printing of the *Payk* series has been discussed above. It is also important to mention the specific roles that the Tehran Branch might have played in the process of *Payk* content production. While we certainly need a more in-depth study of the knowledge produced and distributed by these magazines, below I will outline my observations of the monarchist historiography and Islamic teaching in the *Payk*s.

Monarchist historiography: A textual analysis of the *Payk* series shows that, especially in the *Payk*s for primary and middle schools, each year subject-related articles were systematically published to propagandize the official monarchical narratives—on occasions, for example, such as the end of the Azerbaijan Crisis of 1946, the coup of February 22, 1921,[70] the launch of the "White Revolution,"[71] and the anniversary of the Shah's coronation.[72] Similarly, celebratory articles on personal occasions of the royal family (the birthdays of the Shah, queen, and crown prince) appeared each year in these *Payk*s. The Azerbaijan Crisis of 1946, which I pointed to earlier as one of the early crises of the Cold War era, was taught in the *Payk*s through a monarchist historiography, meaning that each year, day 21 of the month of Azar (December 12) was memorialized as the day of "the Liberation of Azerbaijan" (*nijāt āzarbāyjān*). According to this narrative, reprinted most years in the December issue, a group of malicious people (*mardum badkhwāh*) had occupied Azerbaijan, but on December 12, 1946 Iranian soldiers under the Shah's command and with the help of the people liberated this province.[73] The birthday of the Shah, the anniversary of the coronation, and the birthday of the crown prince (which was formally celebrated by the Pahlavi regime as the Day for Children [*rūz-i kūdak*]) were all taught and celebrated each year in the November issue. Starting from the 1969/70 educational year, an annual competition, the Outstanding Child contest mentioned above, was also awarded on the occasion of the crown prince's birthday.[74]

In addition to the essays and short pieces that presented this monarchist historiography and narration of royal life events, there are numerous stories in *Payk for Children* and other student editions that dramatize kings and princes, and idealize the quest for marrying a prince or princess, such as "The Black Bird and the King's Son" (*murq siyāh va pisar pādishāh*);[75] "A House in the Jungle" (*khānah ʾī dar jangal*);[76] "The Wise Demon and the Healer Angel" (*div dunyā bīn va parī darmāngar*);[77] "The Children of the Woodcutter" (*bachihā-yi mard hizum shikan*);[78] "The Laughing Boy" (*pisar khandān*);[79] and "The Sound of the Nightingale" (*āvāz-i bulbul*).[80] "The Laughing Boy" provides a good example. It narrates the life of a baby who is found in a jungle and raised in a village. When he gets older, he finds a reed in the jungle. The sound of this reed makes any person or even any animal who hears it happy. At the end of the story, it is revealed that this young man is actually the crown prince who had been kidnapped years before. Over the years since his kidnapping, all the people had been depressed, and there was no laughter anymore. The boy arrives at the royal court, and the king recognizes his son. Happiness returns to all the people.

Some stories, in line with the official celebration of the White Revolution, dramatize the crown prince as a just social force who defends the peasants against the cruelty of the landlords. For instance, the story "The Cart and the Pony" (*gārī va kurrah asb*) concerns a landlord who unlawfully seizes the newborn horse of a peasant. The peasant's son, however, correctly answers questions asked by the king's son. Then, the king's son forces the landlord to give the newborn horse back to the peasant. The king's son and the peasant's son become close friends.[81]

Annually, and in a manner similar to *Payk for Children*, *Payk for Primary School Students* also discussed and commemorated the anniversary of the coronation and the births of Queen Farah, the Shah, and the crown prince.[82] Moreover, it expanded on the monarchical historiography of the Azerbaijan Crisis, the 1921 coup, and the White Revolution. As noted before, Mohammad Reza Pahlavi wrote the biography of his father, Reza Shah (r. 1925–41), as an additional chapter to the FBP-sponsored Persian edition of Bolton's *Lives of Poor Boys Who Became Famous*. This chapter, along with excerpts from two books written by the Shah, *Mission for My Country* (*ma'mūriyat barāy-i vatanam*, 1960) and the *White Revolution of Iran* (*inqilāb-i sifīd īrān*, 1966), were used by *Payk for Primary School Students* in the publication of a lengthy celebration of the life and legacy of Reza Shah.[83]

Several stories published in *Payk for Primary School Students* also depict just kings and admirable crown princes. The story "The Mystery of the Letter" (*mu'amā-yi nāmah*) dramatizes the marriage of a crown prince and a peasant girl who is clever enough to answer the prince's riddle.[84] The story "The Shepherd's Judgment" (*qiḍāvat-i chūpān*) is about a king who has always been so just and fair to the people, that the people come to him for their matters in full trust.[85] The story "The Daughter of the Moonlight" (*dukhtar-i mahtāb*) dramatizes a just king who is ready to reject eternal life and love, for the betterment of his people.[86]

Payk for Youth follows the other *Payk*s in memorializing the official monarchical calendar and celebrating the lives of the royal family (the birth of the Shah, the birth of the Queen, the birth of the crown prince, the White Revolution, the marking of the 2500th Year of the Foundation of the Imperial State of Iran, and so on).[87] However, it extended its coverage of the royal family to include photos and reports on Ashraf Pahlavi (the Shah's twin sister) and Farideh Diba (the Queen's mother).

By the early 1970s, a renewed attempt to add to the extent and range of monarchy-related materials in the *Payk*s can be detected, now extending to include memorializing the occasion of the 2500th Year of the Foundation of the Imperial State of Iran, and promoting the ceremony of the fiftieth year of the Pahlavi dynasty. In *Payk for Primary School Students*, as with the other *Payk*s, the celebration of monarchical history and ideology intensified by early 1971. Later in 1974 the concept of fatherland (*mīhan*) was foregrounded in many articles containing monarchical, patriotic and nationalist content, and reformulated in line with the Shah's officially promoted discourse of Iran as a "great civilization." In the context of this reinvigorated monarchist propaganda, *Payk for Youth* and *Payk for Teachers and Parents* also started to publish lengthy articles elaborating on and justifying various educational, economic, and internal and foreign policies of the Shah. *Payk for Youth*, usually in its opening article, defended and promoted a wide range of national, regional, and international policies of the monarchy. As for the regional and international policies of the Shah, the following subjects were covered: the Arab–Israel conflict;[88] the Shah's support for the US role in the Vietnam War;[89]

the Shah's oil policies and his role in OPEC;[90] and the military presence of Iran in Oman against the Dhofar movement.[91]

Further, *Payk for Youth* also contained articles defending and promoting the national educational, social, military, and economic policies of the Shah—such as the White Revolution, with a specific focus on his educational policies;[92] military spending and his vision for Iran's military role in the Middle East and beyond;[93] the establishment of the Rastakhiz Party;[94] the women's issue;[95] and his anti-inflationary policies.[96] *Payk for Youth* also contained reports on the Shah's public lectures, with long passages quoted from him on issues such as women's rights on the occasion of January 7,[97] and on the campaign against illiteracy.[98] In 1976 and 1977, several of the issues of *Payk for Youth* opened to full-page messages from the Shah on various educational events, to the Shah's message to the Rastakhiz Party, or to full-page excerpts from the Party's manifesto. The government's yearly budget and fifth economic and social planning program (1973–8) are also discussed in detail and promoted in several articles.[99]

Islamic teachings: The second set of notable narratives repeated each year in the *Payk*s in a systematic manner was the teachings on Islam according to Twelver Shiʻism.[100] The birthday of Ali ibn Abi Talib (601–61), the first Imam according to Shiʻa Islam; the birthday of Hasan ibn Ali (624–70), the second Shiʻa Imam; the birthday of Husayn ibn Ali (626–80), the third Shiʻa Imam; the birthday of Jaʻfar al-Sadiq (702–65), the sixth Shiʻa Imam; the birthday of Ali al-Reza (766–818), eighth Shiʻa Imam (who is buried in Iran); and the birthday of al-Mahdi (b. 879), the twelfth and last Imam who the Shiʻas believe went into occultation and will reappear at the end of time to bring absolute justice to the world, are all commemorated each year in the *Payk* student editions. Other notable Shiʻa teachings in the *Payk*s concerned the assassination of Ali ibn Abi Talib and the battle which ended in the death of Husayn ibn Ali. The general history of early Islam, shared with other Islamic sects, is also taught through teachings on the life and appointment of Mohammad ibn Abdullah (571–632) to prophecy, and the celebrations of the month of Ramadan and of Eid Fitr.

The Islamicization of *Payk* content extended to include children's stories from the cleric and Muslim thinker Morteza Motahhari (1919–79), generally credited as an influential ideologue of the Islamic Republic. Five stories from his book *Anecdotes of Pious Men* (*dāstān-i rāstān*; 1965) are included in *Payk for Children*. This book, published in 1960, was a collection of ethical Shiʻa stories on the life and personality of the Prophet and the Imams, written for children and young readers. *Payk for Children* in its December 1973 issue contained two Shiʻa Islamic dramatizations of the lives of Imam Ali and Imam Zain al-Abedin (the fourth Imam according to Shiʻism) from *Anecdotes of Pious Men*. Another story from this book, which dramatizes the life of the sixth Shiʻa imam, appeared in October 1975.[101] Three other narratives from the book, all on the life of the Prophet Mohammad, appeared in February 1976.[102] The religious content of *Payk for Primary School Students* also intensified in the 1970s, with full-page pictures of mosques such as Masjid Shah, Masjid Lutfullah, Masjid Jamiʻ Shiraz, Masjid Wakil, Shah Chiraq, and Masjid Sipahsalar as well as the shrines of Maʻsomeh, Masjid Nasir al-mulk, and Masjid Jamiʿ Isfahan appearing on the back cover.[103] Essays by authors such as Morteza Motahhari and Jawad Fazel Larijani (1916–61), a religious writer,[104] also began to appear.

In sum, while there is a need for a thorough textual content analysis of the supplementary-reading materials published by the EPC, it can be noted that the *Payk* series, with the exception of *Payk for Youth*, all followed a mechanical and systematic approach in their content organization—meaning that each year they published pedagogical and propaganda articles, essays, and notes based on the Shiʿa religious calendar and the occasions of monarchical ceremonies. By the early 1970s, a renewed attempt at adding to the extent and range of the monarchy-related materials in the *Payk*s can also be detected.

Relations with Other Organizations in the Field of Education

The FBP was very concerned about the possible involvement and role of other international organizations in the field of education in Iran. It exploited any opportunity to come into contact with the organizations that were working in this field, so as to channel the educational activities of individuals and foundations or to block any attempt at a conflict of interest in this area. For instance, when in 1969 the FBP's New York office became aware that the Raytheon Service Company had contracts in Iran for vocational training projects and was looking to expand its work in Iran, it encouraged Ali Asghar Mohajer to meet their representative, Mr. Tim Wise, in Tehran.[105]

In another case, following FBP concerns over a "scientific apparatus manufacturer who had licensed an Iranian manufacturer," Mohajer reported that he could not find any information on such a company, but a former editor of *Kayhan* (a leading evening daily newspaper) by the name of Mr. Qureishi had established a company named Rotatif and was importing presses, mostly from the Soviet Union. Rotatif was also the sole agent for the distribution of Russian-made projectors. However, Mohajer reassured the FBP that for Rotatif to become involved in producing film strips based on textbooks this would require the support of the Ministry of Education, which it did not have.[106]

The FBP also intended to influence the activities of individuals and foundations that intended to work in the field of Iranian education. The Iran Foundation, Inc. was one of these foundations and was run by Mrs. Grimson, who was interested in health education. The Iran Foundation ran the Namazi Technical School in Shiraz for a period of time before 1964. In 1967, Mohajer wrote to Datus C. Smith criticizing the advice that Torb Mehra, vice-president of the foundation and also president of Gondi Shapur University in Khuzistan, had given the Iran Foundation. In this letter, Mohajer stated that as a result of "opportunist and useless advice," the Iran Foundation was collecting kerosene lamps and school bags containing stationery, and suggesting to US schools that they should adopt a school in Khuzistan. Mohajer argued that "the way the Foundation is performing its part in the Literacy Campaigns will not secure it a good outward appearance for the Foundation," as it was moving against attempts by the Iranian government to convince the world that the government was financially well situated and fitted to address its illiteracy problems. The letter ends with a suggestion from Mohajer to the Iran Foundation that it should go through the "right channels" for its involvement in Iran, which according to Mohajer meant going via the sponsorship of the FBP's translation projects or paying subscription fees for *Payk*s on behalf of 20,000 corpsmen. The letter further asserted that the *Payk*s were the best reference material at the disposal of teachers and corpsmen.[107]

In 1970, following a brief discussion with Rhett Austell in November, Ali Asghar Mohajer wrote a "confidential" letter informing the FBP that Mr. Bahadory (secretary to Queen Farah) was making efforts to "by-pass" FBP by seeking investors from abroad to establish a new printing plant. While Mr. Bahadory had said to an American investor, Rhett Austell, that this new printing plant was desired for new publications, Mohajer contended: "but I am positive that he is aiming at establishing a printing plant for existing textbooks."[108] Mohajer further reported that

> [a] few days before I came to the U.S., Mr. Shamaavari, Director of the Textbook Institute, met me and informed me about an assignment he had been given to collect statistics on textbooks. He told me the Ministry of Education has been ordered to submit a report on all textbooks throughout the country to the secretariat department of H.I.M.Q. [Her Imperial Majesty the Queen].[109]

Mohajer concluded that the motive and the person acting behind the scenes who was encouraging Mr. Bahadory "remains for further investigation," but if this new printing plant were to be established, the Tehran Branch, Offset Printing House, and the company that was in charge of secondary school textbooks would go out of business.[110]

The FBP was also very concerned with new developments in the educational sphere in Iran as proposed by international institutions. For instance, in March 1970, Ali Asghar Mohajer and Harold Munger from the FBP met with Mr. Dimitri Koulourianos (of the World Bank's Education Division) to discuss the World Bank's recent survey of educational needs in Iran. In this meeting, they found out that while the World Bank had proposed a pilot project at a secondary level of education called "guidance schools," the Iranian government still had not approved it, so no loans had been negotiated yet. While the result of this proposal was still not clear, the Tehran Branch had already begun to think about new written materials that it might develop for these guidance schools.[111]

The various initiatives and operations of the Tehran Branch and their developments during its history have been detailed. As shown in Chapter 5, the Tehran Branch developed in the context of the close alliance between Iran and the United States after the coup. During the Cold War, the Iranian state actively blocked any Soviet attempt at achieving cultural and educational influence, while assisting US initiatives in cultural and educational transmission, the most important of which was the Tehran Branch. The current chapter has detailed how the Tehran Branch moved from its early Regular Translation Programs to conducting a variety of Special Projects in Iran. The Tehran Branch further developed an extensive network of intellectual and scholarly affiliations in Iran that endorsed its operations. As noted, it had close relations with the royal family and several political and educational leaders. It can be safely claimed that no national or international organization had a comparable influence in Iran's publication and textbook-writing history. Given such influence, these relations, and the various operations that the Tehran Branch conducted in Iran, it is not surprising that dissident intellectuals were criticizing it.

Reaction to the Tehran Branch: The Case of Jalal Al Ahmad

With the expansion of the Tehran Branch's operations to educational publishing, reactions against it also surfaced, first and foremost by Jalal Al Ahmad. Jalal Al Ahmad (1923–69) was a translator for and advisor to the Tehran Branch (from 1954). He is one of the most controversial thinkers of contemporary Iranian intellectual history. Al Ahmad's intellectual trajectory is complex and very much contested. He has been read differently and in several contradictory manners. In post-revolutionary Iran, Al Ahmad's seminal book *Westoxification* (*qarb zadigī*) (published in 1962) has been sometimes rendered as an advocation for an anti-Western Islamic ideology and a major ideological manifesto of the revolution.[112] Others such as Nabavi (2003) and Matin-Asgari (2018) have argued that *Westoxification* is more complex and also not a coherent argument and that this book and Al Ahmad's intellectual trajectory cannot be reduced to a simple embracing of anti-Western revolutionary Islam.

Within current scholarship on Al Ahmad, there is a general lack of serious engagement with his criticisms of the FBP. This suggests that Al Ahmad's discussions of the Tehran Branch might have been reduced to quarrels and personal issues with this Branch and with San'atizadeh—and this I find very problematic. As I will show below, Al Ahmad's criticisms of the Tehran Branch go beyond a simple personal issue. These criticisms are extensive and have been echoed and reemphasized in several works. A chronological reading of his published works in the 1960s clearly helps in interpreting Al Ahmad's intellectual trajectory as it was influenced by his reflections on the Tehran Branch of the FBP. He started to criticize this institution's involvement in the production of textbooks in his *Chaotic Situation of the Educational Textbooks* (1960), refers to this institution in *Westoxification* (1963), and then vehemently attacks it and its manager in *One Well and Two Hollows* (1965). Finally, certain categorizations in *On the Merits and the Perfidy of the Intellectuals* (1969) might best be understood if we interpret them in the context of the previous decade-long engagements with the Tehran Branch.

Al Ahmad was not the only dissident intellectual who was critical of the educational policies of the Pahlavi era and the influence of the FBP and Tehran Branch's operations. As discussed in Chapter 5, Samad Behrangi was also a teacher who criticized the significant role that the translation of US books was playing in the educational system. However, Behrangi's criticism was not directed toward the FBP and its Tehran Branch per se. He decried the fact that the Tehran Branch-sponsored translations had become textbooks in teacher-training programs, and criticized Iranian educationalists and their inability to produce locally related research on educational needs.

US imperialism and the close cultural, political, and military alliance between the Pahlavi state and the United States was criticized by many dissident intellectuals, activists, and political oppositional groups in samizdats, declarations, and bulletins. Much metaphorical and direct criticism of Iran–US relations and Pahlavi's official monarchist ideology and cultural policy can be traced in Iran's 1960s and 1970s visual arts, films, novels, and poetry.[113] The student movement both inside and outside the country was radicalized during the 1960s. Student journals of the time both inside and outside the country include poetry, fiction, cartoons, and essays, which criticize imperialism and share a call for revolutionizing social relations, nationally, regionally, and internationally.[114] Mehdi Bahar's Marxist criticism of US neocolonialism should also be mentioned. As for criticizing US cultural imperialism per se, several arguments can be traced through the 1960s, such as those developed by Ali Asghar Haj Seyyed Javadi, and Mostafa Rahimi (Matin-Asgari, 2018). These authors, among others, dealt in the details of US imperialism and the role that culture played in it. Still, what makes it important to investigate Al Ahmad's criticism is the fact that he was the most outspoken critic of the Tehran Branch—its structure, organizational practice, and socio-cultural role in Iran.

Jalal Al Ahmad was born in Tehran to a religious family. Influenced by authors such as Ahmad Kasravi,[115] he began to depart from his religious background in high school. In 1944, he officially joined the Tudeh Party. Al Ahmad became an editor of the Tudeh publications, such as *The People* (*mardum*) and *The Leader* (*rahbar*). He earned an MA in Persian literature from Tehran Teachers College in 1946. In 1947, along with the nationalist socialist intellectual Khalil Maleki (1903–69) and a few other members, Al Ahmad left the Tudeh Party, criticizing it as an instrument of Soviet policies and in protest against its late withdrawal of its army from Azerbaijan (Clinton, 1984). Al Ahmad started his PhD in literature, but left university in 1951 before defending the dissertation. Starting from 1950, he actively supported the Mosaddeq government and its policy of nationalizing the oil industry. In 1952, Al Ahmad joined Khalil Maleki to found a nationalist socialist party called the Third Force.

An influential intellectual and prolific author, Al Ahmad wrote more than twenty volumes of books including stories, social criticism, travelogues, and anthropological memoirs, and he also translated several books, such as Albert Camus's *The Stranger*. Famously, in 1963 he had a meeting with Ayatollah Khomeini (1902–89), who later became the first leader of the Islamic Republic; Khomeini endorsed Al Ahmad's book *Westoxification*.

The first time Al Ahmad criticized the FBP's operations in Tehran dates back to 1960. In this year, Al Ahmad, who had contributed to the Tehran Branch as a translator, published an article entitled "Chaotic Situation of the Educational Textbooks" (*balbashū-yi kitābhā-yi darsī*) and argued that due to financially corrupt relations between the Tehran Branch and the Iranian government, the Tehran Branch, which used to be a US "propaganda" agency, had developed to gain a "monopoly" over the cultural products in Iran. He further argued that such a "cultural monopoly" enabled "the [process of] homogenization of the thoughts and beliefs of the people" (Al Ahmad, 1963, p. 86).

Al Ahmad claims that with the state's decision to give the printing of primary school textbooks to the Offset Printing House, the value of this firm's shares increased thirty times in less than three years. He points to the profits that this house gains each year from printing textbooks and claims the costs for printing are much less than the amount it receives from the state (Al Ahmad, 1963, p. 74). Al Ahmad further criticizes the Tehran Branch, noting that given the relations between this Branch and the Iranian state, Tehran is the only one among the FBP branches that is making money beyond its allocated budget from the FBP itself, and the money it receives from certain organizations such as the Ford Foundation, or under Public Law 480. Al Ahmad acknowledges that the establishment of the Tehran Branch has encouraged a better quality of translation and book production in Iran. He also observes that the books sponsored by the Tehran Branch do not fit simply in the category of "propaganda." Still, he argues that the Branch has become so powerful that it has a "tight grip" over the Ministry of Culture (Al Ahmad, 1963, p. 84). Al Ahmad further criticizes the fact that some of "the best and renowned" cultural figures of Iran are working for this institution and endorsing it. He contends that this is so because such figures are not allowed to work in the Ministry of Culture, and have no other career options, and in such conditions the Branch have exploited this fact and attracted them.

To support his claim that the Tehran Branch has gained a hegemonic role in Iran, Al Ahmad notes that from any of a hundred books published in a year, around half of them are sponsored by the Tehran Branch. He further claims secret and close working affiliations between the Tehran Branch and Bungāh Tarjumah va Nashr Kitāb. Al Ahmad strengthens his case by saying that several cultural journals are also published either by the Tehran Branch or rely on its financial support. Al Ahmad concludes:

> I am warning all bookreaders, bookwriters, and booksellers, from now on you are facing a press trust. There is no more space for small, personal and private businesses. From now on, if you want to write something, to publish a poetry collection, to establish a book firm, to write a textbook, even if you are a wandering bookseller, or intend to establish a cultural journal, all and all, in case you don't want to lose interest, and aim for it to remain in operation, you have to first negotiate with the [Tehran Branch of] Franklin.
>
> (Al Ahmad, 1963, p. 85)

Al Ahmad concludes that given the evolvement of the Tehran Branch to a cultural trust, it has become a danger to freedom of thought. Worried about the Branch's capabilities to create intellectual conformity, Al Ahmad suggests that the Tehran Branch should be pushed back to its early objective, to simply translate US books. While at this point in the early 1960s, Al Ahmad was proposing to limit the operations of the Tehran Branch, his ideas soon radicalized in his next book, which called for "socializing" it.

Westoxification (1962) is a "polemic" argument rather than "a reasoned historical study" (Clinton, 1984). In *Westoxification*, Al Ahmad argues for the socialization of the cultural industries by means of the revolt of "the Islamic body" (*kulīyat islāmī*; that is, the Islamic community) as the emancipatory path for countering cultural imperialism. Borrowing the neologism "westoxification" from Ahmad Fardid,[116] Al Ahmad described westoxification as an illness (*bīmārī*), "like being infected with cholera" (Al Ahmad, [1962] 2006, p. 13). According to Al Ahmad, a westoxified human is a faithful consumer of Western products. This person is amazed by the West and is not critical at all of what happens there. Al Ahmad criticizes the knowledge produced in the West concerning the East, and states that even when westoxified people aim to know about themselves, they will not rely on their own knowledge and everyday experience but will recognize themselves only through the language of the Western Orientalists (Al Ahmad, [1962] 2006).

In a footnote to the book, Al Ahmad points out that in its historical analysis his theory is informed by *Conquering the Western Civilization* (*taskhīr tamadun farangī*), a book by Seyed Fakhr al-Din Shadiman[117] published in 1947. To understand Al Ahmad's argumental debt to Shadiman, as well as his divergence from him, it is worth discussing Shadiman's book briefly. Written in the form of a long essay, *Conquering the Western Civilization* is Shadiman's nationalist attempt to criticize those who argue that the Persian language per se, Islam, and the national traditions of Iran are the roots of Iran's underdevelopment. Shadiman vehemently regrets what he considers the decay of the Persian language as a result of cultural submission to the Western civilization. He concludes: "The only exit and only alternative for us is [...] to conquer it [i.e., Western civilization] before we are conquered by it" (Shadiman, 1947). He argues that the Persian language is the only instrument by which Iranians can conquer the Western civilization. He analogizes Western civilization to an army of a hundred million soldiers and argues that each book that is well translated into Persian, and every design, blueprint, example of architecture, machine, and weapon that is brought to Iran, if it is accompanied by a study on it in Persian, is as if Iranians have arrested a foreign soldier (Shadiman, 1947).

Shadiman criticizes the emphasis placed on sending students to Europe that began in the mid-nineteenth century, arguing that these students came back mostly empty-handed and seduced by Europe. Instead, he advocates the pursuit of systematic translation projects conducted by Iranians who are familiar with the Persian language and are able to both use old words and, in case one is needed, construct a new well-crafted neologism. According to him, such translation projects would counter Western cultural domination.

Seven years later, what Shadiman had suggested—that is, a systematic translation project—was already being undertaken in Iran by publishing houses such as the Tehran Branch and Bungāh Tarjumah va Nashr Kitāb. However, contrary to what Shadiman advocated, in the case of the Tehran Branch this systematic translation project was not part of a national effort to conquer the West, but rather was part of US cultural diplomacy in competing against Soviet influence during the Cold War.

Al Ahmad argues that Shadiman adequately distinguished "the social illness"; however, Shadiman's suggestion for a systematic translation project was not adequate for curing it. Al Ahmad claimed that the translation of thousands of Western books in the previous two decades had not cured the problem. Consequently, in a nativist turn toward political Islam, Al Ahmad suggests that mosques should become the backbone of the entire educational system, from kindergarten to university, to replace a reliance on translation projects (Al Ahmad, [1962] 2006).[118]

Through a schematic and reductionist historical account of the colonization of Africa and India, Al Ahmad argues that these regions were more vulnerable to the colonization process in comparison to the Islamic societies of the East because their people had many religions and races. He claims that the Islamic societies of the East were not as vulnerable precisely because they were part of an "Islamic body." He further elaborates on this assertion, claiming that this is the reason the West has historically opposed the Islamic body and tried to divide and rule it (Al Ahmad, [1962] 2006).

Next, Al Ahmad provides a schematic account of the history of the world narrated as a war between Islam and Christianity. He states that starting from the twelfth century, the Christian world became so anxious about the expansion of Islam that it began to adopt Islamic knowledge and techniques, which centuries later made Christians the masters of capital, technology, and machinery. According to Al Ahmad, "[i]t is now just the reverse; it is now Islam which is so much under the threat of the West that it has to wake up" (Al Ahmad, [1962] 2006).[119]

Writing at a time when the increase in oil revenue had led to an increase in the rate of imports in Iran, Al Ahmad criticizes using oil money to buy and import machines, and contends that such imports are internally linked with the importing of foreign advisors and specialists. According to Al Ahmad, Orientalists too are imported into the country and work in close relation with the economic sectors of foreign countries in order to shape the cultural sphere of Iran and so monitor it in case a dangerous argument, such as his position, is being produced (Al Ahmad, [1962] 2006).

Al Ahmad points to the funds that foundations such as Ford and Rockefeller were dispersing to produce and distribute cultural commodities in Iran, and argues that their sponsorship of the FBP's Tehran Branch resulted in that branch's monopoly over educational books—thereby bringing about the devastation of all local publishers (Al Ahmad, [1962] 2006, p. 108). While he does not elaborate more on the Tehran Branch, Al Ahmad refers his readers in a footnote to his essay, "Chaotic Situation of the Educational Textbooks," discussed above.

To counter such social and cultural subjugation, Al Ahmad suggests that in Iran big media, such as television, should not be under the control of companies. Instead, he argues that selected councils of writers and intellectuals, without serving any special economic or promotional agenda, should administer them.

Al Ahmad argues that the exact opposite is happening in Iran and that cultural industries are being administered by big shareholders and trusts. Al Ahmad states:

> What is dangerous nowadays is the ownership of the movable properties, money, shares, bank credits, and the capital which is deposited in the banks abroad, and [also] the personal power of those who are connected to the industrial jobs. The [danger] comes from the power of the big shareholders and [shareholders of] the monopolies, especially, those who are administrating the cultural industries. We must be aware of their danger, and we should come up with a plan to socialize these [cultural industries].
>
> (Al Ahmad, [1962] 2006, p. 137)

Given that these lines were written just a few years after Al Ahmad's detailed criticism of the Tehran Branch, it is clear that he had the Tehran Branch in mind when referring to cultural trusts. This is an important contextual link between this book, and two other books Al Ahmad wrote just before and after it. In a direct attack on the Shah and the royal family's role in cultural organizations, Al Ahmad notes that the duty of culture should be to democratize the leadership of the country and de-monopolize it by rescuing it from a certain family (i.e., royal family) (Al Ahmad, [1962] 2006). In sum, to counteract what it framed as cultural monopolies (as seen in the Tehran Branch) and frightened by the ability of such cultural entities to create hegemony, the theory of westoxification suggests that the cultural industries should be socialized.

Al Ahmad's criticism of the Tehran Branch did not end here. Three years later, he wrote *One Well and Two Hollows* (*yik chāh va dū chālah*) (1965), which is a direct criticism of the Tehran Branch and a personal attack on San'atizadeh. Calling the Tehran Branch a "shop," Al Ahmad writes: "In his [San'atizadeh's] shop, which is essentially a monster created by colonialism, and which is a capital that is expended outside America, […] people are becoming commodities, and their talents remain needy of the deceits of the middle-men." He asserts:

> In a shop such as Franklin, the pen is not even a ladder, it is only a commodity. Just like eggplant, or curd. Its price is something today, and another tomorrow. Today it is used for making a food to celebrate the Russian policy, and tomorrow it is used to decorate the tax exemptions of the American newspapers.
>
> (Al Ahmad, 1964, p. 15)

By the time Al Ahmad wrote *On the Merits and the Perfidy of the Intellectuals* (*dar khidmat va khīyānat rūshanfikrān*) (first printed in 1968), his ideas had changed beyond *Westoxification*, but still the shadow of his earlier observations about the Tehran Branch can be traced. In this book, Al Ahmad, who had moved to become more intellectually cosmopolitan (Matin-Asgari, 2018), presents his theory on the definition and the role of intellectuals in a society. He categorizes and relativizes the intellectuals of his time into two camps: "outsiders" who were assisting the dominant government—that is, intellectually assisting it through justifying its rationales; and the second camp, "insiders" (*rūshanfikr-i khawdī*)—that is, the intellectuals who were searching for a resolution to the deadlocks of imperialism and colonialism in Iran. Outsiders are minimal intellectuals, and insiders are maximal.

In an evaluative categorization, Al Ahmad discusses the distance that each group of intellectuals has from truthful "insider intellectuals." According to this categorization, "most publishers" were the furthest group from the central core and thus the furthest group from the nobility of intellectual thinking. Contextualizing this assertion in Al Ahmad's three previous books, it is clear that his categorization of publishers as the ones with the least ethical and intellectual value might have very well been shaped by the operations of the Tehran Branch, and his vehement criticisms of it.

In sum, in search of a haven in face of Western imperial cultural and economic invasion, Shadiman's *Conquering the Western Civilization* (1947) is a nationalist attempt that foregrounded the necessity of empowering the Persian language, and which suggested that a systematic translation project would assist Iranians in understanding the deep philosophical and scientific roots of modern Western culture. Almost two decades later, Jalal Al Ahmad wrote his seminal book, *Westoxification*. As part of the theory of westoxification, Al Ahmad argued that the cultural production industries should be socialized to counteract the imperialist cultural monopolies. In this book, Al Ahmad further emphasized the role of religion in the war against cultural imperialism. In a sense, Al Ahmad argues that translation projects have not worked, publishers are collaborators, and that religious schools should be founded to defend Iran's culture from Western cultural imperialism. While Al Ahmad's argument is inconsistent in this book, and later changes in the course of his intellectual life, still a specific ideological interpretation of this text was embraced by the post-revolutionary Islamic regime, and has contributed to its attempt at Islamicizing culture, education, and society after the 1979 revolution. In the next section, I will discuss the demise of the Tehran Branch. This section narrates how after the revolution, the remaining properties of the Tehran Branch were confiscated by the Organization for Publication and Education of the Islamic Revolution (*sāzimān āmūzish inqilāb islāmī*). In other words, the ability to create cultural hegemony was appropriated so as to be employed by the new regime, this time for its Islamicization objectives.

Demise of the Tehran Branch

San'atizadeh left the Tehran Branch in 1969 and was succeeded by its second and last manager, Ali Asghar Mohajer. The historians of the publishing industry in Iran and former staff of the Tehran Branch generally consider this change of management as a turning point in the Branch's history, with some attributing the gradual demise to mismanagement by Mohajer. Bayat, a historian of the publishing industry in Iran, points to two factors in his analysis of the decline of the Tehran Branch. First, he explores the change of management from San'atizadeh to Mohajer. Bayat contends that the peak of the Tehran Branch's operations in Iran was during the management of Sanʿatizadeh, who had a vast political and intellectual network that included Iran's President of the Senate, Seyyed Hassan Taqizadeh. According to Bayat, Sanʿatizadeh with his energetic and entrepreneurial capabilities exploited the chance offered by the FBP to develop this branch. Bayat also points out that as the tactics of the Cold War changed and the Soviet–US antagonistic rivalry lessened, the FBP lost its "initial characteristics" (*khāṣiyat avaliyah*). Bayat further criticizes the intellectuals of the time for not "understanding" the developments initiated by the Tehran Branch or the necessity for supporting such endeavors in order to help establish these "innovations." He points to Jalal Al Ahmad's criticism as an example of such intellectually poor judgment (Bayat, 1995).

Jaʿfari, the manager of Amīr Kabīr publishers, emphasizes the role of Ali Asghar Mohajer in transforming the Tehran Branch from its early adherence to a non-competition policy to becoming a publisher competing with other local publishers. Jaʿfari claims that during the years of Mohajer's management, there was commercial competition between local publishers, including Amīr Kabīr publishers and the Tehran Branch.[120] The Tehran Branch began paying higher rates to translators and for publishing rights (Jaʿfari, 2009).

Still, while Sanʿatizadeh's role in building the vast political and intellectual network of the Tehran Branch cannot be neglected, a study of the FBP records as discussed in Chapter 4 shows that the demise of the Tehran Branch was also a consequence of the US's gradual scaling down of its financial and technical aid programs, and the consequent financial and structural crisis that the FBP had been facing since the late 1960s—a crisis that led to a few attempts by the FBP to reframe its operations and reformulate its structure. The article in the *New York Times*, discussed in Chapter 4, which pointed to certain ties between the FBP and the CIA, led to the sudden dissolving of the FBP.[121]

Karim Emami, the chief editor of the Tehran Branch editing bureau, notes that Mohajer was heading in the direction of dissolving the Tehran Branch for a few years before it happened. Around 1976, the FBP headquarters in New York ordered Mohajer to begin selling some of the assets of the Tehran Branch, such as the copyrights of its books, the goodwill (*sarqufli*) of the Pocket Books Company's bookshops, and the copyright for the *Persian Encyclopedia*. The Tehran Branch also started to sell all the books it had in stock. Amīr Kabīr publishers paid around five million tomans to buy all the shares of the Pocket Books Company, the goodwill of its bookshops (including thirteen stores in Tehran,[122] one store in Mehrabad Airport, and one in Mashhad), its book stocks, and copyrights of its books. Amīr Kabīr publishers also bought the copyrights to the *Persian Encyclopedia* (Jaʿfari, 2009). In 1976, as a result of a dispute over misconduct in the distribution of textbooks, Iran's Ministry of Education terminated its collaboration with the Tehran Branch. Consequently, the Tehran Branch lost its most substantial source of income. During the same few months, disorder in the publication of the *Payk* series and other journals also ended the collaboration between EPC and the Tehran Branch.

Furthermore, when Azad University of Iran was established in the mid-1970s, and as this university had a program for publishing textbooks, Mohajer came up with an arrangement with the university's chancellor, Abdulrahim Ahmadi, to transfer the editors of the Tehran Branch there. With the fulfillment of this arrangement, the editing bureau in the Tehran Branch was closed. In January 1978, all the remaining properties, liabilities, projects, and programs of the Tehran Branch were sold to an Iranian institute by the name of Nawmarz Educational Organization (sāzimān āmūzishī nawmarz),[123] and the Tehran Branch was officially dissolved on January 25, 1978 (Yadegar, 1979, p. 12).

Datus C. Smith reports on this final stage of the FBP's operations in Iran:

After twenty-five years in existence the director of Franklin Book Programs, Inc. decided to dissolve the corporation, a process completed in 1979, and the remaining assets of the corporation (only about $8,000) were given to the Center for the Book at the Library of Congress. Before that the Franklin assets in Egypt were given to an Egyptian non-profit organization to continue Franklin work there, and the assets in Persia (valued at about $10 million) to a Persian non-profit organization to continue the Tehran program—which it did until its takeover by the new government at the time of the 1979 revolution.

(Smith, 2000)

A report by the US ambassador to Iran is indicative of the fate of the Tehran Branch-affiliated projects in Iran as the revolutionary movement grew. In December 1977, just before a visit by Jimmy Carter to Iran, "young men calling themselves students" attacked the Branch-affiliated Offset Printing House.[124] Press reports said that the group of students damaged some equipment and shouted provocative slogans; at least some of them were anti-American.[125]

After the revolution, the Interim Government took over Nawmarz Educational Organization and seized the assets of Amīr Kabīr publishers.[126] The Interim Government appointed a conservative Muslim poet, Ali Mossawi Garmarudi (b. 1941), as the manager of Nawmarz Educational Organization on February 26, 1979 (Yadegar, 1979, p. 12). Later, the name of this organization was changed to the Organization for Publication and Education of the Islamic Revolution. In his interview with Yadegar, the newly appointed Ali Mossawi Garmarudi noted that in contrast with the objectives of the Tehran Branch and Nawmarz Educational Organization, which were "to promote national monarchical identity," the objective of the Organization for Publication and Education of the Islamic Revolution would be to promote "Islamic Iranian Culture" (Yadegar, 1979, p. 12). A few days later, on March 10, 1979, Garmarudi was also appointed as the supervisor of the Offset Printing House (Yadegar, 1979). In the 1980s, the Organization for Publication and Education of the Islamic Revolution (formerly the Tehran Branch) lost its legal independence and was absorbed into the Ministry of Culture and Higher Education. Finally, in 1984 the Organization for Publication and Education of the Islamic Revolution and Bungāh Tarjumah va Nashr Kitāb were merged, and

Scientific and Cultural Publications (*intishārāt 'ilmī va farhangī*) was founded as a cultural firm affiliated with the Ministry of Culture and Higher Education.

In Chapters 5 and 6, I have discussed the extensive role of the Tehran Branch in the translation of American books into Persian, in the training of textbook writers, and in the publication of educational and supplementary readings. As shown in these chapters, the "success" of the Tehran Branch as compared to other FBP branches can be best understood when we consider the close relations between the Tehran Branch and the Iranian state, represented in the close relations of the Tehran Branch with the royal family and ministers and senators of the time. The fact that the Shah, his twin sister, and some of the most powerful politicians of the time contributed articles or translations to the Tehran Branch is evidence of friendly relations. Also, the fact that the Shah authorized the Tehran Branch to publish the textbooks for the first four grades of primary school proved to be hugely profitable for both the Tehran Branch and the Offset Printing House. Joint operations between the Tehran Branch and Iran's Ministry of Education, such as the publication of the *Payk* series as discussed above, further indicate how these ties with the Iranian state crucially assisted the Tehran Branch in becoming the most "successful" among FBP's seventeen branches. The close relations between the Tehran Branch and the Iranian state should also be understood in terms of their shared interest in the production and distribution of pro-capitalist, pro-monarchy knowledge after the coup.

After the 1953 coup, both the US and the post-coup regime in Iran were in need of a modern, far-reaching apparatus of production and distribution of bourgeois knowledge. The land reform and the subsequent national literacy and educational campaigns were part of the capitalist policies supported by the United States and embraced by the Shah, which were intended to foster industrialization in Iran. The increase in oil prices in the mid-1960s enabled the Iranian regime to financially assist these educational and publication policies. This revenue further allowed the Iranian state to use educational and supplementary-reading publications, as shown in the case of the *Payk* supplementary readings, to solidify the Pahlavi regime through the promotion of the Iranian state's official historiography and the celebration of the institution of the monarchy. The Tehran Branch of the FBP, having an unprecedented influence among the ruling class and a close affiliation with the Iranian state, achieved an increasingly hegemonic influence over Iran's publishing industry and played a mainstream role in these capitalist educational reforms and knowledge production projects.

Chapter 7

THE COLD WAR, KNOWLEDGE PRODUCTION, AND THE MIDDLE EAST

This book has historicized the twenty-five years of the FBP's operation (1952–77) in the context of US–Soviet cultural and ideological rivalry in the Middle East, and the various international educational initiatives and policies of the United States and their developments during the Cold War. This investigation follows on from scholarship that has discussed the Cold War in relation to its ideological contestations, as well as in terms of cultural diplomacy and educational exchange. It explores the role and methods of knowledge production in a specific historical period of US imperialism and shows how the United States employed education, translation, publications and publishing, and distribution in its international Cold War cultural operations. I employed a Marxist understanding of ideology to investigate who produced what for whom and to analyze how the social relations in which knowledge is produced frame the production and mobilization of knowledge.

The key concern of this research was around the construction rather than the reception of the US cultural and knowledge production. Therefore, my focus has been on the execution of US cultural and ideological strategies through the FBP in the Third World countries. As I argued in Chapter 2 in criticizing Tomlinson's theory of cultural imperialism, an emphasis on the reception and interpretation of cultural commodities by the receivers may assist us in complicating the process of cultural transmission. Still, an appreciation of individual interpretation should not overshadow the social and structural relations of dominance, which form the social context in which individual interpretation takes place. In the case of the FBP, an emphasis on mere individual interpretation of the sponsored titles fails to analyze the international and politically motivated role that the FBP played for more than two decades in knowledge production.

Also, it is essential to employ the Cold War as a framework through which to understand and study the FBP. The FBP was a product of the Cold War and was shaped in various ways by the Cold War's discursive and geopolitical developments. Its origin, finance, missions, objectives, methods, and principles cannot be analyzed without a contextual understanding of the Cold War, US cultural diplomacy, and the geopolitical importance of each of the countries that the FBP operated in within the Cold War.

Understanding the FBP in the context of the global history of the Cold War also calls for a closer attention to the program's structures and principles, rather than an overemphasis of the agency of local nationals. As showed in this study, the scope of local nationals' agency was already defined within the structure of the FBP and in its title selection process. While a close investigation into the intentions of the local agents, their agendas, and decisions can help complicate how and in what ways each branch of the FBP developed, rarely did a branch initiate any project that was not already included in the FBP's developmental prospects and objectives. In the case of the Tehran Branch, several of the operations that the first local manager claims he initiated were already part of the program even before the establishment of that branch. Sanʿatizadeh may have been the first or sometimes the only local manager who activated and fulfilled those objectives, but he did not introduce them into the FBP's missions and functions.[1]

Rather than an emphasis on the agency of local managers, it is crucial to explore the role that national states played in the development of the FBP in each country. As shown in this study, the achievements of the FBP in Iran and Afghanistan primarily occurred on the basis of the close affiliation between the Ministries of Education in each of these countries with the FBP branches. Therefore, the study of the cultural Cold War in the Middle East calls for exploring the role of the state in organizing educational and cultural policies and in promoting or blocking US and Soviet efforts at cultural diplomacy.

The first chapter introduced the FBP and discussed the archives and sources for this study. The second chapter provided a detailed discussion of the key theoretical concepts employed for analysis. Chapter 3 showed how the roots of the FBP in the ideological contestation between the United States and the Soviet Union shaped the FBP's policies and structure. Chapter 4 historicized the FBP's operations over twenty-five years in its various international translation and educational projects. In Chapters 5 and 6, this exploration moved to a historicization of FBP operations in Iran and the role that the national state played in the facilitation and development of the FBP's Special Projects—such as textbook publications, the production of supplementary reading, and in the establishment of a printing plant.

With the end of the Second World War, the United States began to replace Britain to become the new leader of the capitalist bloc. However, there was a significant difference between US imperialism and its predecessor, British colonialism. British colonialism developed in the context of the rise of mercantile capitalism in Britain from the sixteenth to the mid-nineteenth centuries and relied on the presence of a network of British administrative, legal, and political representatives in the colonies. The postwar US leadership of capitalism, however, historically followed the rise of imperialism—that is, it was a monopoly capitalism that arose out of an earlier mercantilism. The rise of imperialism changed the nature of labor, financialization, technology, and capitalist social relations. Indispensable to the rise of this capitalism was education (Carpenter & Mojab, 2017), and this element continued thereafter to play a significant complex role in solidifying imperialist social relations.

By the late 1940s, the US leadership had to respond to an essential gap in its new imperialist role. US imperialism developed foreign policies in education that were ideological, in order to solidify its political, cultural, and economic power, to directly combat communism, and to create an international socio-economic alliance, again primarily against communism. Consequently, the United States developed a network of global and far-reaching cultural, educational, and knowledge production enterprises to influence not only Western Europe and the developed countries, but also countries that extended to the remotest rural areas of the Third World. Books and libraries had already been employed in the fight against fascism during the Second World War. By the end of the war, international education, global literacy, and adult education campaigns had developed in the context of hundreds of thousands of wartime-dislocated books and destroyed libraries on the one hand (Intrator, 2019), and the rising ideological competition between capitalist and socialist blocs on the other. The United States initiated, supported, and developed several book programs to expand on its previous practices in the field of book production, distribution, and knowledge mobilization and to adjust those practices in response to the emerging international context and its new global needs.

One of the important instruments for winning the "hearts and minds" of the people of the world during the Cold War was the translation, production, and publication of reading materials, including textbooks and extracurricular teaching materials for children, youth, and adults. The history of the FBP advances our knowledge of the instruments, measures, and structures by which the United States pursued this policy. The FBP was founded in 1952, concurrent with the operations of other Department of State-financed cultural enterprises of the Cold War era, such as the Congress for Cultural Freedom (CCF). While the CCF has been studied and explored extensively, the FBP has remained understudied; its geographical scope of operations, its structure, administration, and players were different from those of the CCF. Michael Josselson, a former agent in the Intelligence Section of the Psychological Warfare Division (PWD), developed the CCF. The CCF was a transnational organization of intellectuals gathered together in the name of freedom of expression, which was intended to direct intellectual leaders in Western Europe and move the European intellectual and artistic debates away from an orientation toward communism. At the 1951 Strasbourg meeting, the two central questions of the CCF invitees were, first, how to influence the minds of the communist intellectuals and, second, what methods were available to respond to and undermine the theory of historical materialism (Scott-Smith, 2002). By the mid-1950s, the CCF had established a network of intellectual consensus in the United States and Western Europe and had popularized anti-communist discourses, such as that of "the end of ideology." However, while the establishment of a US–Western European network of intellectuals was rather easy and was accomplished by the CCF in the early years of the 1950s, the gap in terms of culture between the West and the Third World countries in Asia, the Middle East, and Africa was much greater (Scott-Smith, 2002). The FBP was one of the major US cultural enterprises to fill this gap and was the most important initiative to address US ideological objectives in the Middle East.

The FBP was established as a not-for-profit US organization and was a result of collaboration between the Department of State and US librarians, publishers, and educational leaders. In contrast to the CCF, the FBP was specific to the Third World countries of the Middle East and Asia. The FBP's objective was to fill the gap in US ideological penetration and knowledge production in these Third World countries through commercial book distribution. These countries lacked a developed national and regional infrastructure of book production, printing, and mass distribution. Therefore, the FBP actively pursued any possibility for establishing or sponsoring the developing print and distribution infrastructure. During its history, the FBP oversaw a variety of programs, from sponsoring the translation of US books into local languages (such as Arabic, Persian, and Urdu) to administering workshops for textbook writers, local publishers, and booksellers, and on to the production of textbooks for Afghanistan (in Persian and Pashto) and Iran (in Persian). The FBP did not consider translating from these other countries into English for American readers. Similarly to the case of US Cold War international educational exchange programs, the objective was not "exchange" or mutual understanding per se, but a "one-way intellectual street"—that is, to portray American exceptionalism (Grieve, 2018, p. 92).

As discussed in Chapter 3, the FBP is another example of how during the Cold War the United States developed state–private networks in its attempts to compete with communism and the Soviet Union's cultural influence. Not only was the FBP established with a seed grant of $500,000 from the Department of State, it also benefited from the clandestine assistance of US missions in the FBP's countries of concern, in terms of locating and then interviewing the local managers-to-be for the FBP branches. Established in 1952, the International Information Administration (IIA) listed the Department of State's financial funding to the FBP as one of the operations undertaken to intensify "psychological" deterrents to aggression on the part of Soviet communism and to combat extremist tendencies particularly in the Near and Middle East and South and Southeast Asia. The IIA further guided the FBP in its publication and distribution of works using funds granted by the Department of State. While the IIA considered the creation of "awareness" of the dangers of Soviet communism a desirable ideological goal, an even more urgent ideological objective was the establishment of attitudes in Third World countries toward close collaboration with the West.[2]

US ideological goals in the Middle East and the IIA's operational objectives shaped the content of the books published by the FBP and also formed the FBP's policies and structure. Similarly to the CCF's practice in knowledge production, the content of FBP-sponsored titles was intended to show US cultural life in a positive light. The FBP's objective was to publish translations of American books in the local languages of targeted countries that historically had rarely been exposed to US cultural products. The FBP concentrated on different types of texts: US books promoting the American way of life; textbooks and reference works presenting non-communist political, social, and economic content; and trade books in an inexpensive format. In all these types of books, three possible levels of audience were targeted: first, the level of the university student and mid-level government officials; second, the level of those with a secondary education; and third, the juvenile level. Consequently, the audience of FBP-sponsored books in the Middle East was broad: college and university students; the bureaucrats in general; government officials and employees; and the "conservative" intellectual community with a traditional Muslim education.[3]

The FBP's policy was to create "good faith" in the Third World countries. Therefore, it avoided open affiliation with US embassies in all of the countries in which it established local branches. Through local managers and advisors, each of the branches actively pursued the establishment of close working relationships with the "effective foci of opinion formulation and dissemination" in the areas concerned, such as political, educational, and intellectual leaders.[4]

The FBP also worked toward the commercial distribution of US books in its regions of operation, as this was recognized as better than propaganda "give-away" practices, both for financial reasons and because commercial distribution ensured greater and more permanent publisher and reader interest.[5] In doing so, the FBP closely cooperated with local publishers, book distributors, booksellers, and printing houses. This practice further assisted in the task of assuring the local publishing industry of the FBP's goodwill. Gradually, a network of local publishers worked closely with the FBP's local branches because the publishers did not consider the FBP to be an instrument of competitive commercial intrusion.

The absence of a US distributing system and overseas promotional activities was another reason behind the lack of a commercial distribution of US books that could compete against the circulation of communist literature. Therefore, another reason for the FBP's establishment was to build relations with the existing local publishing, manufacturing, and distributing facilities in Third World countries and to address their inadequacy. As such, the FBP started to assist in the enlarging and improving of existing publishing channels in the countries concerned. The FBP had to also actively develop new channels for promotional campaigns, regional distribution, and the development of mass distribution methods.

In terms of its structure, the FBP operated within three main rules. First, the operating offices of the FBP had to be staffed entirely by local nationals and not by resident Americans. This was crucial, as it was important for the FBP not to be seen as a propaganda tool linked to US Cold War interests. Similarly to CCF policy, while the general policy of the US cultural Cold War was not to assist communists, nonetheless the FBP's local branches recruited staff from left-of-center groups. The endorsement of such a non-communist left enabled the FBP's sponsored books to gain more credibility in the countries concerned. As discussed in Chapter 5, in the case of Iran the Tehran Branch was a cultural and publishing organization where non-communist leftists could work even if they had a history of political imprisonment. The cultural endeavors of such intellectuals were directed toward translating and editing the titles approved by the FBP and in line with the general objectives of the FBP. Furthermore, the Pahlavi regime's SAVAK could monitor their operations closely.

The second structural rule of the FBP was that each local manager had to choose the books to be translated only from a list of books prepared by the FBP. This title selection process ensured that the book suited the needs of the local market while providing an appearance of freedom of choice. The FBP's title selection policy and procedure resulted in the sponsorship of books that in practice followed the general aims of the US Doctrinal Program during the Cold War.

Third, the FBP was not to act as a publisher; it had to prepare the book, translate and edit the final manuscript and then sell it on to a local publisher. This practice ensured a continuing interest in the book on the part of these publishers. By the mid-1950s, the FBP's sponsored translations had already created a market for US books in the Middle East, and US publishing techniques and crafts were starting to be seen as a model many Middle Eastern publishers and booksellers were looking to adopt.

In a very short time, by means of following through on its sophisticated localized policies and structures, the FBP managed to build a social and educational network among the elites and publishing houses of each country concerned, and this brought it early success. The FBP even managed to quickly take US books to the bookshelves of the religious centers in the Middle East, notably in Mecca's bookshops. As early as 1955, the FBP had "modernized" and "Americanized" the physical production of books in Arab-, Persian-, and Urdu-language publications in the Middle East and Asia, and by 1956 it was publishing and distributing its sponsored books in six languages spoken by about 250 million people, in some of the most critical countries of the time for US anti-communist policy.

The rise of state-sponsored mass literacy programs in the developing countries of the Middle East and Asia in late 1950s and early 1960s enabled the FBP to move its focus away from the translation of US books for an elite audience and toward publishing educational and supplementary readings for the newly literate in rural areas. Chapter 4 traced this gradual move. By the late 1950s, the FBP had consolidated itself through its translation programs and had expanded its social network in the Middle East and Asia. Through its local branches in the Middle East, the FBP began projects in the areas of publishing textbooks, sponsoring encyclopedias and dictionaries, village library development, and mass distribution operations. The most extensive of its textbook production projects were conducted under contracts with the ministries of education in Egypt (for higher-education textbooks), Iran, and Afghanistan (for school textbooks). This expansion toward educational publications and technical aid in the field of textbook production was also strengthened in the 1960s, in the context of the Kennedy administration's focus on the importance of education and technical aid in the US policy of modernizing Third World countries. The FBP's move toward educational projects resulted in closer and open FBP affiliation with the US government and international agencies by the mid-1960s. The FBP further expanded its regions of operation and moved to work actively in Africa and South America. By the late 1960s, the FBP's worldwide staff numbers rose to about 440, and it was conducting its programs through offices in seventeen cities, in twelve countries, on three continents.

The year 1968 marked the beginning of a new period of organizational development for the FBP, both financially and structurally. The United States scaled down its financial and technical aid programs, and the US government's financial support of the FBP was significantly reduced. The economic crisis in Indonesia, the aftermath of the Pakistan–India war, and the civil war in Nigeria pushed the FBP to reduce its staff and curtail its programs in these three countries. In an organizational reframing, the FBP foregrounded its experience in organizing and administering translation programs for university textbooks, general and professional reference books, and supplementary-reading books for young people. With the closure of several local offices, in a shift from its initial structure and policy, the FBP's New York headquarters directly undertook operations in these countries. The FBP further moved away from its initial policies and structures in the following ways: (1) the presence of more FBP technicians in the field offices; (2) an emphasis on its Special Projects at the cost of terminating its Regular Programs; (3) the FBP's evolution into a publisher itself in some offices such as the Tehran Branch; (4) the establishment of solid and open affiliations with US government organizations such as USAID—exemplified in the FBP's role in founding the Book Procurement Improvement and Bibliographic Center, which was responsible for coordinating activities and making recommendations relating to the USAID process of book selection and procurement.

The 1973–5 US recession further exacerbated the already difficult financial conditions for the FBP, which resulted in the closure of some of its local offices. The FBP substantially relied on the US government and private-sector funding for its operations. While the FBP managed to continue working despite the financial strains for a few years, and was searching for funding opportunities to continue its operations, an article published in the *New York Times* in 1977 pointing to certain ties between the CIA and the FBP was the last blow, resulting in the final demise of the FBP that year.

Chapters 5 and 6 historicized the Tehran Branch (1954–77), the most "successful" local branch of the FBP, and showed the role that the close political alliance between the post-coup Iranian regime and the United States played in this "success." Chapter 5 historicized the Tehran Branch in the context of the sociopolitical history of US–Iranian relations and the importance of Iran in the US Cold War policy of containment. Consequently, the Tehran Branch is understood and discussed as a continuation and extension of the Point Four program, the US-centered flow of students from Iran, and the geopolitical history of the rise of international education during the Cold War.

The Iranian Revolution of 1979 and its consequences, especially in terms of the dramatic transformation of US–Iran relations, have led scholars to question the actual effect of US Cold War educational and cultural policies toward Iran. Several scholars ask why the measures that the United States took during the Cold War to influence the states and win "the hearts and minds" of people were not successful. Recent scholarship on US–Iran Cold War cultural and educational relations (e.g., Garlitz, 2012b; Shannon, 2017) has analyzed the ideological functioning of modernization theory as the theoretical framework underlying

US educational policies in relation to the latter's technical assistance and student exchange programs during the Cold War.

Modernization theory was a product of the US Cold War academy, a framework that linked development to education. It was part of US Cold War ideology and the underlying theoretical framework of the US educational aid programs. This theory acted as a non-communist manifesto to compete against the influence of Marxist-Leninist doctrines in the US race for influence in the Third World (Shannon, 2017). Richard Garlitz attributes the failure of the US Cold War educational policy in Iran to the failure of modernization theory. In his analysis of the impact of these educational relations, Garlitz criticizes both the theory and practice of US foreign educational policies. He points to the limitations of modernization theory as the main premise that guided US foreign policy, especially during the early years of the 1960s with Kennedy in office. Modernization theorists such as Walt Rostow and Daniel Lerner articulated several stages of developing countries that were primarily drawn from the history of the rise of capitalism in the West. This process led to a theoretical approach, which defined modernization as Americanization.[6] Garlitz further argues that the application of modernization theory in the educational sphere during the Shah's regime resulted in the rejection of US cultural influence by critical teachers such as Samad Behrangi (1931–67), who categorized these educational reforms as "imitative of America" (*āmrīkāzadah*), and also later by Jalal Al Ahmad (1923–69), an ex-translator for the Tehran Branch who labeled them as "westoxification" (*qarb zadigī*).

As a result of Iran's strategic importance, successive US administrations placed greater emphasis on its stability and regarded the Shah as the key to the US strategic plan in the Middle East. Therefore, US policymakers supported the Shah's vision of modernization and backed him through an escalating sale of military equipment (Offiler, 2015). Garlitz argues that although US university advisors had made some modest improvements in the Iranian education system in the short term, the US support of the authoritarian Pahlavi regime and its inability to push the Shah toward political liberalization greatly undermined the effectiveness of its educational assistance program (Garlitz, 2012b). The close association of US foreign aid with the Shah's increasingly authoritarian regime, coupled with the Iranian intellectual and religious elite's rejection of US cultural influence, resulted in popular dissatisfaction, which contributed to the anti-US character of the 1978–9 Iranian Revolution (Garlitz, 2012b).

Still, the dominant historicizations of US–Iranian educational relations are limited to the role of the US government in these relations and do not investigate the extensive role of joint not-for-profit government–private undertakings such as the FBP and the role of the Iranian state in mediating and sponsoring the knowledge production and educational policies of US imperialism. While there were humanistic impulses involved in the FBP as well, the FBP's production and dissemination of knowledge could not escape the imperatives of imperial domination. As outlined in Chapter 3 and later in Chapter 5, the knowledge produced by the FBP was marked by its origins in the Cold War, the US–Soviet cultural and ideological contestation, and US–Iranian relations—all of which affected the FBP's sponsored content.

No international organization has had an influence comparable to the FBP's Tehran Branch in Iran's publication and textbook-writing history. While the FBP exploited any opportunity to mimic its success in Iran in other countries in which it was operating, no other FBP branch was able to establish such close ties with the ruling class and the ministry of education. Chapter 6 showed the significant role of the Iranian state and Iran's Ministry of Education in sponsoring, facilitating, and cooperating with many of the operations that the Tehran Branch undertook in Iran. It should be noted that this book is not a thorough investigation of print and translation history in Iran; rather I have discussed the role of the FBP within a specific aspect of Iranian modernity, which is the modernization of the publishing industry and the systematic translation of US books to Persian. Also, I have not attempted to detail the history and developments of the Pahlavi regime's cultural planning and policies,[7] but instead to historicize the close affiliation between Iran's Ministry of Education and the FBP in mass production and distribution of textbooks, teaching guides, and extracurricular reading materials.

In his book *Imagined Communities*, Benedict Anderson discusses the manner in which the rise of national consciousness historically owes so much to print capitalism (Anderson, 2006). According to him, the coalition between Protestantism and print capitalism created large new reading publics and simultaneously mobilized them for politico-religious purposes (Anderson, 2006). The rise of print in nineteenth- to early twentieth-century Iran has been studied to some extent (Marashi, 2008; Vejdani, 2015; Tavakoli-Targhi, 2020). The extensive role and effect of the FBP on the publication history of Iran shows that here print capitalism in its industrial phase was introduced and supported by the United States to a considerable degree and was embraced and assisted by the Iranian state in order to distribute far-reaching bourgeois and monarchist knowledge in the aftermath of the 1953 coup. Therefore, although the modernization of the print and publishing industry created new reading publics, this modernization aimed to train them to be capitalist and monarchist subjects and to inoculate them against possible communist influence.

As discussed in Chapter 6, revisiting Al Ahmad and the theory of westoxification through the history of the FBP's Tehran Branch shows that disillusionment with such experiences of print capitalism contributed to the formation of an anti-Occidental discourse, which empowered political Islam for competition against cultural imperialism. Al Ahmad developed an ahistorical and nativist understanding of colonialism, which reduced all the historical socio-political factors to religion. In Al Ahmad's theorization, social spaces become uniform cultural spaces. His argument relies heavily on abstraction, essentialization, homogenization, and cultural reductionism. He reads the history of the world as a product of war among religions, especially Christianity (or the West) and Islam (or the East). Therefore, while Al Ahmad criticizes cultural imperialism and Orientalist knowledge production, his own argument discourages historical inquiry, and he draws content for his argument from pre-existing cultural ascriptions. He too reinforced the ideologically religious and essentialized binaries of West and East, but in new ways. This nativist and anti-Occidental argument became one of the main ideological components of the post-Revolution Islamist ideology in Iran.

With the rise of US imperialism after the Second World War, the active role of the United States in the sphere of knowledge production and in shaping educational theory, practice, and content in the Third World intensified. Exploring the history of the FBP—its complex network of state and private sector, the role of US librarians, publishers, and academics in it, and the joint projects the FBP organized in several countries with the help of national ministries of education, financed by the US Department of State and US foundations as well as local states—helps us to understand the long history of education in the imperialist social order and provides a historical lineage for contemporary developments. There are still questions related to this research, which need to be answered. The FBP's operations and the history of its other programs in Asia, Africa, and Latin America need to be investigated further. Certain aspects of the FBP, such as its role in library development in Pakistan and Afghanistan, are not studied at all. Also, as pointed out in Chapter 6, the specific role of the Tehran Branch in the process of content production for the *Payk*s should be detailed, and historicized. Also, a thorough historical and textual study of these school magazines is much needed. Through an in-depth textual analysis of *Payk* school magazines, we can look at the tensions and contradictions in these journals, to see what social forces were at play in shaping the ideological framework of Iranian educational supplementary readings. I also plan to enrich this study through a comparison of FBP publications with contemporary critical and dissident works, including student journals. I will study the student journals published in Iran—their content, methods of production, and distribution during the 1960s and 1970s—to contribute to the literature on social movements, which looks to revive the knowledge produced within these movements, to uncover lessons relevant to present-day struggles (Choudry, 2015).

The long legacy of imperialism in US global educational programs is also in need of much further investigation. Even after the 1979 revolution, which resulted in the dramatic transformation of US–Iranian relations, the educational contact between the two countries did not come to an end. Although US schools, educational advisors, and organizations at this time cannot be present in Iran, online platforms are quite active. For instance, *Tavaana: E-Learning Institute for Iranian Civil Society* was launched in 2010, which according to its website intends to "support active citizenship and civic leadership in Iran" and envisions "a free and open Iranian society." The *Tavaana* project was launched with a seed grant from the US Department of State's Bureau for Democracy, Human Rights and Labor (DRL). It has also secured funds from the National Endowment for Democracy (NED) and USAID. The role that *Tavaana* plays in translating, and in the online dissemination of neoliberal capitalist knowledge, is clearly observable. *Tavaana* has published many translations defending the desirability of the US political system and is a dedicated supporter of the change of Iran's system to a liberal capitalist one. It also frequently produces content to criticize and undermine socialist knowledge and political practice. A study of such contemporary projects assists in examining the post-Cold War developments of cultural imperialism, as well as the US practice of knowledge production and its content, policies, and digital methods of distribution.

Imperialism throughout its recent history has consolidated itself with capitalist networks of production, mobilization, and dissemination of knowledge—networks that were sponsored, administered, or promoted by national states, private corporations, and state–private sector cooperation. The FBP was one part of a US cultural imperialism during the Cold War that was composed of complicated global networks. Understanding the historical role of education and of knowledge production and dissemination in solidifying capitalist social relations brings up considerations that are essential for any radical anti-imperialist project. Such a project should develop a global and international production and dissemination of revolutionary knowledge. This would include archiving and disseminating activist research and knowledge produced within social movements (Choudry, 2015), as well as organizing and administering global networks of translation, production, and distribution of knowledge between revolutionary forces.

APPENDIX I: THE PRESIDENTS OF THE FBP AND A LIST OF FBP LOCAL BRANCHES

Datus C. Smith, Jr., was the FBP's first president. He was in charge from 1952 to November 1967. Smith was formerly the president of the Association of American University Presses from 1947 to 1949 and director of Princeton University Press from 1942 to 1953. After the FBP, Smith became an associate of John D. Rockefeller III and vice-president of the JDR III Fund. In later years, he was the president of the US Committee for UNICEF and a member of the US National Commission for UNESCO (Pace, 1999).

In 1967, **Michael Harris**, who was formerly deputy secretary-general, Organization for Economic Cooperation and Development (OECD), was elected by the FBP board of directors to succeed Smith; the OECD was an international body that grew out of the operation of the Marshall Plan in Europe (NYT, 1967). Harris was FBP president until 1969, when he was succeeded by **Carroll G. Bowen**, formerly director of the MIT Press. Two years later, at the annual meeting of November 1971, **John H. Kyle**, founding director of the East–West Center Press, was elected as the new president. He continued acting in this position up until the time when the FBP was dissolved in 1977.

The Tehran Branch and its legacy are discussed in detail in Chapters 5 and 6. Here I briefly point to the other branches in their order of establishment and the major areas in which they organized the publication of FBP-sponsored books. The FBP established operating offices in Cairo (1953), Tehran (1954), Lahore (1954), Dacca (1955), Jakarta (1955), Baghdad (1957), Beirut (1957), Tabriz (1959), Kuala Lumpur (1960), Kabul (1964), Lagos (1964), Enugu (1964), Nairobi (1965), and Kaduna (1965). The languages of its operations were Persian (Farsi), Arabic, Urdu, Spanish, Bengali, Indonesian, Malay, Portuguese, and some African languages (Smith, 2000).

Cairo office: This was the most senior of all FBP offices, established in 1953. It was especially influential on and provided assistance to the other Arabic-language offices in Beirut and Baghdad. Its textbook project was the third largest among the offices. Cairo was active in the promotion of children's books throughout the Arab world. It sponsored more than 1,000 translations, including 200 college texts and two encyclopedias.[1]

Lahore office: This office opened in 1954 and conducted a Regular Translation Program, the Urdu encyclopedia project, and an extensive school library project. It translated 448 titles into Urdu.

Dacca office: An FBP office was established in Dacca, the capital of East Pakistan, in 1955, and it was shortly thereafter involved with the educational reconstruction of the capital after the partition of India and Pakistan. It had a Regular Program, the four-volume Bengali encyclopedia, and a large school library project. It sponsored 329 translations and air-lifted 30,000 US textbooks for Bangladesh's six universities in 1974.

Jakarta office: Established in 1955, this office had the largest number of copies per title of any of the FBP programs. Its Special Projects included the Indonesian encyclopedia, an Indonesian–English dictionary (an authorized Jakarta reprinting of a book published in the United States by Cornell University Press), and an English–Indonesian dictionary, and it provided assistance with the establishment of the Indonesian Publishers Association.

Baghdad office: This office opened in 1957. According to FBP internal reports, Iraq was a country with a great interest in books but a small population and a tradition of importing most of its books from other Arabic-speaking countries.[2] The major project of the Baghdad office was for books in vocational education.

Beirut office: This office was established in 1957. The books that this office sponsored were most distinguished in the fields of advanced literary criticism and US literature. It was also the seat of the English–Arabic dictionary project.

Tabriz office: Tabriz was an important region for the FBP for both ideological and logistical reasons. It was the capital of the province of Azerbaijan in northwestern Iran, south of the Soviet Union. The historical presence of communist movements in the northwest of Iran, which had participated in the establishment of the short-lived Azerbaijan People's Government (in power between November 1945 and December 1946) and Kurdish Republic of Mahabad (in power between January and December 1946), called for an active publication of US books there. According to FBP internal reports, no US books had ever been sold in Iran's Azerbaijan province, directly south of the Soviet border, before 1956. In that year, however, the Tehran Branch conducted a provincial promotion campaign in this region and managed to sell 4,000 US books in Persian translation.[3] Three years later, in 1959, the Tabriz Branch was established as the second FBP office in Iran.

The Tabriz Branch was also important in terms of logistics, in the distribution of paper for FBP projects in Iran and regionally. According to Datus C. Smith, FBP president, "[t]he decision to open a Tabriz office came about because of Franklin's effort to import large amounts of book paper for its cooperation publishers, especially those trying to produce the new Franklin-sponsored textbooks." The Tabriz Public Library, with its children's department, was closely associated with this office in Azerbaijan province.

Kuala Lumpur office: This office, in the capital of Malaysia, was opened in 1960. Its manager was Inche' Ghazali Yunus. Other than the Regular Translation Program, the chief Special Project of this office was the production of supplementary readings.

Kabul office: Although the FBP's Tehran Branch started to print textbooks for Afghanistan in 1957, the FBP did not have an office there until 1964, when the Kabul office was established under the management of Atiqullah Maroof, an educator and educational administrator. In its first year, with technical assistance from the Tehran office, it managed and reorganized the Afghanistan Ministry of Education's printing plant and published twenty-eight textbooks (717,000 copies in total) in Persian and Pashto.

Lagos office: The FBP office in Lagos, the capital of Nigeria, was established in 1964. It was active in both Lagos and Ibadan, the capital of Western Nigeria and the seat of the University of Ibadan, the leading institution of higher education at the time in sub-Saharan Africa. This office published in Yoruba. Its projects were financed by the Ford Foundation and were under contract with the US Agency for International Development.

Enugu office: This office was established in 1964 in Enugu, the capital of Eastern Nigeria, under the management of John Iroaganachi. Nsukka, the seat of the University of Nigeria, which was a new American-style institution with connections with the United States, was near Enugu. The office published in Igbo. It was financed by the Ford Foundation and was under contract with USAID.

Nairobi office: This office was established in 1965 in the capital of Kenya, East Africa, for works in English, Swahili, and other East African languages.

Kaduna office: The Kaduna office was established in 1965 in northern Nigeria, where the most widely used vernacular was Hausa. Its first manager was Mallan Mustafa Zubairu. This office was active in book development in English and Hausa. As with the two other FBP offices in Nigeria, the Kaduna office was financed by the Ford Foundation and was under contract with USAID.

The FBP in Latin America: While the FBP never had an office in Latin America, it operated several programs there in collaboration with locally registered organizations. Its first program in Latin America started in Buenos Aires in 1964. It was not a direct operation but was in cooperation with a new non-profit organization established for the purpose, the Fundación Interamericana de Bibliotecología Franklin. An initial grant of $250,000 from the Ford Foundation made the establishment of the Fundación possible. The FBP began to coordinate projects in Rio de Janeiro and Sao Paulo in 1965. Many of the books sponsored by the FBP in Latin America were in the field of demography and ranged from the biological to the economic aspects of the subject. This was because the predicted doubling of South America's population during the coming twenty-five years was considered to be the most serious threat to the continent's economic development.[4]

APPENDIX II: LOCAL PARTICIPATION BY CIVIC AND INTELLECTUAL LEADERS (DEVELOPED BASED ON THE FBP'S ANNUAL REPORT, 15 SEPTEMBER 1960)

United Nations Officers

Bokhari, Patras (1898–1958), also known as Sayyid Ahmed Shah: Pakistani diplomat and writer, former under-secretary-general of the United Nations, wrote the introduction to the Urdu edition of Edward R. Murrow's *This I Believe*.

Malik, Charles Habib (1906–1987): Lebanese diplomat, former president of the United Nations General Assembly, contributed to the Arabic edition of Edward R. Murrow's *This I Believe*.

Prime Ministers and Presidents

Abdel Nasser, Gamal (1918–1970): The second president of Egypt, contributed to the Arabic edition of Edward R. Murrow's *This I Believe* and publicly commended the Cairo office of the FBP on several occasions.

Eghbal, Manucher (1909–1977): Prime Minister of Iran, contributed an original chapter to Noah D. Fabricant's *Why We Became Doctors*.

Farhoodi, Hossein (1906–?): Deputy of the Prime Minister of Iran, translated Norman Sharpe Buchanan and Howard S. Ellis's *Approaches to Economic Development*.

Iskandar Mirza (1899–1969): President of Pakistan, contributed to the Urdu edition of Edward R. Murrow's *This I Believe*.

al-Jamali, Mohammad Fadhel (1903–1997): Prime Minister of Iraq, contributed to the Arabic edition of Edward R. Murrow's *This I Believe*.

Maher Pasha, Aly (1881–1960): Prime Minister of Egypt, wrote the introduction for David Cushman Coyle's *The United States Political System and How It Works*.

Matin-Daftari, Ahmad (1897–1971): Prime Minister of Iran, translated Arthur Nussbaum's *A Concise History of the Law of Nations*.

Naguib, Mohammad (1901–1984): The first president of Egypt, wrote an original contribution and publicly commended the Cairo office of the FBP.

Qasim, Abd al-Karim (1914–1963): Prime Minister of Iraq, authorized newspaper publication of his commendation of the Cairo office's work.

Sharif-Emami, Jafar (1912–1988): Prime Minister of Iran, contributed to the Persian edition of the *Columbia–Viking Desk Encyclopedia*.

al-Solh, Sami (1887–1968): Prime Minister of Lebanon, contributed to the Arabic edition of Edward R. Murrow's *This I Believe*.

Suhrawardy, Huseyn Shaheed (1892–1963): Prime Minister of Pakistan, contributed to the Urdu edition of Edward R. Murrow's *This I Believe*.

Sukarno (1901–1970): The first president of Indonesia, authorized inclusion of some of his comments on Thomas Jefferson (the third president of the US) in the foreword to the translation of John Dewey's *Living Thoughts of Thomas Jefferson*.

Shah and Royal Family

Pahlavi, Mohammad Reza (1919–1980): The last Shah of Iran, wrote the biography of his father, Reza Shah (r. 1925–1941) as an added chapter to the Persian edition of Sarah Knowles Bolton's *Lives of Poor Boys Who Became Famous*.

Pahlavi, Ashraf (1919–2016): The twin sister of Mohammad Reza Pahlavi, the chairwoman of the Imperial Organization for Social Services, translated Benjamin Spock's *Baby and Child Care* and Helen Z. Gill's *Basic Nursing*.[5]

Cabinet Members

Eight Egyptian Ministers of Education, some of whom translated one or more whole books, others of whom wrote introductions to FBP-sponsored translations: **Taha Hussein, Ahmad Amin, Ahmad Zaky, Mohammad Awwad, Mohammad Hosein Heykal, Ibrahim Bayoumi Madkour, Kamaledin Hossein,** and **Abdelrazzak Sanhoury**.

Hedayati, Mohammad Ali (1913–1986): Minister of Justice in Iran, was the Tehran Branch's legal counsel for a period of time.

Hekmat, Ali Asghar (1893–1980): Minister of Foreign Affairs and Minister of Culture in Iran, translated Edward Chiera's *They Wrote on Clay: The Babylonian Tablets Speak Today* and Huston Smith's *The Religions of Man*.

Hussain Khan, Mamoud (1907–1975): Minister of Education in Pakistan, translated Nejla Izzedin's *The Arab World, Past, Present and Future*.

Pringgodigdo, Abdul Karim (1906–1961): Indonesian cabinet minister and director of the office of the president, was on the editorial committee for the Indonesian edition of the *Columbia–Viking Desk Encyclopedia*.

Sadiq, Isa (1894–1978): Minister of Education in Iran, advisor for the Persian edition of the *Columbia–Viking Desk Encyclopedia*.

Shaykh al-Bakuri (?–?): Minister of Awqaf in Egypt, wrote the introduction for the Arabic translation of Abraham Cressy Morrison's *Man Does Not Stand Alone*.

Suwandi (1899–1964): Minister of Education and Minister of Justice in Indonesia, was editor-in-chief of the Indonesian edition of the *Columbia–Viking Desk Encyclopedia*.

Zafar, Amir Hossein Ilkhan (1894–1976): Parliamentary member and one of the chiefs of the Bakhtiari tribe, translated Cora Mason's *Socrates: The Man Who Dared to Ask*[6] and Merian C. Cooper's *Grass*.

Ambassadors, Senators, Justices, Military Educators

Ahmed, Gulzar (?–?): Brigadier of the Pakistan army, translated Harold Lamb's *Genghis Khan: The Emperor of All Men* and Edward Mead Earle's *Makers of Modern Strategy: Military Thought from Machiavelli to Hitler*.

Ahmed, Jamal Mohammad (1915–1985): Sudanese ambassador to Ethiopia and Britain, translated Alexander Hamilton's *The Federalist Papers*.

Erfan, Mahmoud (1900–1975): Justice of the Supreme Court in Iran, translated Harry W. Hazard's *Atlas of Islamic History*.

al-Falaky, Mahmoud (?–?): Egyptian ambassador to France and a member of the National Council for Production and Economic Affairs, translated Abraham Cressy Morrison's *Man Does Not Stand Alone*.

Hassouna, Abdul Khalek (1898–1992): Egyptian diplomat and the second secretary-general of the Arab League, wrote the introduction for David Cushman Coyle's *The United Nations and How It Works*. Also, it was under his leadership that the Arab League gave the FBP $2,900 to aid the publication of George Sarton's *Introduction to the History of Science*.

Ibrahim, Abdel Fattah (?–?): Brigadier of the UAR army, translated Edward Mead Earle's *Makers of Modern Strategy: Military Thought from Machiavelli to Hitler*.

Rahnema, Zainolabidin (1894–1989): Iranian ambassador to France, translated Majid Khadduri's *Law in the Middle East: The Origins and Development of Islamic Law*.

Razmara, Hossein Ali (1893–1985): Military educator in Iran, translated W. Maxwell Reed's *The Stars for Sam*.

Sheikh Abdul Rahman (1903–1990): Chief Justice of Pakistan, wrote the introduction for David Cushman Coyle's *The United States Political System and How It Works* and was chairman of the advisory committee for the Urdu edition of the *Columbia–Viking Desk Encyclopedia*.

Taqizadeh, Seyyed Hassan (1878–1970): President of the senate in Iran, former ambassador and cabinet minister, and a leader of Persian intellectual life, was the FBP's chief editorial advisor in Iran.

Tomeh, George J. (1922–2004): Syrian diplomat who also served as the consul-general of the UAR in New York City, translated John Herman Randall Jr.'s *The Making of the Modern Mind: A Survey of the Intellectual Background of the Present Age*.

Ebrahim Khwajeh Noori (1900–1991), **Mohammad Moti'-al-Dawlah Hejazi** (1901–1974), and **Sadiq Rezazadeh Shafaq** (1890–1971), Iranian senators, each translated two books sponsored by the Tehran office.

Educational Leaders

Alexandria: Mohammad Ahwad, Rector; Mohammad Khalafallah, Dean of the Faculty of Arts; Ahmed Bedawy, Rector; Kamal Hussein, Rector; Abdel Aziz Koussy, Dean of Education; Adel Halim Montasser, Dean of Science; Osman Khalil Osman, Dean of Law.

Cairo: Taha Hussein, Ahmad Amin, Ahmed Zaky (all former rectors).

Damascus: Hikmat Hashim, Rector; Gameel Saliba, Dean of Education.

Khartoum: Mohamad Omar Beshir, provost of the university.

Beirut: Costi Zurayk, vice-president of the American University of Beirut; Fuad Sarruf, vice-president of the American University of Beirut.

Kabul: Mohammad Anas Khan, Rector; Amanalsin Ansari, Dean of the Faculty of Arts.

Tehran: Ali Akbar Siyassi, Rector, was one of the advisors for the Persian edition of the *Columbia–Viking Desk Encyclopedia*; Manucher Eghbal, Rector, contributed an original chapter to Noah D. Fabricant's *Why We Became Doctors*.

Punjab: Afzal Hussain, Vice-Chancellor.

Sind: Raziuddin Siddiqi, Vice-Chancellor.

Dacca: Hamoodur Rahmen, Vice-Chancellor.

Indonesia: Bahder Djohann, Rector; Sadarjoen Siswamartojo, Dean of Education.

Airlangga: Abdul Gafar Pringgodigdo, Rector.

Individuals with Literary Standing (either as translator or writer)

Arabic: Abbas Mahmoud al-Aqqad (1889–1964), Taha Hussein (1889–1973), Tawfiq al-Hakim (1898–1987), Ahmad Amin (1886–1954), Mohammad Hussein Heikal (1888–1956), Mohammad Shafiq Ghurbal (1894–1961), Sahir Kalamawy (?–?), Mahmoud Teymour (1894–1974), Mohammad Farid Abu Hadid (1893–1967).

Persian: Seyyed Hassan Taqizadeh (1878–1970), Mohammad Ali Jamalzadeh (1892–1997), Mohammad Motii'-al-Dawla Hejazi (1901–1974).

Urdu: Sayyid Ahmed Shah (1898–1958), Salahuddin Ahmad (1902–64), C.H. Hasrat (?–?), Abdul Majid Salik (1894–1959), Aziz Ahmad (1914–1978), Hamid Ali Khan (?–?), G.R. Mihr (?–?).

Bengali: M.A. Hafiz (1907–1994), Kobi Ahsan Habib (1917–1985), Ashraf Siddiqui (1927–2020), Golam Wahed Choudhury (1926–1997), Ibrahim Khan (1894–1978).

Indonesian: Achdiat Karta Mihardja (1911–2010), Anas Ma'ruf (1922–1980), Asrul Sani (1927–2004), Sumantri Mertodipuro (?–?).

NOTES

Chapter 1

1 It should be noted that the term "Third World" is rooted in Cold War geopolitics and also in the core–periphery understanding of the international order. While this term is problematic, it will be used in this study to reflect the power relations of the historical period under investigation.
2 One way of handling this misfiling, a method which did not become necessary for this research, is to correlate with the copies of correspondence and cables to and from FBP local offices that are held at the Harry Ransom Center, University of Texas at Austin. Duplicate copies were made in 1978. While the first copies, which are archived in Princeton, were filed alphabetically and by subject, the second copies were filed chronologically. These sets of files, consecutively numbered, include all FBP correspondence with overseas offices. Furthermore, certain series deemed non-archival by the Princeton University Library were later acquired by the Harry Ransom Center.
3 It should be noted that while the FBP records refer to him as "Sanati," I have used his full family name, "San'atizadeh," throughout this book.

Chapter 3

1 Some of the major book programs with international outreach and objectives that were established in the United States during the Cold War: Franklin Book Programs (FBP), the Informational Guaranty Program, USIA Donated Book Programs, USIA Low Priced Books in Translation, Ladder Books in Low Priced Editions, and USIA French for Africa Programs (Benjamin, 1984).
2 For a review of a few other studies that investigate the role of culture in US Cold War diplomacy, see Smulyan, 2009.
3 Nigel Gould-Davies (2003) and Rosa Magnúsdóttir (2010) are authors of other notable articles published recently about the Soviet side of this cultural diplomacy.
4 The National Security Act of July 26, 1947, created the first US peacetime intelligence organization, the CIA. The CIA succeeded the wartime intelligence agency, the Office of Strategic Services (OSS), to coordinate military and diplomatic intelligence. Within a few months, on December 19, 1947, the National Security Council issued a directive, NSC-4. An appendix to this directive, NSC-4A, instructed the CIA director to undertake "covert psychological activities" in support of US anti-communist policies. This directive was later superseded in July 1948 by NSC-10/2, which was more explicit in instructing the CIA to undertake "a plethora of covert operations" ranging from propaganda and economic warfare to "preventive direct actions," including "sabotage" and "subversion against hostile states" (Stonor Saunders, 2000, p. 39). NSC-10/2 further stressed that these activities must be "planned and executed" in such a manner that there would remain no evident relation to the US government and that the US government could "plausibly disclaim any responsibility for them"

(Stonor Saunders, 2000, p. 39). The theoretical foundation of the CIA's political operations against communism from the 1950s to 1970 was the strategy of promoting a non-communist left.
5 For a study of the legacy of the CCF in the Middle East, see Holt, 2017.
6 The US cultural Cold War in Western Europe has also been studied in Giles Scott-Smith and Hans Krabbendam's *The Cultural Cold War in Western Europe, 1945–1960* (2003).
7 On March 1, 1964, the name of the organization changed from Franklin Publications, Inc., to Franklin Book Programs, Inc. The name change, however, did not signify a change in the scope of the FBP's operations. Instead, it placed emphasis on books to avoid suggesting that the FBP was a publisher itself. Furthermore, the term "Programs" was used to indicate that the FBP's works included a variety of forms such as textbook writing training programs and library development (FBPR, Box 15, Annual Report 1964).
8 The US Treasury Department issued a certificate of tax exemption for this corporation, which was confirmed in 1955 and which remained in force throughout the time of the functioning of the FBP.
9 FBPR, Box 15, Annual Report 1963.
10 NSA, Department of State Internal Paper to the United States Legation. Jordan [et al.]. "Franklin Publications," July 22, 1952.
11 NSA, "Franklin Publications," July 22, 1952.
12 The group visited Beirut from November 8 to 15, 1952; Damascus from November 15 to 19, 1952; Cairo from November 19 to 27, 1952; and Baghdad from November 27 to December 2, 1952. Datus C. Smith also went to Amman and Jerusalem on December 4, 1952.
13 NSA, Department of State Cable to the United States Embassy, Jordan, October 30, 1952.
14 NSA, Department of State Airgram from David K.E. Bruce to the United States Embassy, Iraq, November 4, 1952.
15 According to the "Quarterly Status Report, June 30, 1952 to September 30, 1952" (dated October 30, 1952), the tasks of the foreign information and educational exchange that started to be carried out by the IIA were, in order of priority: (1) to multiply and to intensify psychological deterrents to aggression by Soviet communism; (2) to intensify and to accelerate the growth of confidence in and among the peoples and the government of the free world … in their capability to successfully deter aggression of Soviet communism; and (3) to combat "particularly in the Near and Middle East and South and South-east Asia, extremist tendencies threatening the undermining of the cohesion and the stability of the free world and the withdrawal of governments and peoples into neutralism." In listing the actions of an "operational nature," which were taken by October 1952 by IIA to support the actions listed above, this document points to the establishment of the FBP and the sum of $500,000, which had been made available to it by the Department of State (CIAA-RDP80-01065A000500090002-2).
16 Dan Lacy also had a persuasive role in the original establishment of the FBP in the 1951 joint meeting of the American Library Association (ALA) and the American Book Publishers Council (ABPC). In this meeting, Lacy criticized the US government's ineffectual use of books and suggested that book professionals rather than government bureaucrats should direct translation and library building programs (Travis, 2013).
17 NSA, United States. International Information Administration. Information Center Service Letter from Dan Lacy to Datus C. Smith, Jr. "Guidance for Franklin Publications," October 27, 1952.
18 NSA, "Guidance for Franklin Publications," 1952.

19 Ibid.
20 The Institute for International Education was an American not-for-profit organization funded by the Department of State and foundations; it was founded between the two world wars, in 1919. IIE was intended for the international exchange of peoples and ideas. It administered the Fulbright Program and Gilman Scholarships for the US Department of State.
21 NSA, "Guidance for Franklin Publications," 1952.
22 Ibid.
23 Ibid.
24 Ibid.
25 Ibid.
26 Ibid.
27 Ibid.
28 Ibid.
29 NSA, Princeton University Letter from Bayard Dodge to Richard H. Sanger. "Colloquium on Islamic Culture," February 2, 1953.
30 NSA, Letter from Helen M. Anderson to Richard H. Sanger. "Colloquium on Islamic Culture" [Background Information on Islamic Colloquium; Includes Minutes, Letter, and Budget], May 8, 1953.
31 NSA, Department of State Memorandum from Wilson S. Compton to David K.E. Bruce. "Colloquium on Islamic Culture to Be Held in September, 1953, under the Joint Sponsorship of the Library of Congress and Princeton University" [Attached to Cover Note Dated January 16, 1953; Includes Enclosure], January 13, 1953.
32 The Under Secretary of State, the Deputy Secretary of Defense, and the director of Central Intelligence or their designated representatives were members of the PSB. For the archives of the PSB, see Harry S. Truman Papers, Staff Member and Office Files: Psychological Strategy Board Files.
33 PSB, "Memorandum for the Psychological Strategy Board: The U.S. Doctrinal Program," PSB D-33/2, May 5, 1953.
34 In pointing to the Soviet Union's use of "doctrinal warfare," the "Memorandum for the Psychological Strategy Board" admitted that "[b]efore Leninism, much less Stalinism, had developed their major theses, the materialistic philosophy of Karl Marx had become a basic hypothesis of the world intellectuals." Therefore, the memorandum argued that in developing an American "Doctrinal Program," it should be noted that "the initial spread of Marxism was not connected with any Soviet design or objective" (PSB, "Memorandum for the Psychological Strategy Board: The U.S. Doctrinal Program," PSB D-33/2, May 5, 1953).
35 PSB, "Memorandum for the Psychological Strategy Board: The U.S. Doctrinal Program," PSB D-33/2, May 5, 1953.
36 Ibid.
37 Ibid.
38 Ibid.
39 Commissioned by Stalin in 1935, the English translation of the book was published in 1938 as a textbook.
40 PSB, "Memorandum for the Psychological Strategy Board: The U.S. Doctrinal Program," PSB D-33/2, May 5, 1953.
41 Ibid.
42 FBPR, Box 16, President's Annual Reports, "A Memorandum about the Organization, and Its Future Development," 1955.
43 FBPR, Box 16, President's Annual Reports, "Project for Future Development," 1954.

44 Ibid.
45 Ibid.
46 For a study of children's literature during the Cold War, see Grieve, 2018.
47 FBPR, Box 16, President's Annual Reports, "Project for Future Development," 1954.
48 While the FBP's overall policy in the early 1950s was to avoid engagement in textbook writing, it nevertheless discussed the case of Silver Burdett C., which, at the request of the Karachi Federal District in Pakistan, produced texts chiefly in history and geography using local writers and artists under the direction of an American textbook editor and a leading writer of textbooks. Years later, the above case became a model for the FBP when it sponsored textbook-writing workshops for the leading local textbook writers of the Middle East and African countries.
49 FBPR, Box 15, Annual Report 1960.
50 By the late 1950s, in Indonesia, the army was a regular bulk purchaser of FBP books for recreational reading, with about twenty titles being bought in this manner. In Iran in 1959, a request from the army was sent to the FBP for prescribed reading in the fields of world history, international affairs, and so on by the officer corps (FBPR, Box 15, Annual Report 1960).
51 While by early 1955, the head office had not found it necessary to use its veto power if the local advisors suggested the translation of an unsuitable book for the program, they had done so a few times by May 1956. However, they still had not used this veto regularly.
52 FBPR, Box 15, President's Annual Reports, "Memoranda Dealing with Special Aspects of Its Work," 1957.
53 FBPR, Box 15, President's Annual Reports, "Franklin Book Publications" [Staff use only], January 25, 1956.
54 Ibid.
55 FBPR, Box 15, President's Annual Reports, "Franklin Book Publications," May 1, 1956.
56 Ibid.
57 FBPR, Box 15, President's Annual Reports, "Franklin Book Publications," May 1, 1956.

Chapter 4

1 As a diplomat al-Aroussy held posts in Kabul, Beirut, and London.
2 In November 1965, Hassan Galal al-Aroussy died and was succeeded by Ahmed Riad Abaza, his deputy director. In 1976, Kamil Farid succeeded Abaza.
3 FBPR, Box 16, President's Annual Reports, "A Memorandum about the Organization and Its Possible Future Development," August 15, 1954.
4 For instance, while the retail price of the US edition of most of the sponsored titles within the United States was above $2.50 at the time and the retail price of the US edition in Cairo was above $3.50, the FBP's Arabic editions were sold for less than 50 cents.
5 FBPR, Box 16, President's Annual Reports, "Project for Future Development," 1954.
6 Both Sabine's *History of Political Theory* (1937) and Soule's *Ideas of the Great Economists* (1952) had achieved quasi-textbook status at the University of Cairo, and the FBP was hopeful these texts were finding their way to the University of Baghdad. The leading teacher-training institution in Egypt, the Institute of Education of Ibrahim University, was using Gate's *Educational Psychology* (1948), Menninger's *Self-Understanding: A First Step to Understanding Children* (1953), and Leonard's *Why Children Misbehave* (1952). Most of the books in Turkish sponsored by the FBP were

specifically intended for teacher training and were published by the Turkish Ministry of Education (FBPR, Box 16, President's Annual Reports, "A Memorandum about the Organization and Its Possible Future Development," August 15, 1954).
7   FBPR, Box 16, President's Annual Reports, "A Memorandum about the Organization, and Its Possible Future Development," 1954.
8   A US field consultant was appointed to advise the local managers on technical issues. The field consultants were also responsible for making suggestions for improving systems of book distribution.
9   As early as 1955, the Egyptian Minister of Education, Mohammad Awwad, was translating two books for the FBP. Six former Egyptian Ministers of Education were participating in translating or writing introductions to the books. The Minister of Defense in Egypt, Abdel Latif Baghdadi (1917–99), was writing the introduction for Lindbergh's *Spirit of St. Louis* (1953). Taha Hussein (1889–1973), famous Egyptian scholar and Minister of Education, wrote an introduction to a book on US literature. The Minister of Religious Endowments in Egypt, Shaykh Ahmed Hussein al-Bakuri, former leader of the Islamic radical group the Muslim Brotherhood, wrote the introduction for Morrison's *Man Does Not Stand Alone* (1944). Ishtiaq Hussain Qureshi (1903–81), the Minister of Education in Pakistan, also wrote an introduction to an FBP book. In the case of Iran, most notably, Mohammad Reza Shah wrote the biography of his father, Reza Shah (1878–1944), for a special Persian edition of Bolton's *Lives of Poor Boys Who Became Famous* (1885). Hassan Taqizadeh (1878–1970), former president of the Iranian senate and leading Iranian intellectual, was the FBP's chief editorial advisor. Hossein Pirnia (1913–93), president of the Oil Commission in Iran, translated Soule's *Ideas of the Great Economists* (1952). The Lebanese ambassador to the United States, Charles Malik, the Saudi Arabian ambassador to London, Hafez Wahba, and Egypt's ambassador to Paris, Mahmoud Falaki, all participated by writing or translating. While the FBP had not yet opened an office in Baghdad, Mohammad Fadhel al-Jamali (1903–97), the former Prime Minister and Foreign Minister of Iraq, was advising the FBP from the beginning (FBPR, Box 16, President's Annual Reports, "A Memorandum about the Organization and Its Possible Future Development," August 15, 1954).
10 FBPR, Box 16, President's Annual Reports, "A Memorandum about the Organization and Its Possible Future Development," August 15, 1954.
11 For a list of some of the local intellectual, civic, and educational leaders who participated in the FBP, see Appendix II.
12 FBPR, Box 16, President's Annual Reports, "Memorandum about the Organization and Its Possible Future Development," 1954.
13 Ibid.
14 According to San'atizadeh, he personally approached the court to ask the Shah to write this chapter on his father, and Hossein Ala' (1883–1964), the Court Minister, accepted, asking San'atizadeh himself to write the chapter and bring the final manuscript for approval. The Tehran Branch wrote the chapter in the name of Mohammad Reza Shah, and Mohammad Reza Shah approved the final manuscript without any edits (Alinejad, 2016, p. 71).
15 For instance, by 1954, the newspaper *Akhbār Al-Yūm* and the magazine house *Dār Al-Ḥilāl* in Cairo were two of the publishers, which the FBP found beneficial for extending the distribution of its sponsored Arabic books to the provinces, as what the FBP had published in cooperation with them had reached the remote parts of the Arab world (FBPR, Box 16, President's Annual Reports, "Memorandum about the Organization, and Its Possible Future Development," 1954).

16 The Arabic edition of *This I Believe* had sold a total of 8,000 copies in Baghdad and Beirut. One thousand copies of Sabine's *History of Political Theory* were also exported from Egypt (FBPR, Box 16, President's Annual Reports, "A Memorandum about the Organization and Its Possible Future Development," August 15, 1954).
17 FBPR, Box 16, President's Annual Reports, "A Memorandum about the Organization and Its Possible Future Development," August 15, 1954.
18 FBPR, Box 15, President's Annual Reports, "Franklin Book Publications," May 1, 1956.
19 Ibid.
20 In the FBP's 1959 Annual Report, the impact of FBP books on other Arab publishers is reiterated when it points out that in the Arab book trade, attractively presented books are described as of "Franklin design" (FBPR, Box 15, Annual Report 1959).
21 By 1957, ninety conventional bookstores in Baghdad, Mosul, Basra, Beirut, Damascus, Aleppo, Amman, Jerusalem, Cairo, Alexandria, Ismailia, Port Said, Suez, Tripoli, Benghazi, Algiers, Rabat, Casablanca, and Khartoum were handling FBP Arabic books. About 120 bookstores in Tehran, Isfahan, Shiraz, Hamedan, Tabriz, Mashhad, and other cities were selling FBP Persian books. And approximately fifty bookstores in Karachi, Lahore, Rawalpindi, Peshawar, Bahawalpur, Multan, and Hyderabad were selling FBP Urdu books (FBPR, Box 15, President's Annual Reports, "Memorandum Dealing with Special Aspects of Its Work," January 9, 1957).
22 The selling of several FBP titles in Arabic outside Egypt had been raised to 2,500 copies, and in one case as many as 10,000 (FBPR, Box 15, President's Annual Reports, "Memorandum Dealing with Special Aspects of Its Work," January 9, 1957).
23 FBPR, Box 15, President's Annual Reports, "Memorandum Dealing with Special Aspects of Its Work," January 9, 1957.
24 Of the 700,000 total sales, 95 percent were through bookstores, newsstands, or street peddlers, and at prices that were not lower than comparable books in the same language. The majority were individual single-copy sales to local people. Merely 10,000 of these sales had been to the USIS, General Motors, Aramco, and other American purchasers. As the local publishers were obliged to pay royalties to FBP according to their sales, the number of sales was not an exaggeration (FBPR, Box 15, President's Annual Reports, "Memorandum Dealing with Special Aspects of Its Work," January 9, 1957).
25 Three thousand copies of the first printing of the Arabic edition of Sabine's *A History of Political Theory* were sold out and another 5,000 copies were printed. Gilbert Highet's *The Art of Teaching* (1950) similarly went to two more reprints (a total of 9,000 copies) once its initial print run of 3,000 copies sold out (FBPR, Box 15, President's Annual Reports, "Franklin Book Publications," May 1, 1956).
26 This money went to the publication of Erich Schmidt's *Persepolis*.
27 FBPR, Box 15, President's Annual Reports, "Memorandum Dealing with Special Aspects of Its Work," January 9, 1957.
28 Ibid.
29 Ibid.
30 Below is a list of publishers working with the FBP by 1957 in various languages:

   Arabic: Akhbār al-Yūm (Cairo), Anglo-Egyptian Bookshop (Cairo), Zohair Baalebakki (Beirut), Issa al-Halaby (Cairo), Dār al-Ḥilāl (Cairo), Irānī (Cairo), El Khangī (Cairo), Dār al-Kitāb (Casablanca), Lagnet al-Taʾlīf (Cairo), Dār al-Maʾārif (Cairo), Al-Muthanna (Baghdad), Renaissance Bookshop (Cairo), Al-Saḥar (Cairo), Dār al-Sakafa (Beirut)

Persian: Amīr Kabīr, Dānish, Iqbāl, ʾIṭilāʾāt, Ibn Sīnā, Kiyhān, Maʾrifat, Nīl, Ṣafīʾalīshāh, Sukhan, Ṭahūrī, Zavvār

Urdu: Academy Punjab, Ahsan Brothers, Aina-i-Adab, Maktaba Caravan, Darul Ishaat, Ferozsons, Idara-i-Mansour, Maktaba Jadeed, Malik Siraj Din, Markaz-i-Adab, Nawa-i-Waqt, Publisher United, Saqi Book Department, University Book Agency, Maktaba-i-Urdu

Bengali: Azad, Bards & Books, Katha Bitan, Liberty, Majid, Malik, Mullick, Manju, Pakistan Book Co-operative

Indonesian: Endang, Balai Buku, Indira, Pantja Tria, Pembangunan, Tarate, Pembimbing, Putaka Rakjat, Timun Mas, Tinta Mas, Soeroengen

(FBPR, Box 15, President's Annual Reports, "Memorandum Dealing with Special Aspects of Its Work," January 9, 1957)

31 FBPR, Box 15, President's Annual Reports, "Franklin Book Publications" [Staff use only], January 25, 1956.
32 FBPR, Box 15, President's Annual Reports, "Memorandum Dealing with Special Aspects of Its Work," January 9, 1957.
33 FBPR, Box 15, President's Annual Reports, "Franklin Book Publications" [Staff use only], January 25, 1956. The FBP board of directors consisted of the presidents or vice-presidents of the following publishing houses: McGraw-Hill Book Co.; Doubleday & Co.; Macmillan Co.; Harper and Bros; Thomas Y. Crowell Co.; Combat Forces Press; Silver Burdett Co.; John Wiley & Sons, Inc.; D. Van Nostrand Co.; Houghton Mifflin Co.; W.W. Norton & Co., Inc.; Harper & Bros.; American Book Co.; Grosset & Dunlap; Cornell University Press; W.B. Saunders Co.; Simon and Schuster, Inc.; and Houghton Mifflin Co. Datus C. Smith, former director of Princeton University Press and president of the Association of American University Presses, was also a board member and president of the FBP New York office. Among the non-publishers on the board of directors were Arthur S. Adams, president of the American Council on Education; Carl Kraeling, director of the Oriental Institute at the University of Chicago; James R. Killian Jr., president of the Massachusetts Institute of Technology; and Philip E. Mosely, professor of International Relations at Columbia University.
34 FBPR, Box 15, President's Annual Reports, "Franklin Book Publications" [Staff use only], January 25, 1956.
35 FBPR, Box 15, President's Annual Reports, "Memorandum Dealing with Special Aspects of Its Work," January 9, 1957.
36 The Agricultural Trade Development and Assistance Act regulated funds derived from the sale of surplus US agricultural commodities to a number of countries for non-convertible local currency. These funds could be used locally for educational projects by agreement with the purchasing countries.
37 For a detailed report on this project, the people involved, its procedures, and a classified list of books translated, see Jemudd & Garrison, 1975.
38 Also, Afghanistan's Ministry of Education had placed orders for 400 to 600 copies each of several of FBP's Persian books suitable for university use and for 2,500 copies each of eighteen juvenile titles. West Pakistan's Ministry of Education had already approved one FBP title for school use and was processing twelve more (FBPR, Box 15, President's Annual Reports, "Memorandum Dealing with Special Aspects of Its Work," January 9, 1957).
39 CWIHP, "The Ideological Aggression of American Imperialism in the Orient," January 13, 1959.
40 Ibid.

41 The manager was Mohammad Y. Najm, Assistant Professor of Arabic at the American University of Beirut.
42 Under the management of Mahmud el Amin, archeologist.
43 Under the management of Abdulali Karang, Associate Professor of Persian at Teachers College, Tabriz.
44 FBPR, Box 15, Annual Report 1959.
45 The FBP had published 759 titles with 3,224,000 total copies. It had also published 11,966,000 copies of thirty-five Iranian textbook titles and 1,491,000 copies of sixty-two titles for the Afghanistan textbook project.
46 FBPR, Box 15, Annual Report 1959.
47 FBPR, Box 15, Annual Report 1960.
48 Ibid.
49 A total of 1,017 book titles and 135 textbooks had been published, with total copies numbering 21,000,000, including textbooks. In its Regular Program, the number of copies produced during 1961 (968,000) was nearly a quarter of the total for all nine years of the FBP's existence. The FBP had also published forty-seven textbooks for Iran, with a total of 15,617,000 copies, eighty-five textbooks for Afghanistan, with a total of 1,781,200 copies, and three textbooks for the United Arab Republic, with 30,000 copies. Lawson's *Robbut: A Tale of Tails* (1948) was reprinted in an edition of 165,000 copies for supplementary reading in Egyptian schools (FBPR, Box 15, Annual Report 1961).
50 Ellen Clayton Garwood (1903–93) was the daughter of William L. Clayton. William L. Clayton, a wealthy cotton merchant-turned-government official, played an important role in the development of the Marshall Plan while serving as Under Secretary of State for Economic Affairs during the Truman administration. See Truman Library, Ellen Clayton Garwood Papers.
51 FBPR, Box 15, Annual Report 1961.
52 In 1961, the FBP sent two teams for a preliminary survey to be finished by January 1962, which was to report to the board of directors as well as making information available to foundations, publishers, and government agencies. Its book surveys soon extended to include India, Burma, Thailand, and so on (FBPR, Box 15, Annual Report 1961).
53 Kennedy Library, President's Office Files, Departments and Agencies Series, Box 91, USIA 1/62-6/62, April 16, 1962.
54 FBPR, Box 15, Annual Report 1962.
55 Ibid.
56 By this time it had published ninety editions of Iranian textbooks, totaling 24,808,500 copies; ninety editions of Afghanistani textbooks, totaling 1,813,400 copies; and thirty-three editions of Egyptian textbooks, totaling 379,000 copies. Its total Regular Program had also reached 1,707 editions and a total of 6,754,000 copies (FBPR, Box 15, Annual Report 1963).
57 By the end of June of the following year, 340,000 books, which were reprints of previously published translations of American books, had gone to about 8,000 schools in Pakistan, and an additional 300,000 copies were scheduled to be added.
58 FBPR, Box 15, Annual Report 1963.
59 At this time, the largest project specifically intended for vocational education was being organized in Iraq.
60 FBPR, Box 15, Annual Report 1963.
61 FBPR, Box 15, Annual Report 1964. This year for the first time, three honorary directors were appointed; Ghasem Khiradjou, president of the Industrial & Mining Development Bank of Iran, was among them.

62 The list of the other non-profit organizations, professional and trade groups, and private companies, which cooperated with the training division, includes the American Book Publishers Council, the American Textbook Publishers Institute, the Children's Book Council, the American Booksellers Association, the Association of American University Presses, the Teachers College (Columbia), the School of Education of Harvard University, the Asia Society, and the Africa–America Institute (FBPR, Box 15, Annual Report 1964).
63 Under the management of Atiqullah Maroof, an educator and educational administrator.
64 The programs in Nigeria were supported by a three-year grant totaling $365,000 from the Ford Foundation.
65 FBP representatives also visited India, Guinea, Kuwait, Algeria, Tunisia, Venezuela, Peru, Chile, and Mexico for special consultation (FBPR, Box 15, Annual Report 1964).
66 FBPR, Box 15, Annual Report 1964.
67 FBPR, Box 15, Annual Report 1965.
68 Dariush Homayoun (1928–2011) was an Iranian politician and journalist. Later, in 1977, Homayoun became Iran's Minister of Information and Tourism.
69 In 1965, the new board chairman was W. Bradford Wiley, president of American Textbook Publishers and president of John Wiley & Sons. He visited the FBP offices in Buenos Aires, Lagos, Cairo, Beirut, Baghdad, Tehran, Kabul, Lahore, Dacca, Kuala Lumpur, and Jakarta between October and December of 1964, the longest trips ever undertaken by an FBP officer. The FBP president, Datus C. Smith, Jr., visited fourteen FBP offices during this same year and made surveys in Saudi Arabia, Nepal, and the Philippines. The FBP had affiliations with forty-six countries throughout the year; either it had undertaken surveys through its representative in those countries, or else it had hosted nationals of those countries for training under FBP supervision. The FBP had prepared and was distributing special reports on subjects such as Books in East Africa, Books and Economic Development, Children's Books in Developing Countries, and University Presses in Asia (FBPR, Box 15, Annual Report 1965).
70 In one case, an educational writer's workshop was conducted in Nigeria, jointly sponsored by the FBP (with financing provided by USAID) and the British Book Development Council, on the subject of preparation of educational materials (FBPR, Box 15, Annual Report 1965).
71 FBPR, Box 15, Annual Report 1965.
72 Ibid.
73 Start-up costs, including new press equipment, were covered by an interest-free loan from the FBP and from the Asia Foundation (FBPR, Box 15, Annual Report 1972).
74 FBPR, Box 15, Annual Report 1965.
75 The representation of the FBP at the UNESCO meeting on Asian Book Publishing, held in Tokyo in May 1966, clearly shows the stature of this organization and its officials on the international educational scene of the mid-1960s. In this meeting, the official delegates of Indonesia and Afghanistan were the FBP directors in these two countries (Hassan Sahdily and Atiqullah Pazhwak). Homayun San'atizadeh (manager of the Tehran Branch) was technical advisor to the Iranian delegation, which also included Dariush Homayoun (the Asian field consultant of the New York office). Robert MacMakin, FBP printing advisor, was with the Afghanistan delegation; Austin J. McCaffrey, an FBP board member, was advisor to the UNESCO secretariat; and Datus C. Smith, Jr., FBP president, was also a member of the US National Commission for UNESCO (FBPR, Box 15, Annual Report 1966).

76 FBPR, Box 15, Annual Report 1966.
77 Ibid.
78 Ibid. Each of the libraries contained 500 volumes in Persian, with the volumes purchased from the Tehran office.
79 Ibid.
80 Ibid.
81 Other writers' groups were organized in Lagos, Enugu, and Kaduna to prepare materials for new literates, primarily in Yoruba, Hausa, Igbo, and English.
82 FBPR, Box 15, Annual Report 1967.
83 FBPR, Box 15, Annual Report 1968.
84 Ibid.
85 Ibid.
86 Ibid.
87 Ibid.
88 The US Commission on International Education and Cultural Affairs, 1969.
89 Ibid.
90 Franklin Book Programs, 1969.
91 FBP activities in Indonesia are reported in Homayoun, 1964 and Sahdily, 1964.
92 FBPR, Box 15, Annual Report 1969.
93 Later, with the establishment of UNESCO's International Copyright Information Center, UNESCO's center also passed on requests received from member countries for US rights to INCINC.
94 Of the twenty-six titles in this project, twenty-two were translation adaptations from the series "What Research Says to the Teacher" published by the National Educational Association in Washington, DC. By June 1969, copies of eight titles had been distributed to 8,000 institutions in East Pakistan (FBPR, Box 15, Annual Report 1969).
95 FBPR, Box 15, Annual Report 1970.
96 Ibid.
97 Ibid.
98 FBPR, Box 15, Annual Report 1971.
99 Ibid.
100 Ibid.
101 Ibid.
102 Ibid.
103 FBPR, Box 15, Annual Report 1972.
104 Ibid.
105 Ibid.
106 The Ministry of Education's press in Nepal had been established a few years before with USAID assistance.
107 Houshang Pirnazar was director of the center and made several trips to Europe and the United States for consultation and observation. Bahman Forsi, previously managing director of Pocket Books, was the director of operations at the center; he also visited the United States for consultations with producers of audiovisual materials (FBPR, Box 15, Annual Report 1973).
108 FBPR, Box 15, Annual Report 1972.
109 FBPR, Box 15, Annual Report 1973.
110 Ibid.

111 FBPR, Box 15, Annual Report 1974. The FBP's former president and last chairman of the board of directors, Datus C. Smith, completed this study, *The Economics of Book Publishing in Developing Countries*. It was published by UNESCO early in 1977.
112 FBPR, Box 15, Annual Report 1974.
113 Ibid.
114 Ibid.
115 Ibid.
116 CIAA, Document number 1975Kabul00391.
117 FBPR, Box 15, Annual Report 1974.
118 FBPR, Box 15, Annual Report 1976.
119 FBPR, Box 15, Annual Report 1977.
120 "Worldwide Propaganda Network," *New York Times*, December 26, 1977.
121 FBPR, Smith to Board, December 28, 1977; also see Auerbach & Castronovo, 2013.
122 CIAA, file no: 200-135-26/5, October 20, 1963.
123 Ibid.

Chapter 5

1 For studies on this crisis, see Atabaki, 2000; Hasanli, 2006.
2 The Shah also undertook official tours of the Soviet Union in 1965, 1972, and 1974.
3 See document number 311/15202, dated May 23, 1964, in *Chap dar īrān*, 2003, p. 134. According to Amanat, the Iranian state's "rapprochement with the Communist bloc" helped it in the geopolitical setting of the Cold War dominated by the two antagonistic superpowers. On the one hand, following this rapprochement, Soviet propaganda pressure on Iran was decreased, and on the other hand Iran's relations with the communist bloc counterbalanced American primacy—which eventually assisted the Iranian state in its objective of purchasing high-tech weapons from the United States (Amanat, 2017, p. 630).
4 Document number 326/1255 in *Chap dar īrān*, 2003, p. 94. Another SAVAK document dated May 19, 1965, also shows that SAVAK was concerned about the correspondence between Radio Moscow, Radio Baku, and Radio Romany and the Iranians who had written letters to them; therefore, it seized all such dispatched packages (*Chap dar īrān*, 2003, p. 227).
5 For instance see document number 326/1792 in *Chap dar īrān*, 2003, p. 110.
6 *Chap dar īrān*, 2003, p. 133.
7 SAVAK consisted of ten offices; the Third Office was responsible for internal security.
8 *Chap dar īrān*, 2003, pp. 140–1.
9 *Chap dar īrān*, 2003, p. 144.
10 Document number alif/6074 in *Chap dar īrān*, 2003, p. 145.
11 *Chap dar īrān*, 2003, pp. 151–4.
12 Reported in the letter dated June 8, 1965, document number 7526-1-201/13.
13 Document number 324/14452 in *Chap dar īrān*, 2003, p. 223.
14 See *Chap dar īrān*, 2003, p. 306.
15 Ibid.
16 Ibid., p. 310.
17 Ibid., p. 311.
18 See document dated July 3, 1966, in *Chap dar īrān*, 2003, p. 237.
19 *Chap dar īrān*, 2003, p. 251.

20 See document number 324/8356 in *Chap dar īrān*, 2003, p. 286. Unfortunately, there has not yet been any substantial study of the circulation of translations of books published by Progress Publishers in Iran.
21 The Eighth Office of SAVAK was responsible for counter-espionage activities.
22 *Chap dar īrān*, 2003, p. 345.
23 NSA, United States Embassy, Iran Cable from Loy Henderson to the Department of State. [Closure of Foreign Information and Cultural Centers], February 3, 1952.
24 Fazlollah Zahedi (1892–1963) was an Iranian general who replaced Prime Minister Mohammad Mosaddeq after the coup. He was the prime minister from August 19, 1953, to April 7, 1955.
25 NSA, United States Information Service, Tehran, Despatch from Edward C. Wells to the United States Information Agency, 1953.
26 In 1967, the New Left magazine *Ramparts* reported for the first time that AFME was a front organization for the CIA (Shannon, 2017, p. 34).
27 The total number of titles including the reprints was 1,154 (Yadegar, 1979, p. 82).
28 American Presbyterian missionary education in Iran has been the subject of a few studies such as Zirinsky, 1993; Rostam-Kolayi, 2008.
29 For more info on Parviz Khanlari, see Azarang & EIr, 2000.
30 NSA, Department of State Cable to the United States Embassy, Jordan. [Travel Arrangements], October 30, 1952.
31 San'atizadeh claims that after only a year, the Tehran Branch became financially independent from the headquarters in New York (Alinejad, 2016). LeClere reports the year 1959 as the time when the Tehran Branch became financially independent (LeClere, 1973, p. 8). In 1977, the Tehran Branch had 200 full-time clerks with a monthly budget of $660,000 (Yadegar, 1979, p. 7).
32 Dānishjūyān musalmān, n.d., vol. 2, p. 817. For a study of the Shah regime's policy of co-opting intellectuals in the 1960s, see Ansari, 2003.
33 For more information on the National Front and student activism in the United States during the 1960s, see Shannon, 2017.
34 In a confidential US embassy document recording the conversation between Dariush Homayoun and Martin F. Hertz dated January 26, 1967, Hertz pointed out that Homayoun, who had returned from his Neiman Fellowship at Harvard University, intended to use his position in the Tehran Branch (where he began working in 1959) as a jumping board to return to journalism. In this meeting, Homayoun informed Hertz that he had recently had a conversation with the prime minister, Amir Abbas Hovayda (in office 1965–77), and intended to establish a newspaper entitled *āyandigān*. In a following meeting on March 4, 1967, Homayoun stated to Hertz that he would be resigning from the Tehran Branch on the same day (i.e., March 4) to devote all his time to establishing his newspaper. However, the Tehran Branch would "generously" continue to keep him on payroll for a few months (Dānishjūyān musalmān, n.d., vol. 8, pp. 780–1).
35 Such inquiries should be seen as the "identification" process, which was part of the guiding principles of selection in the US educational exchange programs. Kramer finds the following three interlocking principles of selection in the US educational exchange programs to be resilient across time and across private and state sponsorship. First, the process of selection was commonly understood as a process of "identification" of future directing and leading intellectuals and elites of another society. Second, the principle of "diffusion" assumed that these identified elites would then go back to their countries and spread US practices and values

consciously or unconsciously. Third, the principle of "legitimation" was based on the expectation that these foreign students would then play a vital role in supporting the United States by aligning public opinion toward it. These principles and considerations understood US educational institutions "as nodes" in global US-centered networks of power (Kramer, 2012).
36   Dānishjūyān musalmān, n.d., vol. 8, pp. 773–4.
37   FBPR, Box 167, Folder 1 [Sanati Luncheon], 1967.
38   FBPR, Box 167, Folder 1 [Sanati Luncheon], 1967. It is noteworthy that—while this luncheon is revealing in terms of the complex relations between international education, government–private networks, and the social and economic role of the FBP—it was not the only instance in which the FBP sought to address US and foreign corporations in Iran. A letter from Ali Asghar Mohajer to Jack Kyle, the president of the FBP, on February 1, 1972, shows that US, Israeli, European (Belgian, British, Danish, Dutch, French, German, Greek, Italian, Norwegian, Swedish, Swiss), Japanese, and Indian firms with economic activities in Iran were on the mailing list of the Tehran Branch to receive copies of their annual reports, the *Franklin Newsletters*, and other informational materials (FBPR, Box 167, Folder 6, Tehran, 1973).
39   Ali Sadr claims that he was also a candidate to succeed Sanʿatizadeh yet was not chosen by the FBP headquarters because of a pro-Mosaddeq comment he had made in 1966 during his FBP-sponsored stay in the United States. According to Sadr, following his success as the Tehran Branch's representative in Kabul for the technical assistantship project, the FBP headquarters sponsored his US stay for a year to study industrial accounting. During his stay, Sadr was invited for a vacation to a place where personnel from other FBP branches were also staying. During this vacation, he was asked by his host about his ideas on Mosaddeq. Sadr claimed that, years later, he met one of the deputies of the FBP New York offices, who revealed to him that the reason why the FBP did not choose Sadr to succeed Sanʿatizadeh had been a report of his pro-Mosaddeq sentiments (Alinejad, 2016). Sanʿatizadeh, however, noted that it was he himself who suggested Mohajer to the FBP headquarters (Alinejad, 2016, p. 107).
40   For more information on Mohammad Qazvini, see Omidsalar, 2016.
41   For more studies on the history of Iran's publishing industry during the Pahlavi era, see Ahmadi, 1958; Sahib al-Zamani, 1968; Bakhash, 1973.
42   As discussed before, the majority of the US publishers with books on the FBP-sponsored list forfeited the translation rights.
43   In the 1970s, this institute published three manuals on writing articles, on the translation of articles, and as a supplement to both in connection with the launching of *The Encyclopedia of Iran and Islam* (*dānishnāmah īrān va islām*) (Emami, 1997).
44   For more information on Hamid Enayat, see Ashraf, 1998.
45   For more information on Karim Emami, see Emami, 2001; also see Azarang & EIr, 2009.
46   Ahmad Mirʿalaei joined the Tehran Branch in 1969. He was the editor of the Persian translations submitted for publication between 1969 and 1972 and also the chief editor of the *Book of the Day* (*kitāb ʾimrūz*), a book-review journal sponsored by the Tehran Branch (Doostkhah, 2008).
47   Mahdokht Sanʿati worked for the Tehran Branch from 1963 to 1969 (Sanʿati, 2014).
48   The children's section of the Tehran Branch was first launched with the publication of Manuchehr Anwar's *Spinning Gourd* (*kadūy-i qilqilih zan*) [1960]. Later, Mahshid

Amirshahi became the supervisor of this section; Mahdokht San'ati succeeded Amirshahi in this role (San'ati, 2014).
49 For more information on Mohammad Ali Eslami Nadushan, see the special issue of *Iran Namag* dedicated to his intellectual contribution (*Iran Namag*, 3(4), 2019).
50 In 1975, she joined as a librarian the newly founded Farabi University, where she purchased 9,000 books for the university's library (Anvari, 2018).
51 For a study of Persian in India and Indo-Iranian modernity, see Tavakoli-Targhi, 2001.
52 For a discussion of Shirazi and the rise of print capitalism in Iran, listen to Tavakoli-Targhi, 2020.
53 FBPR, Box 15, President's Annual Reports, "Memoranda Dealing with Special Aspects of Its Work," 1957.
54 The first few books were *Animals We Know* (1955), translated by A.M. Ameri (Tehran: Ibn Sīnā & Dānish); *Electricity* (1955), translated by A.M. Ameri (Tehran: Ibn Sīnā); *Heat* (1955), translated by A.M. Ameri (Tehran: Ibn Sīnā); *Light* (1955), translated by A.M. Ameri (Tehran: Ibn Sīnā); *Living Things* (1956), translated by A.M. Ameri (Tehran: Ibn Sīnā); and *You as a Machine* (1955), translated by A.M. Ameri (Tehran: Ibn Sīnā & Dānish).
55 FBPR, "Memoranda Dealing with Special Aspects of Its Work," 1957.
56 In his interview with Alinejad, Parham, who joined the Tehran Branch as early as 1955 as a translator and editor, claims that this title was originally translated by Thamin Baghtcheban but that San'atizadeh published it under the name of Ashraf Pahlavi to build a connection with her and that he also offered Pahlavi a radiogram valued at 7,000 tomans as royalty (Alinejad, 2016, p. 147).
57 FBPR, "Memoranda Dealing with Special Aspects of Its Work," 1957.
58 FBPR, Box 15, Annual Report 1960.
59 Behrangi's theory of education is discussed in Jahani Asl, 2007; Fereshteh, 1993.
60 This list is accessible at https://www.loc.gov/rr/rarebook/pdf/FBPPersian.PDF
61 As noted by Haddadian-Moghaddam, from a translation studies' point of view, the history of the FBP helps us to see the creation of "World Literature" from a cultural Cold War perspective. In its translation of literature as part of the Regular Translation Programs, the FBP introduced "a narrow form of world literature" into local cultures, and non-English literature was rarely included (Haddadian-Moghaddam, 2016, p. 387).

Chapter 6

1 In addition to these major operations, the Tehran Branch assisted some projects financially. For instance, it offered funding to IIDCYA, provided financial assistance to a few public library developments in Iran, and assisted with the establishment of Aryamehr University. The Tehran Branch paid one million tomans in cash to this university and also bought books for it, to a total value of $200,000 (Alinejad, 2016, p. 212).
2 The content of this literacy campaign has been criticized by some scholars; for instance, Amanat argues that the nature of this state-sponsored education was uncritical "in the cities as well as in the countryside" and that the school curriculum

"glorified the state" and demanded "conformity and compliance" (Amanat, 2017, p. 587).

3 There is an inconsistency between the total amount claimed here by Sanʿatizadeh and the total amount of $50,000 recorded in the FBPR; see FBPR, Box 15, Annual Report 1959.
4 The financial relations between the Tehran Branch and Ashraf Pahlavi is the subject of a few other controversies. For instance, Ali Sadr in his interview with Alinejad claimed that during the operation of the Tehran Branch, every year a check was drawn in the name of Sanʿatizadeh but given to Ashraf Pahlavi. He further claimed that the last of these checks was in the amount of 20 million tomans, which Sanʿatizadeh, having quit the Tehran Branch, did not pass on to Ashraf Pahlavi. Consequently, Ali Asghar Mohajer, who had succeeded Sanʿatizadeh, attempted to sue Sanʿatizadeh for this amount. Sadr claims that Datus C. Smith and Ashraf Pahlavi had a meeting in Paris, during which Ashraf Pahlavi reassured Smith that the amount was deposited to her. Smith then asked Mohajer to withdraw the legal claim against Sanʿatizadeh (Alinejad, 2016, p. 204).
5 Kamran Fani, however, provides another account of the total entries. According to him, of a total of approximately 43,000 entries in the *Persian Encyclopedia*, about 30,000 were translated from the *Concise Columbia–Viking Desk Encyclopaedia* and other reference materials, supplemented by approximately 13,000 original articles on Iran (in Alinejad, 2011).
6 FBPR, Box 15, Annual Report 1960.
7 Ibid.
8 It should be noted that according to Ali Sadr, Taqizadeh was not on the Tehran Branch's payroll; he was affiliated, but not in a financial sense (see the interview with Sadr in Alinejad, 2016, p. 200).
9 The 2500th Year of the Foundation of the Imperial State was marked by a series of ceremonies organized by the Pahlavi regime over October 12–16, 1971, that commemorated the anniversary of the establishment of Achaemenid Empire by Cyrus the Great.
10 FBPR, Box 15, Annual Report 1965.
11 FBPR, Box 15, Annual Report 1963.
12 FBPR, Box 15, Annual Report 1971.
13 FBPR, Box 116, Folder 14, "Letter from Mohajer to Byron Buck," March 6, 1963.
14 FBPR, Box 15, President's Annual Reports, "Franklin Book Publications," May 1, 1956.
15 FBPR, Box 15, President's Annual Reports, "Memorandum Dealing with Special Aspects of Its Work," January 9, 1957.
16 Later in this chapter, I will discuss the Tehran Branch's role in the publication of textbooks in Iran in more detail.
17 FBPR, Box 15, President's Annual Reports, "Memorandum Dealing with Special Aspects of Its Work," January 9, 1957.
18 FBPR, Box 15, Annual Report 1963.
19 FBPR, Box 15, Annual Report 1964.
20 Sanʿatizadeh counts a total of seventy specialists, thirty-five from each of the two countries (Alinejad, 2016); Datus C. Smith gives the numbers of twenty-five Iranians and twenty-five Afghans (Smith, 2000). However, the Annual Report of the FBP counts twenty from each country.
21 CIAA, CS file no: 200-135-26/5, October 20, 1963.

22 FBPR, Box 15, Annual Report 1977.
23 FBPR, Box 15, Annual Report 1965.
24 For a study of women and education in Afghanistan in this period, see Sharif, 1994.
25 It is also called the Society for the Founding of National Elementary Schools in Iran (*anjuman ta'sīs maktab-i milliyah īrān*).
26 The Society of Education also supervised Rushdiyeh schools for a period of time. Later, it assisted with establishing other schools, such as ʿIlmīyih (in 1898), ʾIftitāhīyih, Dānish, Sharaf (1898), and Muzaffarīyih (1898) (Anwar, 1985).
27 The Society of Education further established a Western-type Public Library (*kitābkhānah millī*), later renamed the Education Library (*kitābkhānah maʿārif*) (Anwar, 1985).
28 FBPR, Box 15, Annual Report 1959.
29 This geography textbook was later criticized in Iran's parliament (in November 1966) by a member who pointed out that in the textbook for the sixth grade, Bahrain was not included in the map of Iran. It should be noted that Iran had a historic claim to Bahrain until March of 1970. The deputy of the Ministry of Education who was present at this parliament session replied that none of the islands in the Persian Gulf were discussed in the textbook, so the exclusion was not done to undermine Iran's claim over Bahrain. See Iran's Parliament Proceedings in the session of November 15, 1966.
30 See also FBPR, Box 15, Annual Report 1960.
31 FBPR, Box 15, Annual Report 1959.
32 Ibid.
33 FBPR, Box 15, Annual Report 1960.
34 Ibid.
35 It took three years for this code, proposed by the Ministry, to be approved in the National Assembly. See Iran's Parliamentary Proceedings for the session held on November 15, 1966.
36 This code also divided the twelve years of public education into primary, middle, and secondary stages.
37 Sirous Parham, in his interview with Alinejad, claims that the FBP-sponsored book *Masterpieces of Persian Art* by Pope was actually translated by Houshang Pirnazar but published under the name of Natel Khanlari (Alinejad, 2016, p. 156).
38 According to Karim Emami, as a result of these arrangements a committee of scholars compiled a new set of orthographic rules for authors, editors, and proofreaders, which were followed at both the Organization for Textbooks and the Tehran Branch (Emami, 1997).
39 Its editors were Mashayikh Faridani (ed. 1948–50), Yamin Sharifi (ed. 1950–3), and Eghbal Yaghmaei (EIr, 1991).
40 The first and second prizes went to Mahmoud Kianoush (later a notable author of children's books) and Gholamhossein Saedi (later a notable fiction writer).
41 Kalantari joined IIDCYA in 1968 as the director of the Center for Visual Arts (Madinei, 2017).
42 Firuz Shirvanlu (1938–89) finished his high school education at Alborz College. In 1958, he left for Europe to pursue his post-secondary studies in the Sociology of Arts at the University of Leeds. In Europe, Shirvanlu became affiliated with the Confederation of Iranian Students. In 1963, Shirvanlu returned to Iran and started working for the Tehran Branch. In April of 1965, Shirvanlu was arrested on the charge that he was plotting an attempt on the life of the Shah. During the interrogations,

Shirvanlu never admitted to any role in the plot. He was sentenced to five years in prison but was released on December 5, 1965, and returned to work for the Tehran Branch (EIr, 2009).

43 The IIDCYA maintained a "delicate balance" in its operations. The IIDCYA marginalized socialist realist children's literature and replaced it with progressive literature that was not openly critical of the regime (Moezi Moghadam, 2010a). Similar to the Tehran Branch, the IIDCYA recruited leftist intellectuals, and worked with leftist writers, but refrained from publishing leftist literature. A noteworthy exception to this, however, was the publication of Samad Behrangi's *Little Black Fish*. The IIDCYA transformed children's books in Iran in the sense that it "marginalized" pedagogical socialist realist literature. The IIDCYA became a center for apparently "avant-garde" prose and imagery, establishing the dominant avant-garde mode of expression seen as suitable for children (Aslani, 2017).

44 Mohammad Reza Aslani quotes Manuchehr Anwar to the effect that this agreement was reached in a meeting between Lily Amirarjomand and San'atizadeh (Aslani, 2017).

45 FBPR, Box 15, Annual Report 1974.

46 FBPR, Box 15, Annual Report 1965.

47 *payk dānishāmūz*, December 1969, Issue 6.

48 In the educational year 1971/2, *Payk for Primary School Students* was used for the newly established middle schools and *Payk for Teens* was published for the high school students. However, starting from the 1972/3 educational year, *Payk for Teens* was distributed among the middle schools, and a new journal, *Payk for Youth*, was established for the sake of the high school students.

49 *payk muʿallim va khānivādih*, October 1968, Issue 2, p. 15.

50 The students were encouraged to present class lectures based on the materials in *Payk*; see *payk naw āmūz*, April 1968, Issue 14, p. 12.

51 *payk naw āmūz*, October 1967, Issue 1, p. 15.

52 This book, written by Houshang Porkarim, was published by the Ministry of Culture in 1969; see Porkarim, 1969.

53 An initiative of Queen Farah Pahlavi, the Shiraz Arts Festival was an annual international summer arts festival held in Shiraz, Iran, from 1967 to 1977.

54 FBPR, Box 15, Annual Report 1969.

55 *payk dānishāmūz*, December 1969, Issue 6, pp. 2–3.

56 For the Dacca Branch and its school magazine project, see FBPR, Box 15, Annual Report 1971.

57 *payk javānān*, September 1973, Issue 1.

58 *payk javānān*, October 1977, Issue 1.

59 FBPR, Box 15, Annual Report 1967.

60 FBPR, Box 15, Annual Report 1968.

61 FBPR, Box 15, Annual Report 1969.

62 FBPR, Box 15, Annual Report 1971.

63 Ibid. In the first issue of *Payk for Primary School Students*, a similar estimation on the educational use and circulation of *Payk* magazines in the 1971/2 educational year is recorded. However, it gives the total publication number as more than 12 million copies of *Payk* journals in addition to the monthly *Education and Training*. This report further asserts that, based on the statistics and comments of officials in

the Ministry of Education, an average of five students had used each copy (*payk dānishāmūz*, October 1972, Issue 1).
64 *payk dānishāmūz*, December 1972, Issue 7.
65 FBPR, Box 15, Annual Report 1973.
66 FBPR, Box 15, Annual Report 1974.
67 *payk dānishāmūz*, September 1972, Issue 1.
68 *payk dānishāmūz*, May 1971, Issue 15.
69 *payk javānān*, November 1971, Issue 4, p. 37.
70 The 1921 coup was conducted by the Persian Cossack Brigade led by Reza Khan (later to become Reza Shah Pahlavi) and eventually resulted in the establishment of the Pahlavi regime.
71 The "White Revolution," also known as "the Shah and People's Revolution," was a series of reformist campaigns and policies (including land reform and later the establishment of literacy campaigns) launched by Mohammad Reza Shah in 1963. It was composed of six principles: land reform, nationalization of the forests, profit-sharing for industrial workers, the sale of state factories, votes for women, and the foundation of a literacy corps. The principles were later extended to twelve points and, by the late 1970s, to a total of seventeen points (Ansari, 2003).
72 The Shah's official coronation ceremony was held on October 26, 1967, twenty-six years into his reign.
73 For an example, see *payk naw āmūz*, 1967, Issue 5, p. 3. The same framing of the Azerbaijan Crisis appears in *Payk for Teens*, December 1968, Issue 5. However, this issue further adds that the "malicious group" intended to separate that province from Iran. The same content reappears in December 1969 (Issue 5, p. 3), along with a picture of a series of battle tanks; also in December 1970 (Issue 5, p. 4), December 1971 (Issue 5, p. 3), December 1972 (Issue 5, p. 4), December 1973 (Issue 6, p. 2), and December 1975 (Issue 5, p. 4).
74 For a report on the first year of this competition, accompanied with images of the crown prince delivering the awards to the children, see *payk naw āmūz*, March 1970, Issue 12.
75 *payk naw āmūz*, March 1971, Issue 12, pp. 10–11.
76 *payk naw āmūz*, January 1971, Issue 8, pp. 4–7.
77 *payk naw āmūz*, April 1971, Issue 14, pp. 12–15.
78 *payk naw āmūz*, October 1971, Issue 3, pp. 10–11.
79 *payk naw āmūz*, November 1971, Issue 4, pp. 4–6.
80 *payk naw āmūz*, December 1971, Issue 7, pp. 12–14.
81 *payk naw āmūz*, February 1972, Issue 10.
82 On October 1969 (Issue 2), four pages of *Payk for Primary School Students* were devoted to a report on the crown prince's primary school, a royal class in the Niawaran palace, intended for the study of the crown prince and his sisters. The report details the subject of the crown prince's paintings and writings. The report ends by concluding that while this is a small school, it is doing the most crucial job—that is, educating the crown prince.
83 *payk dānishāmūz*, February 1973, Issue 11.
84 *payk dānishāmūz*, October, Issue 1. For another dramatization of the marriage of the crown prince, see "The Flying Horse" (*asb-i parandah*; May 1970, Issue 15).
85 *payk dānishāmūz*, November 1969, Issue 4.
86 *payk dānishāmūz*, April 1970, Issue 14.

87 There are several reiterations of the official ideology of the monarchy embedded in the section for letters received by *payk javānān*, for instance: December 1971, Issue 7, p. 36; January 1972, Issue 9, p. 36; January 1973, Issue 8, pp. 3–4.
88 *payk javānān*, October–November 1970, Issue 2; also see December 1973, Issue 7; November 1974, Issue 4.
89 *payk javānān*, December 1970–January 1971, Issue 4.
90 *payk javānān*, February–March 1971, Issue 5; also November 1974, Issue 4.
91 *payk javānān*, January 1975, Issue 8.
92 *payk javānān*, October 1974, Issue 2; October 1974, Issue 3; November 1974, Issue 5; October 1975, Issue 1; January 1976, Issue 8.
93 *payk javānān*, December 1974, Issue 6.
94 *payk javānān*, February 1975, Issue 10; March 1975, Issue 11. Mohammad Reza Shah founded the Rastakhiz Party (literally, "Resurgence Party") in 1975 as Iran's single legal political party.
95 *payk javānān*, October 1975, Issue 2.
96 *payk javānān*, November 1975, Issue 4.
97 *payk javānān*, November 1974, Issue 7. This day is a reference to January 8, 1936, when Reza Shah Pahlavi embarked on the policy of unveiling women in Iran, officially commemorated as Women's Day during the Pahlavi regime.
98 *payk javānān*, September 1976, Issue 1.
99 *payk javānān*, February 1976, Issue 9.
100 It is also notable that there was only one reference throughout the *Payk*s to other religions in Iran; on the occasion of Christmas, Iranian Christians are mentioned in December 1969 (Issue 6) and December 1974 (Issue 7).
101 *payk naw āmūz,* October 1975, Issue 2.
102 *payk naw āmūz,* February 1976, Issue 10.
103 For instance, see September 1974, Issue 1 (Masjid Shah); October 1974, Issue 2 (Masjid Shaykh Lutfullah); November 1974, Issue 4 (Masjid Jami˙ Shiraz).
104 See October 1974, Issue 2, pp. 4–5.
105 FBPR, Box 116, Folder 14, "Letter from Michael Harris to Ali Asghar Mohajer," July 23, 1969.
106 FBPR, Box 116, Folder 14, "Ali Asghar Mohajer to Carroll Bowen," June 7, 1970.
107 FBPR, Box 116, Folder 14, "Letter from Ali Asghar Mohajer to Datus C. Smith," January 8, 1967.
108 Ibid.
109 FBPR, Box 116, Folder 14, "Letter from Ali Asghar Mohajer to Carroll Bowen, Confidential," December 12, 1970.
110 FBPR, Box 116, Folder 14, "Letter from Ali Asghar Mohajer to Datus C. Smith," January 8, 1967.
111 FBPR, Box 116, Folder 14, "Harold Munger to Bowen," March 20, 1970. The FBP was also involved in the process of locating professors for colleges in Tehran—one example of which occurred when the Tehran Branch asked Franklin New York to help them locate a professor of mathematics to teach topology, modern algebra, and symbolic logic at the Institute of Mathematics of the National Teacher Training College in Tehran, in late 1969. The New York office consequently contacted the dean of the School of Education at the State University of New York (SUNY) at Albany to see if he could assist in locating such a professor

(FBPR, Box 116, Folder 14, "Letter from R.S. Gardner to Esther Walls," August 7, 1969).
112 For instance in Dabashi, 1993.
113 For instance, one influential genre of poetry in the 1970s, known as "poetry of resistance" and "guerilla poetry," followed the tradition of social criticism in modern Persian literature to mobilize revolutionary sentiments and dramatize the life of an anti-Pahlavi guerrilla fighter (Vahabzadeh, 2015).
114 For example, in the student journal *An zamān in zamān* (*Those Days, These Days*) published by a literary club of the Faculty of Science in Mashhad University in February 1973, the author Ni'mat Mirzazadeh, under the pseudonym Sohrab Dadsitan, criticizes a recent publication (referring to Huquqi, 1972) on the history of modern Persian poetry by Jībī publishers. Mirzazadeh argues that this anthology excluded revolutionary and socially committed poets and instead included "poets of submission" (*sha'irān taslīm*), a phrase he uses to frame formalist poetry and poetry that is not calling for social change. Without further elaboration, Mirzazadeh points out that such an exclusion of revolutionary poets in this anthology is not "accidental" and that the author has done what he has been "paid" by the Tehran Branch to do. For a study of this student journal, see Ganjavi & Mojab, 2018.
115 Ahmad Kasravi (1890–1946) was a prominent Iranian historian, lawyer, and religious reformer. Kasravi was a former seminarian who criticized the Iranian adoration of Europe, calling it Europism (*'urūpāyīgarī*). According to Kasravi, the idea of "European superiority" was a device deceptively assisting colonialism and capitalism. Kasravi's criticism of Europism and Orientalism shaped the works of later intellectuals such as Ahmad Fardid, Fakhr al-Din Shadiman, Jalal Al Ahmad, and Ali Shari'ati (Tavakoli-Targhi, 2015).
116 Ahmad Fardid (1909–94) was an Iranian philosopher and professor at the University of Tehran. He had considerable influence on many intellectuals from the 1950s onward. For a study on the intellectual life and legacy of Fardid, see Mirsepassi, 2017.
117 Seyed Fakhr al-Din Shadiman (1907–67) earned his PhD in Law from the Faculty of Law at the Université de Paris. During his life, he held several government positions, such as Minister of Economics (in 1948, also in 1953), Minister of Agriculture (1948), and Minister of Justice (1954) (Milani, 1995).
118 For a study of the reintroduction of Islamic values to modern education in Iran, and the role of Al Ahmad in the formation of this discourse, see Paivandi, 2012.
119 Mehrzad Boroujerdi has analyzed the rise of nativism among Iranian intellectuals in the context of Iran–Western encounters; see Boroujerdi, 1996.
120 A few of the former staff members of the Tehran Branch also accuse Ali Asghar Mohajer of financially abusing his power. For instance, Ali Sadr claims that once Mohajer succeeded San'atizadeh, he intended to secretly withdraw $200,000 from an account the Tehran Branch had in Finland that was used to purchase paper; see Alinejad, 2016, p. 207. It is not the intention of this study to substantiate or invalidate such claims.
121 Ali Sadr asserts that the reason the FBP and consequently the Tehran Branch was shut down was that a high-ranking CIA agent wrote a book in the late 1970s in which he presented the FBP as a CIA operative (Alinejad, 2016, p. 208). To my best knowledge, his intended reference must be the article "Propaganda Network Built by the C.I.A." in the *New York Times*.

122 The location of some of these bookshops were in front of Tehran University, on Vesal Street, on College Crossroad, and on Naderi Avenue.
123 The latest reference to the Tehran Branch appears in a top-secret document from the US embassy in Tehran to the Department of State, dated January 11, 1979—that is, just a month before the revolution. This document points to the political views of Ali Shapourian, the manager of Nawmarz Publications, which the document claims was a publishing house under the administration of the Tehran Branch. According to this document, Shapourian was the press advisor of Iran's embassy in the United States and later in London. He later worked as the public relations officer for Ashraf Pahlavi. In November 1978, Shapourian became manager of Nawmarz Publications (Dānishjūyān musalmān, n.d., vol. 3, p. 358).
124 NSA, United States Embassy, Iran Cable from William H. Sullivan to the Department of State. "Attack on U.S.-supported Publishing House," December 26, 1977.
125 Ibid.
126 Abdulrahim Ja'fari, the manager of Amīr Kabīr publishers, was arrested and imprisoned for eight months. Amīr Kabīr was seized by order of the Islamic court and was later passed on to the Organization for the Promotion of Islam (*sāzimān-i tabliqhāt-i islāmī*) (EIr, 2002). For more information on Amīr Kabīr publishers and its manager, see the special issue of *Bukhārā* dedicated to this subject (*Bukhārā*, 109, 2016).

Chapter 7

1 In the politicized condition of post-Revolution Iran, when any clue to possible ties with the US state or its cultural diplomacy would and still can put an individual's life and career in danger, the local's narrative, which asserts and writes their agency into the history of the Tehran Branch is completely understandable. Yet such a narrative should not replace a rigorous historical analysis of the program in its entirety.
2 NSA, "Guidance for Franklin Publications," 1952.
3 Ibid.
4 Ibid.
5 PSB, "Memorandum for the Psychological Strategy Board: The U.S. Doctrinal Program," PSB D-33/2, May 5, 1953.
6 For a detailed study of the post-coup Americanization of Iran's universities, see Mojab, 1991. As noted by Mojab, while the Americanization of the universities was part of the general policy of the Pahlavi regime, that regime also aimed to depoliticize higher education in Iran and weaken the academic authority of the University of Tehran. The change in the administrative structure of the universities with the introduction of the board of trustees in Pahlavi University in Shiraz, headed by the Shah himself, was one of the major administrative reforms recommended by US advisors. For more on the developments of higher education in Iran during the Pahlavi regime, see Manzoor, 1971; Shahlapour, 1978; Hakim, 1979; Taban, 1979.
7 For studies on Pahlavi cultural planning, see Matin-Asgari, 2018; Mirsepassi, 2017; Shakibi, 2019; Gholipour, 2018.

Appendix

1 The numbers recorded here as final outcomes of the offices' activities are extracted from FBPR, Box 15, Annual Report 1977. For detailed studies on this office see Arrabai, 2019; Asiri, 2021.
2 FBPR, Box 15, Annual Report 1977.
3 FBPR, Box 15, President's Annual Reports, "Franklin Book Publications," May 1, 1956.
4 FBPR, Box 15, Annual Report 1968.
5 According to Manuchehr Anwar, this book was actually translated by Thamin Baghtcheban and edited by Anwar himself but then published under the name of the Shah's twin sister, Ashraf Pahlavi (Alinejad, 2016).
6 Al Ahmad argues that Zafar's draft translation of Cora Mason's *Socrates: The Man Who Dared to Ask* was so poorly done that the editor, Simin Daneshwar (1921–2012), a prominent novelist and translator, actually retranslated the whole manuscript (Al Ahmad, 1964).

REFERENCES

Abdul Razak, R. (2018). Convenient comrades: Re-assessing the relationship between the Soviet Union and the Tudeh Party during the British–Soviet occupation of Iran 1941–5. In R. Matthee & E. Andreeva (eds.), *Russians in Iran: Diplomacy and Power in the Qajar Era and Beyond* (pp. 276–96). London: I.B. Tauris.

Abrahamian, E. (1982). *Iran between Two Revolutions*. Princeton, NJ: Princeton University Press.

Ahmadi, A. (1958). Nazarī bah āmār-i kitābhā-yi chāpī dar īrān. *Sukhan*, 9 (2): 168–78.

Al Ahmad, J. (1963). *Sih maqālah digar*, 2nd edn. Tehran: Jāvīd.

Al Ahmad, J. (1964). *Yik chāh va dū chālah*. Tehran: Ravāq.

Al Ahmad, J. (1979). *Dar khidmat va khīyānat rawshanfikrān*. Tehran: Shirkat Sahāmī Intishārāt Khawrazmī.

Al Ahmad, J. ([1962] 2006). *Qarbzadigī*. Tehran: Khurram.

Al Dawud, S.A. (1997). Education ix. Primary schools. In *Encyclopaedia Iranica*. Retrieved from www.iranicaonline.org/articles/education-ix-primary-schools (accessed on January 10, 2020).

Alinejad, S. (2011). Sanʿatizadeh Kermani, Homayun. In *Encyclopaedia Iranica*. Retrieved from www.iranicaonline.org/articles/sanatizadeh (accessed on January 10, 2020).

Alinejad, S. (2016). *Az firānklīn tā lālahzār, zindigīnāmah humāyūn sanʿatīzādah*. Tehran: Quqnūs.

Allen, F.L. (1952). *The Big Change: America's Transformation 1900–1950*. New York: Harper and Row.

Allman, P. (2007). *On Marx: An Introduction to the Revolutionary Intellect of Karl Marx*. Rotterdam: Sense.

Amanat, A. (2017). *Iran: A Modern History*. New Haven, CT: Yale University Press.

Amuzigar, S. (1977). *Kitāb wa kitābkhwānī: dar davrān panjāh sāl shāhanshāhī pahlavī*. Tehran: Vizārat Farhang wa Hunar.

Anderson, B. (2006). *Imagined Communities: Reflections on the Origin and Spread of Nationalism*. London & New York: Verso.

Ansari, A.M. (2003). *Modern Iran since 1921: The Pahlavis and After*. New York: Longman.

Anvari, H. (2018). Translating life in Iran. *Roads and Kingdoms*. Retrieved from https://roadsandkingdoms.com/2018/translating-life-in-iran/ (accessed on January 10, 2020).

Anwar, ʿA. (1985). Anjoman-e Maʿāref. In *Encyclopaedia Iranica*. Retrieved from www.iranicaonline.org/articles/anjoman-e-maaref (accessed on January 10, 2020).

Arianpour, Y. (1971). *Az ṣabā tā nīmā, tārīkh-i ṣad-u panjāh sālah adab fārsī*. Tehran: Jībī.

Armajani, Y. (1985). Alborz College. In *Encyclopaedia Iranica*. Retrieved from www.iranicaonline.org/articles/alborz-college (accessed on January 10, 2020).

Arrabai, A.M. (2019). The Franklin Book Program: Translation and image-building in the Cold War. Unpublished doctoral dissertation, Kent State University, Ohio.

Ashraf, A. (1998). ʿEnāyat, Ḥamīd. In *Encyclopaedia Iranica*. Retrieved from www.iranicaonline.org/articles/enayat (accessed on January 10, 2020).

Ashuri, D. (1994). Dāyerat Al-Maʿāref-e Fārsī. In *Encyclopaedia Iranica*. Retrieved from www.iranicaonline.org/articles/dayerat-al-maaref-e-farsi (accessed on January 10, 2020).

Asiri, A.M. (2021). The Franklin Book Program: Translation and the projection of the American soft power in the Cold War. Unpublished doctoral dissertation, Binghamton University, New York.

Aslani, M.R. (2017). Yik ʾulgū-yi mudīrīyat farhangī. *Āngāh*, 2: 20–4.

Atabaki, T. (2000). *Azarbaijan: Ethnicity and the Struggle for Power in Iran*. London: I.B. Tauris.

Auerbach, J., & Castronovo, R., eds. (2013). *The Oxford Handbook of Propaganda Studies*. Retrieved from https://doi.org/10.1093/oxfordhb/9780199764419.001.0001 (accessed on January 10, 2020).

Azarang, A. (2002). Nashr kitāb dar īrān: sayr-i ʾijmālī taḥavvul, maʿānī hā va chālishhā. *Nāmah Farhang*, 44: 92–111.

Azarang, A., & EIr (2000). Khanlari, Parviz. In *Encyclopaedia Iranica*. Retrieved from www.iranicaonline.org/articles/khanlari-parviz (accessed on January 10, 2020).

Azarang, A., & EIr (2009). Emami, Karim. In *Encyclopaedia Iranica*. Retrieved from www.iranicaonline.org/articles/emami-karim-translator-editor (accessed on January 10, 2020).

Bakhash, S. (1973). Chashmandāz ṣanʿat-i nashr-i kitāb dar īrān. *Kitāb Imrūz*, 5: 44–52.

Bannerji, H. (2003). Tradition of sociology and the sociology of tradition. *Qualitative Studies in Eucation*, 16 (2): 157–73.

Bannerji, H. (2015). Ideology. In S. Mojab (ed.), *Marxism and Feminism* (pp. 163–80). London: Zed.

Barghoorn, F.C. (1960). *The Soviet Cultural Offensive: The Role of Cultural Diplomacy in Soviet Foreign Policy*. Princeton, NJ: Princeton University Press.

Barnhisel, G. (2015). *Cold War Modernists: Art, Literature, and American Cultural Diplomacy*. New York: Columbia University Press.

Bayat, K. (1995). Tajrubah firānklīn. *Guftugū*, 7: 57–64.

Behrangi, S. ([1965] 1969). *Kand wa kāw dar masāʾil tarbiyatī īrān*. Tehran: Bāmdād.

Benjamin, C.G. (1984). *U.S. Books Abroad: Neglected Ambassadors*. Washington: Library of Congress. Retrieved from http://catdir.loc.gov/catdir/toc/becites/cfb/83022245.html#about (accessed on January 10, 2020).

Birashk, A., & EIr (1997). Education xvi. School textbooks. In *Encyclopaedia Iranica*. Retrieved from www.iranicaonline.org/articles/education-xvi-school-textbooks (accessed on January 10, 2020).

Blake, K. (2009). *The U.S.–Soviet Confrontation in Iran, 1945–1962: A Case in the Annals of the Cold War*. Lanham, MD: University Press of America.

Bolton, S.K. (1885). *Lives of Poor Boys Who Became Famous*. New York: Thomas Y. Crowell.

Boroujerdi, M. (1996). *Iranian Intellectuals and the West: The Tormented Triumph of Nativism*. Syracuse, NY: Syracuse University Press.

Boyd-Barrett, O. (2015). *Media Imperialism: Continuity and Change*. Thousand Oaks, CA: Sage.

Bu, L. (2004). *Making the World Like Us: Education, Cultural Expansion, and the American Century*. Westport, CT: Praeger.

Carnoy, M. (1974). *Education as Cultural Imperialism*. New York: David McKary.

Carpenter, S., & Mojab, S., eds. (2017). *Revolutionary Learning: Marxism, Feminism and Knowledge*. London: Pluto.

Chap dar Īrān, ravābiṭ Īrān va shawravī bih rivāyat-i ʾasnād sāvāk (2003). Tehran: Markaz Barrisiy-i Asnād Tārīkhī.
Choudry, A. (2015). *Learning Activism: The Intellectual Life of Contemporary Social Movements*. Toronto: University of Toronto Press.
Clinton, J.W. (1984). Al-E Ahmad, Jalal. In *Encyclopaedia Iranica*. Retrieved from www.iranicaonline.org/articles/al-e-ahmad-jalal-1302-48-s (accessed on January 10, 2020).
Clough, S. (1953). *The American Way: The Economic Basis of our Civilization*. New York: Thomas Y. Crowell.
Cole, J.Y. (1986). *The Community of the Book: A Directory of Selected Organizations and Programs*. Washington: Library of Congress.
Coyle, D.C. (1957). *The United States Political System and How It Works*. London: Hansard Society.
Dabashi, H. (1993). *Theology of Discontent: The Ideological Foundation of the Islamic Revolution in Iran*. New York: New York University Press.
Dānishjūyān musalmān payruv khaṭ-i ʾimām. (n.d.). *Asnād-i lānah jāsūsī*. Tehran: n.p.
Dimand, M.S. (1947). *A Handbook of Mohammedan Decorative Arts*. New York: Hartsdale House.
Dmytryshyn, B., & Cox, F. (1987). *The Soviet Union and the Middle East: A Documentary Record of Afghanistan, Iran and Turkey 1917–1985*. Princeton, NJ: Kingston.
Doostkhah, J. (2008). Mirʿalāʾi, Aḥmad. In *Encyclopaedia Iranica*. Retrieved from www.iranicaonline.org/articles/miralai-ahmad (accessed on January 10, 2020).
EIr (1991). Children vii. Children's literature. In *Encyclopaedia Iranica*. Retrieved from www.iranicaonline.org/articles/children-vii (accessed on January 10, 2020).
EIr (2002). Amir Kabir Publishers. In *Encyclopaedia Iranica*. Retrieved from www.iranicaonline.org/articles/amir-kabir-publishers (accessed on January 10, 2020).
EIr (2008). Jamalzadeh, Mohammad-Ali. In *Encyclopaedia Iranica*. Retrieved from www.iranicaonline.org/articles/jamalzadeh (accessed on January 10, 2020).
EIr (2009). Shirvanlu, Firuz. In *Encyclopaedia Iranica*. Retrieved from www.iranicaonline.org/articles/shirvanlu-firuz (accessed on January 10, 2020).
EIr (2016). Taqizadeh, Sayyed Hasan. In *Encyclopaedia Iranica*. Retrieved from www.iranicaonline.org/articles/taqizadeh-sayyed-hasan-parent (accessed on January 10, 2020).
Emami, K. (1997). Editing. In *Encyclopaedia Iranica*. Retrieved from www.iranicaonline.org/articles/editing- (accessed on January 10, 2020).
Emami, K. (1998). English v. translation of English literature into Persian. In *Encyclopaedia Iranica*. Retrieved from www.iranicaonline.org/articles/english-5-translation-into (accessed on January 10, 2020).
Emami, K. (2001). Darbārah karīm imāmī. (A. Azarang, interviewer). *Bukhārā*, 21 & 22.
Ezrahi, C. (2012). *Swans of the Kremlin: Ballet and Power in Soviet Russia*. Pittsburgh, PA: University of Pittsburgh Press.
Falk, A.J. (2010). *Upstaging the Cold War: American Dissent and Cultural Diplomacy 1940–1960*. Amherst, MA: University of Massachusetts Press.
Fejes, F. (1981). Media imperialism: An assessment. *Media, Culture and Society*, 3 (3): 281–9.
Fereshteh, M.H. (1993). International rural education teachers and literacy critics: Samad Behrangi's life, thoughts, and profession. Retrieved from https://files.eric.ed.gov/fulltext/ED364542.pdf (accessed on January 10, 2020).
Filstrup, J.M. (1976). Franklin Book Programs/Tehran. *International Library Review*, 8: 431–50.

Franklin Book Programs (1969). *Books for Developing Countries: A Guide for Enlisting Private-Industry Assistance*. New York: Franklin Book Programs.
Galtung, J. (1971). A structural theory of imperialism. *Journal of Peace Research*, 8 (2): 81–117.
Gamow, G. (1958). *Biography of the Earth*. (M. Behzad, trans.). Tehran: Nīl.
Ganjavi, M. (2017). Critique of the structural theory of imperialism. In L. Lane (ed.), *Conference of the Canadian Association for the Study in Adult Education (CASAE)*, Ryerson University, Ontario, May 28–May 31: 137–41.
Ganjavi, M., & Mojab, S. (2018). A lost tale of the student movement in Iran. In A. Choudry & S. Vally (eds.), *Reflections on Knowledge, Learning and Social Movements: History's Schools* (pp. 55–69). Abingdon: Routledge.
Garlitz, R. (2012a). Introduction: Exploring the intersection of international education and foreign affairs. In R. Garlitz & L. Jarvinen (eds.), *Teaching America to the World & the World to America: Education and Foreign Relations since 1870* (pp. 1–9). New York: Palgrave Macmillan.
Garlitz, R. (2012b). U.S. university advisors and education modernization in Iran, 1951–1967. In R. Garlitz & L. Jarvinen (eds.), *Teaching America to the World & the World to America: Education and Foreign Relations since 1870* (pp. 195–216). New York: Palgrave Macmillan.
Gate, A.I. (1948). *Educational Psychology*. London: Macmillan.
Gholipour, A. (2018). *Parwarish ḍawq-i 'āmmih dar 'ṣr-i pahlawī*. Tehran: Naẓar.
Gilroy, H. (1966). Group hailed for supporting publishers abroad. *New York Times*, October 27.
Golan, G. (1990). *Soviet Policies in the Middle East: From World War II to Gorbachev*. Cambridge: Cambridge University Press.
Gould-Davies, N. (2003). The logic of Soviet cultural diplomacy. *Diplomatic History*, 27 (2): 193–214.
Grieve, V.H. (2018). *Little Cold Warriors: American Childhood in the 1950s*. Oxford: Oxford University Press.
Haddadian-Moghaddam, E. (2016). The cultural Cold War and the circulation of world literature: Insights from Franklin Book Programs in Tehran. *Journal of World Literature*, 1 (3): 371–90.
Hakim, M. (1979). Education and modernization in Iran: Planning and impact of educational policy. Unpublished doctoral dissertation, State University of New York.
Hanieh, A. (2013). *Lineages of Revolt: Issues of Contemporary Capitalism in the Middle East*. Chicago: Haymarket.
Harvey, D. (2003). *The New Imperialism*. New York: Oxford University Press.
Hasanli, J. (2006). *At the Dawn of the Cold War: The Soviet–American Crisis over Iranian Azarbaijan, 1941–1946*. Lanham, MD: Rowman and Littlefield.
Hazan, B.A. (1976). *Soviet Propaganda: A Case Study of the Middle East Conflict*. London: Transactions.
Hazard, H.W. et al. (1952). *Atlas of Islamic History*. Princeton, NJ: Princeton University Press.
Hazard, H.W. et al. (1959). *Atlas of Islamic History*. (M. Erfan, trans.). Tehran: Ibn Sīnā.
Hemphill, R.R. (1964). The role of Franklin Book Programs, Incorporated, in book development in the Middle East and Southeast Asia. Unpublished master's dissertation, Catholic University of America, Washington, DC.
Hendershot, C. (1975). *Politics, Polemics and Pedagogs*. New York: Vantage.
Highet, G. (1950). *The Art of Teaching*. New York: Alfred A. Knopf.
Hitti, P.K. (1937). *History of the Arabs*. London: Macmillan.

Hixson, W.L. (1997). *Parting the Curtain: Propaganda, Culture and the Cold War, 1945–1961*. New York: St. Martin's.
Hobson, J.A. (1902). *Imperialism: A Study*. London: James Nisbet & Co.
Holt, E.M. (2017). Cold War in the Arabic press: Hiwar (Beirut, 1962–67) and the Congress for Cultural Freedom. In G. Scott-Smith & C.A. Lerg (eds.), *Campaigning Culture and the Global Cold War: The Journals of the Congress for Cultural Freedom* (pp. 227–43). New York: Palgrave Macmillan.
Homans, J. (2010). *Apollo's Angels: A History of Ballet*. New York: Random House.
Homayoun, D. (1964). *Mass Distribution of Low-priced Books in Indonesia, a Report for Franklin Book Programs, Inc*. Tehran: n.p.
Humāyūn ṣanʿatīzādah. (n.d.). Retrieved from www.cgie.org.ir/fa/don/</occ>2838 (accessed on January 10, 2020).
Huquqi, M. (1972). *Shiʿr naw, āz āqāz tā ʿimrūz 1301–1350*. Tehran: Jībī.
Intrator, M. (2019). *Books Across Borders: UNESCO and the Politics of Postwar Cultural Reconstruction, 1945–1951*. New York: Palgrave Macmillan.
Jaʿfari, A. (2009). Dar risā-yi humāyūn ṣanʿatīzādah. *Bukhārā*, 73: 453–74.
Jahani Asl, M.N. (2007). A democratic alternative education system for Iran: An historical and cultural study. Unpublished master's dissertation, Simon Fraser University, Burnaby, BC.
Jemudd, B.H., & Garrison, G.L. (1975). *Language Treatment in Egypt: Notes*. Cairo: Ford Foundation.
Khalidi, R. (2009). *Sowing Crisis: The Cold War and American Dominance in the Middle East*. Boston: Beacon.
Kraidy, M.M. (2005). *Hybridity, or the Cultural Logic of Globalization*. Philadelphia, PA: Temple University Press.
Kramer, P.A. (2012). Is the world our campus? International students and U.S. global power in the long twentieth century. In R. Garlitz & L. Jarvinen (eds.), *Teaching America to the World & the World to America: Education and Foreign Relations since 1870* (pp. 11–50). New York: Palgrave Macmillan.
Kushner, M.S. (2002). Exhibiting art at the American National Exhibition in Moscow, 1959: Domestic politics and cultural diplomacy. *Journal of Cold War Studies*, 4 (1): 6–26.
Laugesen, A. (2012). Books for the world: American book program in the developing world, 1948–1968. In C. Turner (ed.), *Pressing the Fight: Print, Propaganda, and the Cold War* (pp. 126–44). Amherst: University of Massachusetts.
Laugesen, A. (2017). *Taking Books to the World: American Publishers and the Cultural Cold War*. Boston: University of Massachusetts Press.
Lawson, R. (1948). *Robbut: A Tale of Tails*. New York: Viking.
LeClere, M.N. (1973). *Let Us All Share in the World of Books*. Tehran: Franklin Book Program.
Lenin, V. (1962). *The National Liberation Movement in the East*. (M. Levin, trans.). Moscow: Foreign Languages Publishing House.
Leonard, C.W. (1952). *Why Children Misbehave*. Chicago: Science Research Associates.
Lindbergh, C. (1953). *Spirit of St. Louis*. New York: Charles Scribner's.
Madinei, N. (2017). Kalāntari, Parviz. In *Encyclopaedia Iranica*. Retrieved from www.iranicaonline.org/articles/kalantari-parviz (accessed on January 10, 2020).
Magnúsdóttir, R. (2010). "Mission impossible?": Selling Soviet socialism to Americans, 1955–1958. In J. Gienow-Hecht & M.C. Donfried (eds.), *Searching for a Cultural Diplomacy* (pp. 50–72). New York: Berghahn.

Manzoor, C. (1971). University reform in Iran: Problems and prospects. Unpublished doctoral dissertation, Tufts University.
Marashi, A. (2008). *Nationalizing Iran: Culture, Power and the State 1870–1940*. Seattle & London: University of Washington Press.
Marx, K., & Engels, F. (1998). *The German Ideology*. New York: Prometheus.
Matin-Asgari, A. (2013). The impact of imperial Russia and the Soviet Union on Qajar and Pahlavi Iran: Notes towards a revisionist historiography. In S. Cronin (ed.), *Iranian Russian Encounters: Empires and Revolutions since 1800* (pp. 11–47). London: Routledge.
Matin-Asgari, A. (2018). *Both Eastern and Western: An Intellectual History of Iranian Modernity*. Cambridge: Cambridge University Press.
McDaniel, C.P. (2015). *American–Soviet Cultural Diplomacy: The Bolshoi Ballet's American Premiere*. Lanham, MD: Lexington.
McNally, D. (2005). Understanding imperialism: Old and new dominion. Retrieved from http://solidarity-us.org/site/node/255 (accessed on January 10, 2020).
Menninger, W.C. (1953). *Self-understanding: A First Step to Understanding Children*. Chicago: Science Research Associates.
Milan, M. (2016). Violence and structural imperialism. In I. Ness & Z. Cope (eds.), *The Palgrave Encyclopedia of Imperialism and Anti-imperialism* (pp. 1392–5). London & New York: Palgrave Macmillan.
Milani, A. (1995). Siyyid fakhr al-dīn shādimān va masʾalah tajadud. *Īrān Shināsī* (2): 261–79.
Mirsepassi, A. (2017). *Transnationalism in Iranian Political Thought: The Life and Times of Ahmad Fardid*. New York: Cambridge University Press.
Mitgang, H. (1978). Poor countries helped with books. *New York Times*, June 25.
Mobin Shorish, M. (1997). Education xxvii. In Afghanistan. In *Encyclopaedia Iranica*. Retrieved from www.iranicaonline.org/articles/education-xxvii-in-afghanistan (accessed on January 10, 2020).
Moezi Moghadam, F. (2010a). Kānun-e Parvareš-e Fekri-e Kudakān va Nowjavānān i. Establishment of Kanun. In *Encyclopaedia Iranica*. Retrieved from www.iranicaonline.org/articles/kanun-e-parvares-e-fekri-e-kudakan-va-nowjavanan-establishment-of-kanun (accessed on January 10, 2020).
Moezi Moghadam, F. (2010b). Kānun-e Parvareš-e Fekri-e Kudakān va Nowjavānān iii. Book publishing. In *Encyclopaedia Iranica*. Retrieved from www.iranicaonline.org/articles/kanun-e-parvares-e-fekri-e-kudakan-va-nowjavanan-book-publishing (accessed on January 10, 2020).
Mohajer, A. (1962). *Zīr āsimān kavīr*. Tehran: Jībī.
Mojab, S. (1991). The state and university: The "Islamic Cultural Revolution" in the institutions of higher education of Iran, 1980–87. Unpublished doctoral dissertation, University of Illinois.
Mojab, S. (2011). Adult education in/and imperialism. In S. Carpenter & S. Mojab (eds.), *Educating from Marx: Race, Gender, and Learning* (pp. 167–91). New York: Palgrave Macmillan.
Monzawi, A., & Monzawi, A.N. (2000). Bibliographies and catalogues ii. In Iran (continued). In *Encyclopaedia Iranica*. Retrieved from www.iranicaonline.org/articles/bibliographies-iia (accessed on January 10, 2020).
Morrison, A.C. (1944). *Man Does Not Stand Alone*. New York: Fleming H. Revell.
Mossaki, N., & Ravandi-Fadai, L. (2018). A guarded courtship: Soviet cultural diplomacy in Iran from the late 1940s to the 1960s. *Iranian Studies*, 51 (3): 427–55.

Motahhari, M. (1965). *Dāstān-i rāstān*. Tehran: Shirkat sahāmī ʿintishār.
Moʾtamedi, E. (2003). Kitābhā-yi darsī dar īrān: az taʾsīs dār al-funūn tā inqilāb islāmī (1230–357). *Tārīkh Muʿāsir*, 27: 111–38.
Mozafari Savuji, M. (2010). *Guftigū bā najaf daryābandarī*. Tehran: Murvārīd.
Mūʾasisah intishārāt firānklīn, fihrist ʾintishārāt az 1333 tā 1340 (n.d.). Tehran: Jībī.
Murrow, E.R. (1953). *This I Believe: Selections from the 1950s Radio Series*. n.p.
Nabavi, N. (2003). *Intellectuals and the State in Iran: Politics, Discourse and the Dilemma of Authenticity*. Gainesville, FL: University of Florida Press.
Nasrabadi, M., & Matin-Asgari, A. (2018). The Iranian student movement and the making of global 1968. In C. Jian et al. (eds.), *The Routledge Handbook of the Global Sixties, between Protest and Nation-building* (pp. 443–56). London: Routledge.
NYT (1967). Nonprofit publishing group elects Michael Harris. *New York Times*, November 2.
NYT (1977). Worldwide propaganda network built by the C.I.A. *New York Times*, December 26.
Offiler, B. (2015). *US Foreign Policy and the Modernization of Iran: Kennedy, Johnson, Nixon and the Shah*. Basingstoke: Palgrave Macmillan.
Olmstead, A.T. (1948). *History of the Persian Empire*. Chicago: University of Chicago Press.
Omidsalar, M. (2016). Qazvini, Moḥammad. In *Encyclopaedia Iranica*. Retrieved from www.iranicaonline.org/articles/qazvini-mohammad (accessed on January 10, 2020).
Pace, E. (1999). Datus C. Smith Jr., 92, leader of Princeton University Press. *New York Times*, December 11.
Paivandi, S. (2012). The meaning of the Islamization of the school in Iran. In M. Ahmed (ed.), *Education in West Asia* (pp. 79–102). London: Bloomsbury.
Pickett, J. (2015). Soviet civilization through a Persian lens: Iranian intellectuals, cultural diplomacy and socialist modernity 1941–55. *Iranian Studies*, 48 (5): 805–26.
Pope, A.U. (1945). *Masterpieces of Persian Art*. New York: Dryden Press.
Porkarim, H. (1969). *ʾilāsht, zādgāh-i aʿlā ḥazrat riẓā shāh kabīr*. Tehran: Vizārat Farhang wa Hunar.
Possony, S.T. (1953). *A Century of Conflict: Communist Techniques of World Revolution*. Chicago: Henry Regnery.
Prevots, N. (1998). *Dance for Export: Cultural Diplomacy and the Cold War*. Middletown, CT: Wesleyan University Press.
Rider, T.C. (2016). *Cold War Games: Propaganda, the Olympics and U.S. Foreign Policy*. Urbana, IL: University of Illinois Press.
Robbins, L.S. (2007). Publishing American values: The Franklin Book Program as Cold War cultural diplomacy. *Library Trends*, 55 (3), 638–50.
Rosenberg, V. (2005). *Soviet–American Relations, 1953–1960: Diplomacy and Cultural Exchange during the Eisenhower Presidency*. Jefferson, NC: McFarland.
Roshangar, M. (2010). Khāṭirāt kitābhā-yi jībī. *Mihrnāmah*, 7. Retrieved from www.mehrnameh.ir/article/1257/ (accessed on January 10, 2020).
Rostam-Kolayi, J. (2008). From evangelizing to modernizing Iranians: The American Presbyterian mission and its Iranian students. *Iranian Studies*, 41 (2): 213–39.
Rostow, W.W. (1960). *The Stages of Economic Growth: A Non-communist Manifesto*. New York: Cambridge University Press.
Sabine, G.H. (1937). *A History of Political Theory*. New York: Holt, Rinehart and Winston.
Sabine, G.H. (1958). *History of Political Theory*. Vol. 1 & 2. (B. Pazargad, trans.). Tehran: Amīr Kabīr.

Saccarelli, E., & Varadarajan, L. (2015). *Imperialism: Past and Present*. New York: Oxford University Press.
Sahba, F. (2017). Tirūr na, tiruvā. *Āngāh*, 2: 226–36.
Sahdily, H. (1964). *Franklin's Role in the Development of Book Publishing in Indonesia* [mimeograph]. Jakarta: n.p.
Sahib Al-zamani, M. (1968). *Iqtiṣād-i bīmār-i kitāb*. Tehran: ʿAṭāʾī.
Said, E. (1994). *Culture and Imperialism*. New York: Vintage.
Salih, M.A. (2020). Internal cultural imperialism: The case of the Kurds in Turkey. *The International Communication Gazette*. Retrieved from https://doi.org/10.1177/1748048520928666 (accessed on March 16, 2022).
Sanʿati, M. (2014). Hīchkas nimīdānist darūnash chah khabar ast. (P. Mawsawi, interviewer). *Sharq*, June 22, 1031.
Sanʿatizadeh, H. (1995). Safar barāy-i fuẓūlīhāy-i bi ḥad. (S. Alinehad, interviewer). *Faṣlnāmah Kirmān*, 17 and 18: 63–7.
Sanʿatizadeh, H. (2004). Bunakdārī kitāb. In I. Afshar & A. Azarang et al. (eds.), *Kitābfurūshī: Yādnāmah bābak afshār*, vol. 1 (pp. 357–65). Tehran: Shahāb sāqib.
Sarton, G. (1948). *The Life of Science: Essays in the History of Civilization*. New York: Henry Schuman.
Schiller, H.I. (1976). *Communication and Cultural Domination*. Armonk, NY: Sharpe.
Scott-Smith, G. (2002). The Congress for Cultural Freedom, the end of ideology and the 1955 Milan Conference: "Defining the parameters of discourse." *Journal of Contemporary History*, 37 (3): 437–55.
Scott-Smith, G., & Krabbendam, H. (2003). *The Cultural Cold War in Western Europe, 1945–1960*. London: Frank Cass.
Scott-Smith, G., & Lerg, C.A. (2017). Introduction: Journals of freedom? In G. Scott-Smith & C.A. Lerg (eds.), *Campaigning Culture and the Global Cold War: The Journals of the Congress for Cultural Freedom* (pp. 1–24). New York: Palgrave Macmillan.
Shadiman, S.F. (1947). *Taskhīr tamadun farangī*. Tehran: Self-published.
Shahlapour, P. (1978). Development of higher education and high level manpower needs in Iran. Unpublished doctoral dissertation, University of Missouri-Columbia.
Shakibi, Zh. (2019). *Pahlavi Iran and the Politics of Occidentalism: The Shah and the Rastakhiz Party*. London: I.B. Tauris.
Shannon, M.K. (2017). *Losing Hearts and Minds: American–Iranian Relations and International Education during the Cold War*. Ithaca: Cornell University Press.
Sharif, S. (1994). Education behind the veil: Women in Afghanistan. *Women's Education des Femmes*, 11 (2): 4–9.
Shepard, R.F. (1965). U.S. books leading in translations: Franklin Programs assess scope of distribution. *New York Times*, May 28.
Smith, D.C. (1956). American books in the Middle East. *Library Trends*, 5: 46–72.
Smith, D.C. (1963). Ten years of Franklin Publications. *American Library Association Bulletin*, 57 (6): 507–12.
Smith, D.C. (1977). *The Economics of Book Publishing in Developing Countries*. Paris: UNESCO.
Smith, D.C. (1983). Books for the developing world. *Quarterly Journal, Library of Congress*, 40 (3): 254–65.
Smith, D.C. (2000). Franklin Book Program. In *Encyclopaedia Iranica*. Retrieved from www.iranicaonline.org/articles/franklin-book-program (accessed on January 10, 2020).

Smith, D.E. (1987). *The Everyday World as Problematic: A Feminist Sociology*. Toronto: University of Toronto Press.

Smith, D.E. (1990). *The Conceptual Practices of Power: A Feminist Sociology of Knowledge*. Boston: Northeastern University Press.

Smith, D.E. (1999). *Writing the Social: Critique, Theory, and Investigations*. Toronto: University of Toronto Press.

Smith, D.E. (2011). Ideology, science, and social relations: A reinterpretation of Marx's epistemology. In S. Carpenter & S. Mojab (eds.), *Educating from Marx: Race, Gender, and Learning* (pp. 19–40). New York: Palgrave Macmillan.

Smulyan, S. (2009). The Cultural Turn in U.S. diplomatic history. [Review of *Satchmo Blows Up the World: Jazz Ambassadors Play the Cold War* by P.M. Von Eschen. Harvard University Press, 2004.] *Diplomatic History*, 33 (3): 539–42.

Soule, G.H. (1952). *Ideas of the Great Economists*. New York: Viking.

Spock, B. (1946). *The Common Sense Book of Baby and Child Care*. New York: Duell, Sloan and Pearce.

Staley, E. (1954). *The Future of Underdeveloped Countries: Political Implications of Development*. New York: Harper.

Stonor Saunders, F. (2000). *Who Paid the Piper? The CIA and the Cultural Cold War*. London: Granta.

Taban, H. (1979). Higher education and its development in Iran. Unpublished doctoral dissertation, University of Northern Colorado.

Tavakoli-Targhi, M. (2001). *Refashioning Iran: Orientalism, Occidentalism and Historiography*. Hampshire & New York: Palgrave.

Tavakoli-Targhi, M. (2015). Ahmad Kasravi's critiques of Europism and Orientalism. In Kamran Talattof (ed.), *Persian Language, Literature and Culture: New Leaves, Fresh Looks* (pp. 228–38). London: Routledge.

Tavakoli-Targhi, M. [Guest] (2020). *A 19th Century Travelogue Chronicles a World on the Cusp of Modernity* [Radio]. In N. Mustafa (producer), *Ideas*. CBC Radio, March 9.

Tomlinson, J. (1991). *Cultural Imperialism*. London: Pinter.

Travis, T. (2013). Books in the Cold War: Beyond "culture" and "information." In J. Auerbach & R. Castronovo (eds.), *The Oxford Handbook of Propaganda Studies* (pp. 180–200). Retrieved from https://doi.org/10.1093/oxfordhb/9780199764419.001.0001 (accessed on January 10, 2020).

US Commission on International Education and Cultural Affairs (1969). *Sixth Annual Report of the US Advisory Commission on International Education and Cultural Affairs*, Document No. 91–63. Retrieved from https://www.state.gov/wp-content/uploads/2020/04/6th-annual-report-ACIECA.pdf (accessed on January 10, 2020).

Vahabzadeh, P. (2015). Rebellious action and "guerrilla poetry": Dialectics of art and life in 1970s Iran. In Kamran Talattof (ed.), *Persian Language, Literature and Culture: New Leaves, Fresh Looks* (pp. 103–23). London: Routledge.

Van Loon, H.W. (1921). *The Story of Mankind*. New York: H. Liveright.

Vaughan, J.R. (2005). *Failure of American and British Propaganda in the Arab Middle East, 1945–1957: Unconquerable Minds*. New York: Palgrave Macmillan.

Vejdani, F. (2015). *Making History in Iran: Education, Nationalism and Print Culture*. Stanford: Stanford University Press.

Weathersby, W.H. (1989). Interview with William Henry Weathersby. (J.R. O'Brien, interviewer). August 1. Retrieved from the Library of Congress, www.loc.gov/item/mfdipbib001236/ (accessed on January 10, 2020).

Werner, E.J. (1952). *The Golden Geography: A Child's Introduction to the World*. New York: Simon and Schuster.
Williams, R. (1983). *Keywords: A Vocabulary of Culture and Society*. New York: Oxford University Press.
Yadegar, Zh. (1979). Barisi-yi faʿāliyat muʾasisah intishārātī firānklīn. Unpublished master's dissertation, University of Tehran, Tehran.
Zirinsky, M.P. (1993). A panacea for the ills of the country: American Presbyterian education in inter-war Iran. *Iranian Studies*, 26 (1): 119–37.

Archives

Central Intelligence Agency Archives. Retrieved from https://www.cia.gov/readingroom/docs/. Cited as CIAA.
Cold War International History Project. Retrieved from https://digitalarchive.wilsoncenter.org/. Cited as CWIHP.
Documentation on Early Cold War U.S. Propaganda Activities in the Middle East. National Security Archive. (2002). Retrieved from http://nsarchive.gwu.edu/NSAEBB/NSAEBB78/. Cited as NSA.
Franklin Book Programs Records; 1920–78 (mostly 1952–77), Public Policy Papers, Department of Rare Books and Special Collections, Princeton University Library. Cited as FBPR.
Harry S. Truman Papers, Staff Member and Office Files: Psychological Strategy Board Files. Cited as PSB.
Iran's Parliamentary Proceedings, accessible at: www.ical.ir/fa/MashroohMozakerat.
Kennedy Library, President's Office Files, Departments and Agencies Series, USIA Files.
Truman Library, Ellen Clayton Garwood Papers. Retrieved from www.trumanlibrary.gov/library/personal-papers/ellen-clayton-garwood-papers.

INDEX

1979 revolution 4, 6, 8, 64, 86, 95, 125, 131, 133, 141–4, 174 n.123, 174 n.1
2500th Year of the Foundation of the Imperial State of Iran 58, 97, 121, 168 n.9

Abaza, Ahmed Riad 35, 157 n.2
Abdel Nasser, Gamal 34, 40, 149
Abu Hadid, Mohammad Farid 37, 152
adult education 29, 137
Afghanistan
 government 45, 101
 Ministry of Education 31, 48, 51, 56, 59, 60, 93, 97, 100–4, 147, 160 n.38
 textbook project 44, 100–3, 161 n.45
Africa 21, 38, 100, 129, 137
 FBP operations in 3, 43, 46, 51, 52–4, 81, 140, 144, 147, 148
Africa–America Institute 162 n.62
Aḥrām 36
Akhbār Al-Yūm 36, 158 n.15, 159 n.30
Ala', Hossein 158 n.14
Al Ahmad, Jalal 5, 6, 78, 93, 94, 125–31, 142–3, 173 n.115, 173 n.118, 175 n.6
 Chaotic Situation of the Educational Textbooks 125, 126, 129
 One Well and Two Hollows 125, 130
 On the Merits and the Perfidy of the Intellectuals 125, 130–1
 Westoxification 6, 125, 126, 128–30, 130–1, 142–3
Alam, Asadollah 50, 79
Allied Forces 2, 65, 66, 76, 87, 111
American Book Publishers Council (ABPC) 155 n.16, 162 n.62
American books 27, 28, 36, 39, 40, 50, 53, 54, 61, 101, 134, 138
American Booksellers Association (ABA) 162 n.62
American Friends of the Middle East (AFME) 7, 75, 165 n.26
American Library Association (ALA) 155 n.16
American Textbook Publishers Institute (ATPI) 7, 108, 162 n.62
American way of life 20, 23, 25, 28, 41, 44, 138
Amin, Ahmad 35, 37, 150, 152
Amin, Mahmud el- 161 n.41
Amirarjomand, Lily 113, 170 n.44 (*see also* IIDCYA)
Amīr Kabīr publishers 9, 76, 84, 87–9, 95–9, 102, 107, 117, 132, 133, 160, 174 n.126 (*see also* Jaʿfari, Abdulrahim)
Amman 22, 38, 155 n.12
Andīshah 76, 87
Ankara 22
Ansari, Abdolreza 57
anti-communist 1, 31, 140, 154 n.4
anti-US 5, 8, 22, 36, 38, 41, 73, 133, 142
Anwar, Manuchehr 77, 84, 112, 170 n.44, 175 n.5
Aqsa, Reza 95, 109, 110
Arabic
 distribution of books in 23, 159 n.21
 encyclopedias 28, 46, 49, 94
 FBP in 5, 34, 38, 50, 101, 146, 147, 158 n.5, 159 n.30
 FBP translations to 5, 34, 36, 37, 39, 91, 138, 149–52
 sales of books in 40, 157 n.4, 159 n.16, 159 n.22, 159 n.25
 textbooks in 48, 51
Arab world 5, 23, 36, 40, 44, 50, 146, 158 n.15
Aram, Ahmad 94, 95, 109
Aroussy, Hassan al- 34, 157 n.1
Aryamehr University of Technology (AMUT) 82, 167 n.1
Asia Foundation 46, 48, 51, 58, 59, 62–4, 103, 162 n.73

Association for Supervision and
    Curriculum Development (ASCD)
    7, 109
Association nationale du livre français à
    l'étranger 50
Association of American University
    Presses (AAUP) 7, 146, 160 n.33,
    162 n.62
Azad University of Iran 61, 133
Azerbaijan Crisis 66, 68, 120, 121,
    171 n.73

Baghdad 22, 39, 40, 45, 49, 55, 71, 155,
    159 n.16, 159 n.21, 159 n.30, 162
Baghdad office 146, 147, 158 n.9
Baghdad Pact 67
Bahrain 44, 169 n.29
Behrangi, Samad 90, 125, 142
Behzad, Mahmood 85, 89, 109, 110
Beirut 35, 38, 45, 49, 94, 155 n.12, 157 n.1,
    159 n.16, 159 n.21, 159 n.30,
    162 n.69 (see also Beirut office;
    Lebanon)
Beirut office 46, 55, 146, 147, 152 (see also
    Beirut; Lebanon)
biographies 28, 29, 37, 79, 88, 89, 95, 111,
    121, 150, 158 n.9
Bolton, Sarah K., *Lives of Poor Boys Who
    Became Famous* 30, 37, 40, 88, 121,
    150, 158 n.9
book
    commercial distribution 26–8, 33, 139
    development 4, 53, 148
    exhibits 38, 41, 42, 109
    gap 47, 101, 138
    promotion 39, 41, 83, 99, 146, 147
    regional distribution 10, 24, 38, 139
    trade 22, 25, 27, 39–41, 47–8, 99, 138,
    159 n.20
Book Procurement Improvement and
    Bibliographic Center 55–60, 141
bookseller-publishers 82, 83, 99
bookselling 1, 36, 41, 83, 97
bookstores 39, 41, 83, 98, 102, 159 n.21,
    159 n.24
Bowen, Carroll G. 53, 56, 146
Brigham Young University (BYU) 75
British Book Development Council 51,
    162 n.70

Buck, Byron 48, 99, 108, 109
Buenos Aires 2, 48, 148, 162 n.69
Bungāh Tarjumah va Nashr Kitāb 76,
    82, 84, 87, 112, 113, 127, 128, 133
    (see also Yarshater, ehsan)
Bureau for Democracy, Human Rights
    and Labor (DRL) 144
Burma 161 n.52

Cairo 22, 24, 36, 39, 43, 152, 155 n.12, 157
    n.4, 158 n.15, 159 n.21, 159 n.30,
    162 n.69 (see also Arabic; Egypt)
Cairo office 2, 29, 34, 38, 39, 49, 50, 51, 60,
    65, 89, 101, 146, 149, 150 (see also
    Arabic; Egypt)
capitalist bloc 19, 66, 136
Center for Educational Technology (CET)
    59, 60
Center for Producing Reading Materials
    for New-literates 111, 113
Central Intelligence Agency (CIA) 3, 6, 8,
    20, 27, 62–4, 65, 66, 74, 103, 132,
    141, 154 n.4, 165 n.26, 173 n.121
children's books 29, 41, 47, 49, 51, 71, 82,
    91, 112, 113, 146, 169 n.40, 170 n.43
Children's Book Council 162 n.62
civic leaders 31, 35, 144 (see also
    intellectual leaders)
Clayton Garwood, Ellen 46, 47, 113,
    161 n.50
Cold War International History Project
    (CWIHP) 6, 7, 44
Colloquium on Islamic Culture 25
Columbia University Teachers College
    (CUTC) 108
Columbia–Viking Desk Encyclopedia 28,
    46, 94, 95, 150, 151, 152
Commonwealth Fund 51
Confederation of Iranian Students (CIS)
    84, 169 n. 42
Congress for Cultural Freedom (CCF)
    20–1, 137–9
Council on Books in Wartime 7, 51
crown prince 116, 120, 121, 171 n.74,
    171 n.82, 171 n.84
cultural exchange 19, 67, 68, 75
cultural imperialism 3, 4, 5, 6, 13–8, 33,
    126, 128, 131, 135, 143–5 (see also
    cultural influence)

cultural influence 3, 69, 101, 138, 142
    (*see also* cultural imperialism)

Dacca office 38, 59, 60, 116, 146, 162 n.69, 170 n.56
Damascus 22, 152, 155 n.12, 159 n.21
Daneshwar, Simin 175 n.6
Dār al-Ḥilāl 36, 158 n.15, 159 n.30
Daryabandari, Najaf 9, 84, 85, 117
Day for Children 120
Dhofar movement 67, 122
Diba, Farah 51, 78, 82, 113, 170 n.53
    (*see also* Royal family)
dictionaries 28, 43, 46, 49, 58, 140, 147
Doctrinal Program 26–7, 140, 168 n.34
doctrinal warfare 26, 31, 42, 156 n.34
Dowlatabadi, Yahya 76, 105

educational
    aid 75, 142
    exchange programs 22, 75, 135, 138, 155 n.15, 165 n.35
    modernization 72, 75, 89
    reform 3, 4, 105, 111, 134, 142
    system 3, 44, 63, 90, 101, 103, 106, 110, 114, 126, 129
Educational Materials Laboratory (EML) 109
Educational Publications Center (EPC) 9, 93, 113–18, 123, 132
Education and Training 114, 116, 118, 119, 170 n.63
Egypt (*see also* Cairo; Cairo office)
    FBP operations in 5, 7, 34, 38, 39, 41, 50, 62, 64, 133, 149–151, 158 n.9, 159 n.16, 159 n.22, 161 n.49
    Ministry of Education 2, 35, 43, 49, 140
    textbook project 44, 45, 48, 51, 161 n.56
Emami, Goli 85
Emami, Karim 9, 84, 85, 89, 90, 117, 132, 169 n.38
encyclopedias 28, 43, 45, 46, 94, 140, 146
    (*see also Persian Encyclopedia*; see under Arabic)
Enugu office 148
Eslami Nadushan, Mohammad Ali 78, 85, 167 n.49

Fardid, Ahmad 128, 173 n.115. 173 n.116
Farid, Kamil 157 n.2

Farjam, Farideh 112, 113
fascism 2, 19, 66, 71, 137
Ford Foundation 43–49, 51, 53, 62, 89, 94, 108, 127, 147, 148, 162 n.64
Forsi, Bahman 163 n.107
Franklin, Benjamin 21, 29, 37, 87, 88, 112, 150
Franklin's Organization for Production and Writing of Textbooks 110, 111
Fulbright Program 34, 75, 155 n.20
Fundación Interamericana de Bibliotecología Franklin 148

Galtung, Johan 13, 15, 16
globalization 13, 16

Harris, Michael 72, 146
Hausa 148, 163 n.83
Hejazi, Mohammad 78, 152, 153
Hendershot, Clarence 72–4
Hertz, Martin F. 79, 165 n.34
Highet, Gilbert, *The Art of Teaching* 159 n.25
Hobson, John A., *Imperialism: A Study* 13–14
Homayoun, Dariush 49, 78, 79, 97, 162 n.68, 162 n.75, 163 n.91, 165 n.34
Hussein, Taha 25, 150, 152, 158 n.9

Ibn Sīnā 76, 87, 88, 96, 99, 160, 167 n.54
ideological 1–4, 10, 15, 19, 20–6, 30–3, 36–8, 41, 71, 125, 131, 135–44, 147
ideology 13, 16–7, 19, 20, 69, 121, 125–6, 135, 137, 142–3, 172 n.87
Igbo 148, 163 n.81
Imperial Organization for Social Services 43, 45, 47, 52, 56, 96, 107, 111, 150
India 38, 53, 57, 59, 67, 86, 129, 141, 146, 161 n.52, 162 n.65, 167 n.51
Indonesia 7, 38, 41, 47, 49, 51, 53–9, 141, 150–2, 157 n.50, 162 n.75, 163 n.91
Information Center Service (ICS) 7, 22, 23
    (*see also* Lacy, Dan)
Institute for International Education (IIE) 24, 108, 155 n.20
Institute for the Intellectual Development of Children and Young Adults (IIDCYA) 51, 112, 113, 119, 167 n.1, 169 n.41, 170 n.43 (*see also* Amirarjomand, Lily)

intellectual leaders 7, 137, 139, 149
    (*see also* civic leaders)
International Copyrights Information
    Center (INCINC) 55-9, 163 n.93
international education 72, 75, 137, 141,
    155 n.20, 166 n.38
International Information Administration
    (IIA) 22-6, 138, 155 n.15
Iran
    Ministry of Education 2, 3, 9, 10, 43-9,
        61, 72-8, 82, 89, 93, 104-19, 123,
        132, 134, 143, 169 n.29, 170 n.63
    Oil Nationalization 74
    post-coup regime 3, 36, 65-8, 74, 78,
        81, 87, 112, 124, 134, 141, 143, 165
        n.24, 186 n.6
    government 66, 71, 72, 74, 76, 97, 100,
        105, 124, 127
Isfahan steel mill 70, 79
Islam 23, 25, 88, 122, 125, 128, 129, 143
Israel 23, 121 (*see also* Jerusalem)

Ja'fari, Abdulrahim 9, 84, 96, 99, 102, 107,
    132, 174 n.126 (*see also* Amīr Kabīr
    publishers)
Jahanshahi, Iraj 113, 117
Jakarta 38, 146, 162 n.69 (*see also* Jakarta
    office)
Jakarta office 56, 57, 58, 147 (*see also*
    Jakarta)
Jamali, Mohammad Fadhel al- 149,
    158 n.9
Jerusalem 155 n.12, 159 n.21 (*see also*
    Israel)
Johnson, Malcolm 22
Jordan 37, 38, 44, 76
Jumhūrriya 36
juvenile reading 25, 29, 35, 44, 101, 139,
    160 n.38

Kabul
    FBP operations in 50, 58, 61, 103, 104,
        162 n.69, 166 n.39
    office 48, 59, 60, 102, 103, 146, 147
Kaduna office 49, 146, 148
Kalantari, Pirouz 9, 110, 113, 169 n.41
Karang, Abdulali 99, 161 n.43 (*see also*
    Tabriz office)
Kasravi, Ahmad 126, 173 n.115
Kennedy, John F. 46, 47, 140, 142

Khiradjou, Ghasem 161 n.61
Khwajeh Noori, Ebrahim 78, 152
Kuala Lumpur office 45, 55, 146, 147
Kuwait 44, 49, 52, 71, 162 n.65
Kyle, John H. 7, 59, 61, 146, 166 n.38

Lacy, Dan 22-6, 155 n.16 (*see also* ICS)
Lagos office 48, 49, 146, 147, 162 n.69, 163
    n.81
Lahore (*see also* Pakistan; Urdu)
    FBP operations in 38, 116, 159 n.21,
        162 n.69
    office 34, 59, 146
Latin America 2, 43, 46, 47, 51, 52, 54, 81,
    144, 148
Lebanon 7, 41, 44, 49, 50, 150 (*see also*
    Beirut; Beirut office)
Lenin, Vladimir, *Imperialism, the Highest
    State of Capitalism* 13-14
Library of Congress 64, 91, 133, 156 n.31
library development 43, 52, 55-60, 82, 89,
    140, 144, 155 n.7
Libya 44
Lincoln, Abraham 37, 112
literacy campaigns 29, 93, 123, 171 n.71
Literacy Corps 47, 51, 61, 171 n.71
local advisors 30, 31, 35, 87, 157 n.51
local publishing 3, 24, 34, 86, 139
local redaction 28, 29, 37

MacMakin, Robert 102, 104, 162 n.75
Mahdavi, Hosein 78-9
Ma'rifat 87, 160
Maroof, Atiqullah 147, 162 n.63
Marx, Karl, *The German Ideology* 17
mass book distribution 3, 43, 47, 97-8,
    138-40, 143 (*see also* Pocket Books)
Mexico City 2
military aid 29
Mirzazadeh, Ni'mat 173 n.14
modernization theory 3, 4, 7, 141-2
Mohajer, Ali Asghar 79, 81, 95, 99, 113,
    117, 118, 123-24, 131-3, 166 n.38,
    166 n.39, 168 n.4, 173 n.120
Monthly Publication 41
Morrison, A. Cressy, *Man does not Stand
    Alone* 37, 87, 88, 151, 158 n.9
Mosaddeq, Mohammad 3, 65, 66, 73, 74,
    78, 126, 165 n.24, 166 n.39
Mosaheb, Gholamhosayn 94, 95

Mosaheb, Mahmood 94, 117
Mossawi Garmarudi, Ali 133
Motahhari, Morteza 122, 123
Murrow, Edward R., *This I Believe* 30, 37, 149, 150
Muslim Brotherhood 36, 37, 158 n.9

Naguib, Mohammad 37, 40, 149
Nairobi office 49, 146, 148
Najm, Mohammad Y. 50, 161 n.41
Natel Khanlari, Parviz 77, 78, 110, 169 n.37
National Committee for the International Campaign against Illiteracy 79
National Council of Churches 52
National Endowment for Democracy (NED) 144
National Security Council (NSC) 154 n.4
Nawmarz Educational Organization 133, 174 n.123
Nepal 57, 162 n.69, 163 n.106
neutralism 26, 155 n.15
newly literate 1, 29, 46, 49, 51, 152
New York Office 4, 30, 34, 35, 45–53, 60, 81, 99, 102, 123, 132, 141, 160 n.33, 162 n.75, 165 n.31, 166 n.39, 172 n.11
New York Times 62–4, 132, 141, 173 n.121
Nigeria 48, 50, 51, 53, 141, 147, 148, 162 n.64, 162 n.70
North Africa 38 (*see also* Africa)

Offset Printing House 49, 50, 93, 96–7, 104, 111, 114, 124, 127, 133, 134
Organization for Economic Cooperation and Development (OECD) 146
Organization for Publication and Education of the Islamic Revolution 6, 131, 133
Organization for Textbooks 110, 111, 169 n.38
Outstanding Child contest 116, 120

Pahlavi, Ashraf 30, 40, 78, 87, 88, 94, 107, 121, 150, 167 n.56, 168 n.4, 174 n.123, 175 n.5
Pahlavi, (Shah) Mohammad Reza 37, 65, 70, 78, 82, 88, 121, 150, 158 n.9, 158 n.14, 171 n.71, 172 n.94

Pahlavi regime 1, 6, 8, 65, 67, 75, 82, 90, 106, 115, 116, 120, 121, 125, 126, 134, 139, 142, 143, 168 n.9, 171 n.70, 172 n.97, 174 n.6, 174 n.7
Pakdaman, Naser 85, 98
Pakistan
  FBP operations in 7, 34, 38, 40, 41, 46, 47, 49, 51, 56, 58, 59, 60, 93, 116, 144, 146, 161 n.57, 163 n.94 (*see also* Lahore)
  Ministry of Education 2, 57, 158 n.9
  government 57
pan-Arab distribution 37–9
Parham, Sirous 84, 167 n.56, 169 n.37
Pars Paper Company 93, 99–100
Pashto 48, 51, 56, 103, 138, 147
Payk 3, 9, 49, 51, 93, 111, 113–23, 132, 134, 144
Pazhwak, Atiqullah 162 n.75
Peace Corps 50, 52
Penguin publishing house 99
Persian Encyclopedia 47, 78, 83, 88, 93–5, 132, 168 n.5
Pirnazar, Houshang 110, 163 n.107, 169 n.37
Pocket Books 48, 89, 93–9, 132, 163 n.107 (*see also* mass book distribution; Roshangar, Majid)
Point Four 25, 67, 72–4, 102, 104, 112, 141 (*see also* Hendershot, Clarence)
policy of containment 2, 3, 72, 141
Princeton University 4, 6, 22, 25, 146, 160 n.33
Progress Publishers 71, 165 n.20
propaganda 5, 20, 21, 27, 30, 31, 38, 44, 54, 62, 69, 70, 71, 87, 121, 123, 127, 139, 154 n.4, 164 n.3
Prophet Mohammad 114, 122
Psychological Strategy Board (PSB) 7, 8, 26–8, 156 n.32
public affairs officers 22, 24
Public Law 480 44–7, 51, 100, 102, 108, 127
Publisher's Weekly 41

Qazvin 80, 114
Quran 40, 61, 111
Qutb, Sayyid Ibrahim Husayn 36

Rastakhiz Party 122, 172 n.94
Reza Shah 37, 65, 116, 121, 150, 158 n.9, 171 n.70, 172 n.97
Rio de Janeiro 2, 52, 148
Rockefeller Foundation 7, 44, 46, 49, 129
Roshangar, Majid 97, 98, 99 (*see also* Pocket Books*)
royal family 76, 78, 86–8, 120–1, 125, 130, 134 (*see also* Diba, Farah; Pahlavi, Ashraf; Pahlavi, Mohammad Reza)
Royalty 25, 28, 78, 97, 167 n.56

Sabine, George H., *A History of Political Theory* 30, 42, 88, 89, 157 n.6, 159 n.16, 159 n.25
Ṣafī ʿalīshāh 87, 88, 99, 160
Sahdily, Hassan 162 n.75
Sanʿati, Mahdokht 77, 85, 166 n.47, 167 n.48
Sao Paulo 2, 148
Saudi Arabia 38, 44, 52, 162 n.69
sāzimān-i ʿiṭilāʿāt va amniyat-i kishvar (SAVAK) 6, 8, 9, 67, 69–72, 84, 139, 164 n.4, 164 n.7, 165 n.21
Schmidt, Erich, *Persepolis* 159 n.26
school library 43, 47, 49, 51, 56, 60, 89, 146
School of Education at the State University of New York (SUNY) 172 n.111
School of Education of Harvard University 162 n.62
Shadiman, Seyed Fakhr al-Din, *Conquering the Western Civilization* 128–9, 173 n.115, 173 n.117
Shirvanlu, Firuz 113, 169 n.42 (*see also* IIDCYA)
socialist bloc 2, 3, 6, 100, 137
Society for Cultural Relations between Iran and the Soviet Union (Society) 68, 69
Soule, George, *Ideas of the Great Economists* 87, 157 n.6, 158 n.9
Soviet Azerbaijan Fair 69, 70
Soviet Union
  cultural diplomacy 20, 68–72, 136, 154 n.3
  embassy 69–71
  Iran relations 66, 68–72, 75
Spaulding, John 108, 113

sponsored titles 39, 42, 87, 88–90, 135, 138, 157 n.4
state–private network 20, 138, 145
Suez Canal 66, 100
survey teams 35, 42

Tabriz office 45, 99, 100, 146, 147 (*see also* Karang, Abdulali)
Taqizadeh, Seyyed Hassan 77, 78, 96, 107, 132, 152, 153, 158 n.9, 168 n.8
teacher training 7, 29, 48, 51, 56, 61, 73, 89, 90, 106, 110, 118, 126, 157 n.6
technical assistantship 2, 3, 103, 104, 166 n.39
Thailand 57, 161 n.52
title listing 10, 28–31
title selection 5, 28–31, 42, 136, 140
translation rights 28, 34, 42, 54, 55, 84, 166 n.42
translators 35, 76, 78, 84, 87, 94, 132
Tripoli 22, 159 n.21
Truman, Harry S. 66, 72, 75, 161 n.50
Tudeh Party 65, 66, 69, 70, 77, 84, 112, 112, 126
Tunisia 44, 162 n.65
Turkish 34, 38, 40, 80, 90, 157 n.6

United Arab Republic 45, 47, 49, 50, 51, 56, 57, 161 n.49
United States
  cultural diplomacy 6, 8, 19, 20 129, 135, 174 n.1
  Department of State 7, 9, 21–4, 27, 29, 137–8, 144, 155 n.15, 155 n.20, 174 n.123
  embassy 6, 8, 22, 43, 57, 61, 63, 77, 79, 103, 165 n.34, 174 n.123
  Iran relations 67, 72–6, 141–4
  publishers 38, 41, 52, 54, 55, 166 n.42
United States Agency for International Development (USAID) 7, 48–63, 72, 116, 141, 144, 148, 162 n.70, 162 n.106
United States Information Agency (USIA) 7, 19, 21, 44–7, 55, 154 n.1
United States Information Service (USIS) 27, 34, 66, 74, 159 n.24
United States Treasury Department 155 n.8

United Nations Educational, Scientific and Cultural Organization (UNESCO) 7, 48, 50, 53, 60, 79, 99, 146, 162 n.75, 164 n.111
University of Pennsylvania (UPenn) 75
Urdu (*see also* Lahore; Pakistan)
  distribution of books in 38, 159 n.21
  encyclopedias 28, 46, 94, 146
  FBP in 39, 46, 47, 51, 116, 140, 146, 159 n.30
  FBP translations to 34, 38, 59, 138
  sales 40
Utah State Agricultural College (USAC) 75

veto power 30, 157 n.51
Vietnam War 67, 71, 121

Village and Industrial Development (VAID) 46
Vsesoyuznoe obschestvo kul'turnoi svyazi c zagranitsei (VOKS) 68

White Revolution 120–2, 171 n.71
W.K. Kellogg Foundation 2, 44, 51, 52
World Bank 53, 60, 62, 101, 124

Yarshater, Ehsan 112 (*see also* Bungāh Tarjumah va Nashr Kitāb)
Yoruba 147, 163 n.81

Zafar, Amir Hosssein 78, 151
Zahir Shah, Mohammed 102, 103
Zarrinkelk, Nur al-Din 113

www.ingramcontent.com/pod-product-compliance
Lightning Source LLC
Chambersburg PA
CBHW061831300426
44115CB00013B/2331